[6—0]
Kerria japonica

[6—0a]
Russel Lupines
(Lupinus polyphyllus varieties)

[6—1]
Iris Garden

NEW *ILLUSTRATED* ENCYCLOPEDIA OF GARDENING

UNABRIDGED

EDITED BY T. H. Everett

Assistant Director (Horticulture) and Curator of Education
The New York Botanical Garden

WITH CONTRIBUTIONS FROM

TWENTY HORTICULTURISTS AND AUTHORITIES
IN THE UNITED STATES AND CANADA

Growers, Breeders, Exhibitors, Plantsmen, Writers, Lecturers, Professors, Editors and Superintendents of Famous Estates, who are Experts in all Fields of Horticulture, including Pests and Their Control.

VOLUME SIX—Ina-Mah

 GREYSTONE PRESS · NEW YORK

INARCHING. This is one of the oldest known methods of propagating certain plants, shrubs and trees, but is rarely practiced nowadays. Inarching is often known as Approach Grafting and depends upon the same principles as grafting for success, i.e. the close contact of the cambium layers of the scion and the stock. When the usual methods of grafting are carried out, a shoot is entirely detached from the parent plant and placed on another; in inarching, the shoot used as the scion is not severed from the parent plant until it is united with the stock; both stock and scion are nourished by their own roots until the union is complete.

Inarching is now employed chiefly as a means of propagating certain exotic plants that cannot readily be increased by other means, but it is occasionally adopted with the Grape and Fig, with Orange, Lemon and other Citrus fruits, and sometimes with the Walnut. It may be used to replace an unsuitable variety without removing the old plant or tree; or to test the value of a seedling or new variety. Inarching is also the method that was employed in greenhouses to graft certain weak-growing varieties of Grapes on a more vigorous variety, while light-cropping varieties may be induced to bear heavier crops by inarching them on a free-cropping variety used as the stock.

Methods of procedure vary in detail under different conditions and the kind of material available, but the principle of inarching is the same in all cases.

A variegated leaved Geranium (Pelargonium) being inarched on to a green-leaved one.

How Inarching Is Carried Out. The scion (the plant to be perpetuated and grafted on the stock) and the stock plant may be planted in a border and grown in close proximity to one another, or, as is more usual, the scion plant is grown in a pot which may be moved to the place and position most convenient for bringing it near the stock. Or both may be pot plants. In the greenhouse, stock and scion plants should be started into growth together and given similar treatment, so that they are in the same stage of development when inarching is done. The season for inarching begins with the flow of sap in spring, and the operation is best carried out when the shoots have four or five leaves.

Inarching is performed by bringing the stock and scion shoots close together, and, at the point where they meet, a strip of bark about 2 in. long is pared off the scion, and a piece corresponding exactly in size is pared from the stock shoot. The two cut surfaces are then fitted together and secured with soft tying material and a tape bandage. Rarely is grafting wax required to cover the union. Under favorable conditions the two cut surfaces rapidly knit together and within a week or two will have united sufficiently to permit the removal of the tying material, to prevent strangulation and its replacement with new ties of raffia or soft string.

When growth becomes vigorous the part of the scion plant below the union must be gradually cut away, first ringing the stem at that point, then cutting it half way through, and finally severing it completely. The stock will supply the moisture and nourishment required to enable the young scion growth to develop strongly. Growth from the stock plant above the union must be pinched back, but not completely stripped—so as to encourage the concentration of its energies upon the scion shoot. When the two have knit firmly together and the scion is separated from its root, then the growth on the stock above the union may be removed entirely.

Sometimes a tongue is cut in the shoot forming the scion and a corresponding tongue in the stock growth (just as in the Whip or Tongue graft described under Grafting); the two fit exactly together and hold the cut surfaces on scion and stock close together.

Bottle Grafting. Another form of grafting sometimes referred to as inarching is Bottle Grafting, where a young scion or shoot of the desired variety is cut off and the end inserted in a bottle filled with rain water. This is suspended from the trellis wires at a convenient spot or placed on the bench alongside the stock plant and the inarching is carried out in the manner described. This is not rightly inarching, since the scion shoot is severed from the parent plant before any union with the stock plant is effected.

INCARVILLEA (Incarvil′lea). Hardy and nearly hardy perennials with thick, fleshy rootstocks, they are chiefly natives of China and Turkestan. Incarvillea is named after Père Incarville, a Chinese Jesuit who was interested in botany about the middle of the eighteenth century. About a dozen kinds are known. They belong to the Bignonia family, Bignoniaceae.

Incarvillea Delavayi, a somewhat tender perennial from China, bears large, rose-purple, yellow-throated, trumpet-shaped flowers in early summer.

Needs Protection in Winter. Incarvillea thrives best in a sunny border in rather light, well-drained loamy soil enriched with decayed manure. In cold districts mounds of old coal ashes should be placed round the crowns in winter as protection, or the plants should be covered with leaves or salt hay. Planting should be done in October or early in March.

Propagation is by division of the clumps or crowns, early spring being the best time for this work, so that any roots broken or damaged quickly make new growth. If the plants are lifted in fall there is the possibility of the roots being damaged and if that happens they may decay in winter. Seeds are sown in early spring in sandy soil in a cold frame. Or the seeds may be sown in flats of soil set in a sheltered position out of doors and covered with sheets of glass.

The best-known kind is Incarvillea Delavayi. It has pinnate leaves, 1-1½ ft. long, and large, trumpet-shaped rose-purple flowers with yellow throat, eight to ten in a bunch, in early summer. This kind was first introduced from China by the French missionary, Père Delavay, in 1893.

I. grandiflora, also from China, has shorter leaves than I. Delavayi, and larger rose-crimson flowers with golden throat, two or three in a bunch: the variety brevipes is stronger in growth and has large purplish-crimson flowers. I. Olgae, a native of Turkestan, is taller, 2-3 ft. high, and has divided leaves and rose-purple flowers. I. variabilis, from western China, grows 1-1½ ft. high, has pinnate leaves and rose-colored flowers. It is less hardy than I. Delavayi.

INCENSE CEDAR. Libocedrus decurrens, which see.

INCENSE PLANT. Humea elegans, which see.

INCH WORM. See Pests and Diseases.

INCINERATOR. The destruction of woody and diseased plant refuse is a necessary part of the routine work of a garden, and an incinerator not only enables rubbish to be burned, but serves as a place of storage for the material which can thus be kept dry; if left out of doors exposed to rain it is difficult to make a bonfire with it. Incinerators of various types or sizes can be purchased, or one can be made from a steel drum of the kind used to contain oil.

The top should be taken off and if the interior is then burned out it will make the drum much cleaner to handle. The bottom should be perforated with a number of holes about 1 in. in diameter, not so close together so as to weaken the bottom. A piece must then be cut away at the base. This should be no longer than 6 in. by 4 in.; it will serve as the grating so that ash can be drawn away when the fire has been burning for a considerable time.

If desired, a permanent foundation can be made, but if set on four bricks, to create an undercurrent of air, the purpose will be served. If a strong drum is secured, the incinerator will last for years and give invaluable service.

INCURVED. A term used to distinguish a certain type of Chrysanthemum having blooms made up of symmetrical florets which curve inwards towards the center. See Chrysanthemum.

INDIANA, GARDENING IN. See Regional Gardening.

INDIAN ALMOND. Terminalia Catappa, which see.

INDIAN AZALEA. See Azalea.

INDIAN BEAN TREE. See Catalpa.

INDIAN CUCUMBER ROOT. See Medeola.

INDIAN CUP. Silphium perfoliatum, which see.

INDIAN CURRANT. Symphoricarpos orbiculatus, which see.

INDIAN DATE. Tamarindus indica, which see.

INDIAN LILAC. See Lagerstroemia.

INDIAN MALLOW. Abutilon Avicennae, which see.

INDIAN PAINT BRUSH. See Castilleja.

INDIAN PHYSIC. See Gillenia.

INDIAN PINK. Dianthus chinensis, Silene laciniata and Lobelia cardinalis, which see.

INDIAN SHOT. Canna, which see.

INDIAN TURNIP. Arisaema triphylla, which see.

INDIGO. Indigofera, which see.

INDIGO, BASTARD. Amorpha fruticosa, which see.

INDIGO, FALSE. A name applied to both Amorpha and Baptisia, which see.

INDIGOFERA—*Indigo* (Indigof'era). Herbaceous plants and leaf-losing trees and shrubs, widely distributed in the warm and cool parts of Africa, Asia, America and Australia. A few only are of value for cultivation, those few being shrubs or subshrubs. Some are of importance from a commercial point of view, notably I. tinctoria, I. arrecta and I. sumatrana, for it is these plants that give us the true Indigo dye of commerce, a dye of much greater importance in the past than now, owing to the present great use of aniline in preference to natural dyes. Indigofera belongs to the Pea family, Leguminosae, and the name is taken from *indigo*, a blue dye, and *fero*, to bear, an allusion to the dyeing propensities of some kinds.

Most Indigoferas are not hardy in the North. Hardy ones include I. amblyantha, I. Kirilowii, and I. Potaninii. All give best results when planted in well-drained loamy soil in a sunny position. They can be increased by cuttings of young shoots taken in July and inserted in a cold frame kept close, or, better still, by seeds when they are obtainable. The seeds should be sown in spring in fine soil placed in a cold frame.

The Best Kinds. In many gardens these plants may be cut down to the ground by frost in winter, but they produce annual shoots which flower freely in summer. This is particularly the case with the Himalayan I. Gerardiana, which will grow and form thick, woody branches from which long, slender shoots are produced each year. From these shoots rosy-purple flowers are borne freely from July–September. In the open ground it may grow 4-6 ft. high, or it may die to the ground each year. Even when it is not killed down it is wise, in spring, to cut the shoots back to within a bud or two of the base of the previous year's growth.

I. amblyantha attains a height of about 6 ft., and has pink flowers. I. incarnata is an attractive bush, 1-1½ ft. high, with white, pink-flushed flowers, from China and Japan; its variety alba has white flowers. I. hebepetala, from the Himalayas, grows about 4 ft. high; it bears long racemes of crimson and rose flowers. I. Kirilowii, 4 ft. tall, bears rose-colored flowers. I. Potaninii, from China, grows 3-4 ft. high and has lilac-pink flowers.

INDIGO, WILD. Baptisia, which see.

INFLORESCENCE. A term used to describe

Inflorescences: (left to right)
Panicle, umbel, raceme.

Inflorescences: (left to right)
Cyme, spike, catkin, corymb.

N.H.D.

the flowering parts of a tree, shrub or plant. There are many kinds of inflorescences—e.g., spike, panicle, umbel, corymb, and so on.

INKBERRY. Ilex glabra, which see.

INSECTIVOROUS PLANTS. Plants which are specially adapted for catching insects. The majority are grown as curiosities, although most possess real beauty and flower attractively.

Various methods are adopted by the different kinds for catching insects. The Drosera (Sundew) and Drosophyllum have cylindric, round or oval leaves, sometimes forked, bearing sticky glands to which the insects adhere. The leaves of the Venus's-Flytrap (Dionaea) are in the form of a snap trap which closes on the alighting insects.

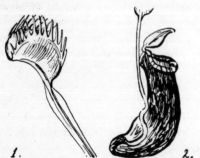

Insectivorous leaves: 1. Venus's Flytrap. 2. A pitcher of a Nepenthes.

The Butterwort (Pinguicula) catches its prey on its sticky leaves and the Nepenthes has large pitchers on the ends of the leaves from which the insects which have entered cannot escape. In Sarracenia (Pitcher Plant) and Darlingtonia (California Pitcher Plant) the leaves also form pitchers in which insects are trapped. The Bladderwort (Utricularia), a submerged water plant, is furnished with minute bladders with trap doors which allow insects to enter but prevent their exit. Once the prey is captured, the plants emit a fluid containing enzymes which decompose their bodies into a suitable form in which they are utilized, by absorption, as plant food. For details, reference should be made to the various plants mentioned.

INSECTICIDES. See Pests and Diseases.

INSECTS. See Pests and Diseases.

INTERCROPPING. The practice of planting and cultivating quick-growing vegetables among others of slower growth for the purpose of cropping the ground to the best possible advantage.

INTERNODE. That part of the stem of a plant which lies between two nodes or joints.

INULA (In'ula). Herbaceous perennial plants of somewhat coarse growth which bear large, yellow, daisy-like flowers in late summer. They are natives of Europe, Africa, and Asia and belong to the Daisy family, Compositae. The name Inula is an old Latin one.

These plants flourish in ordinary garden soil in sun and may be planted in autumn or spring. They vary a good deal in height; some are suitable for the rock garden, others for the herbaceous border or wild garden. They are easily propagated by lifting and separating the clumps into rooted pieces in autumn, or by sowing seeds outdoors or in a cold frame in April. Pieces of root, if set in sandy soil in a cold frame in October, will form new roots.

The Chief Kinds. Inula glandulosa, 18-24 in., which bears large deep-yellow flowers, is the best for the herbaceous border, and I. Hookeri, I. Royleana and I. Oculus-Christi may also be planted there. I. Helenium, which reaches a height of 6-7 ft., is suitable for the wild garden, and I. ensifolia, 9 in., should be planted in the rock garden. All bear yellow flowers in summer.

INVOLUCRE. A collar of one or more rows of small leaves or leaflike organs which stands close beneath a flower or cluster of flowers. Involucres are clearly evident in members of the Daisy family, Compositae, such as Asters, Chrysanthemums and Sunflowers.

INVOLUTE. A botanical term meaning rolled inwards, as a leaf, in such a manner that the underside of the plant part is exposed to view.

IOCHROMA (Iochro'ma). Plants from the warmer parts of South and Central America that belong to the Nightshade family, Solanaceae. They are shrubs and small trees that are suitable for growing outdoors in the warmest parts of the world only and are sometimes grown in warm greenhouses. The name is taken from *ion,* violet, and *chroma,* color, and refers to the flower color of some kinds.

Iochromas thrive in any fairly good soil and require the same culture as Ixora, which see. They are easily propagated by seeds and cuttings. Among kinds likely to be grown are I. coccinea, with scarlet flowers; I. fuchsioides, with flowers of an orange-scarlet hue; I. grandiflora, which has bright purple flowers; I. lanceolata, with flowers that vary in color from blue to purple; and I. tubulosa, which has flowers of a deep blue-purple. All of these are shrubs that grow to a height of about 8 ft.

IONOPSIDIUM ACAULE — *Violet Cress* (Ionopsid'ium). This small annual is a native of Portugal, and is well-suited for climates that are not extremely severe. It is seldom more than 1½-2 in. in height and diameter, forming a neat dome of little green leaves, and bearing a profusion of charming blossoms of pale lilac or white. It belongs to the Mustard family, Cruciferae. The name is derived from *ion,* a Violet, and *opsis,* appearance.

The Violet Cress is one of the daintiest and prettiest hardy annuals available for the rock garden, and is also invaluable for sowing in the crevices of paved paths. The seed may safely be sown at almost any time of year in the place where it is to flower; for so frail-looking and dainty a plant it is surprisingly hardy, withstanding moderately hard weather and often giving a show of flowers during mild days in earliest spring. For this reason it is a good plan to make sowings at intervals in spring and autumn.

In some gardens this beautiful and accommodating little plant will reproduce itself by self-sown seeds, and yet it never becomes a nuisance.

IONOPSIS (Ionop'sis). Small, tufted evergreen epiphytal Orchids from Central America and closely allied to Oncidium. The pseudobulbs are very small and almost hidden by the narrow, rather stiff leaves, which are only 3-6 in. in height. The tall-branching panicles grow from the base of the bulbs and bear numerous flowers with small sepals and petals and comparatively large lips. Ionopsis is derived from *ion,* a Violet, and *opsis,* like, possibly in reference to the color of some species. Ionopsis belongs to the family Orchidaceae.

Hothouse Orchids. These Orchids should be grown in pans suspended near the glass in a warm greenhouse with a moist atmosphere and a minimum temperature of 70 degrees in summer and 60-65 degrees in winter. Water must be given throughout the year, less, of course, in winter than summer. The compost should consist of two parts cut osmunda fiber and two parts sphagnum moss. A second method is to attach the plants to small blocks of wood and suspend them in the greenhouse. Shading is necessary in bright summer weather but should be removed early in autumn. Repotting, when required, should be done in March.

I. paniculata in summer bears beautiful white, rose-flushed flowers, the lip marked with violet-purple; utricularioides, a native of tropical America and Florida, blooms January–July. Its flowers are white to pink, often veined purple. The plant will grow to about 30 in. in height.

IOWA, GARDENING IN. See Regional Gardening.

IPOMOEA: MORNING GLORY
Quick-growing Vines for Handsome Garden Effects

(Ipomoe'a). These are perennial and annual climbing plants with attractive flowers. They are natives of the West Indies, tropical America, North America, Asia, and South Africa and belong to the Convolvulus family, Convolvulaceae. One, I. Batatas, is the Sweet Potato (see Sweet Potato). Most of those grown for their flowers are quick-growing climbers which cling to any available supports with their twining stems. The leaves are ovate, heart-shaped, and the flowers are large and funnel-shaped, white, blue, rose or purple.

The flowers of most kinds open early in the morning and, although they last but a few hours, others are produced in quick succession to keep up the display. The name Ipomoea is derived from *ips,* bindweed, and *homoios,* similar, alluding to the similarity of these plants to the Bindweed (Convolvulus). The nomenclature is much confused.

Management of the Greenhouse Kinds. Those suitable for the greenhouse are grown in large pots or tubs or in a prepared bed of soil in the greenhouse: a minimum winter temperature of 45 degrees is necessary. The potting compost consists of two parts loam, one part peat moss or leaf mold, and one part well-decayed manure with a free scattering of sand. The shoots are trained to wires or a trellis fixed to the wall or roof of the greenhouse. Early in spring the soil is top-dressed with rich compost, and straggling shoots are cut off to prevent overcrowding. From April to September an abundance of water is required, and occasional applications of liquid fertilizer are necessary. During the winter the soil is moistened only when it becomes dry.

The greenhouse perennials can be propagated by sowing seeds in pots of sandy soil in spring, by cuttings inserted in a propagating case in spring, or by layering the shoots in summer.

Annual Morning Glories. Seeds of the annuals are sown out of doors, where the plants are to grow, in ordinary garden soil. The shoots are allowed to twine around wires, strings, trellis or other suitable supports. Quicker results can be obtained by sowing the seeds in small pots, 2 or 3 in each, of sandy soil in a greenhouse, temperature 55 degrees, in March. The seedlings are planted, with their root balls intact, out of doors in May. The seeds germinate more surely if a notch is filed through the skin of each before sowing.

The Chief Kinds. For the greenhouse and for outdoors in the far South: I. Horsfalliae, 10 ft., rose, winter; I. Leari, Blue Dawn Flower, perennial, clear blue, turning red, summer; I. melanotricha, a vigorous kind with purple blooms; I. setosa, with rose-purple flowers. I. Nil, with

This garage is festooned with annual Morning Glories, which provide a brave show of bloom throughout the summer.

The common blue Morning Glory, Ipomoea purpurea, makes a magnificent pot plant for the greenhouse and for growing in the open garden in summer. Seeds are sown in spring and the plants trained up supports.

blue, purple or rose-colored flowers is the progenitor of the Japanese Morning Glories. It may be grown as an annual although it is actually a perennial.

Ipomoea purpurea, the Common Morning Glory, 15 ft., purple, has numerous varieties in pale blue, crimson, purple and rose. I. tricolor (rubro-caerulea), with varieties bearing blue, purple, white and pink flowers, is truly a perennial in its native tropical America but it is easily grown as an annual.

I. pandurata, Wild Sweet Potato Vine, which bears white flowers with purple throats, is a native hardy perennial. I. leptophylla, Bush Morning-Glory, is a hardy native of the drier parts of the central United States and is very attractive. It grows 4 ft. tall and has pink or rosy-purple blooms.

IPSEA (Ip'sea). One species of terrestrial Orchid, family Orchidaceae, from Ceylon. The name is derived from *ips,* a gall fly, from a fancied resemblance.

Ipsea speciosa needs a humid greenhouse with a minimum temperature of 50-55 degrees. A mixture of loam, leaf mold, coarse sand and sphagnum moss is a suitable potting soil.

IRESINE (Iresi'ne; Ir'esine). Tender plants with richly colored leaves which are chiefly used in summer flower beds. The name Iresine is from the Greek *eiros,* wool, and refers to the woolly appearance of the seeds. Between twenty and twenty-five species have been described, but few are cultivated. They are natives of tropical and subtropical America, and belong to the Amaranth family, Amaranthaceae.

When to Take Cuttings. Iresine is easily propagated by cuttings in February–April; the shoots are inserted in sand in a propagating case in a greenhouse, temperature 60 degrees. When rooted, they should be potted separately in 3-in. pots in a compost of loam, two thirds, and leaf mold or peat moss and decayed manure, one third. So rapidly do the young plants grow that cuttings inserted during March and April furnish good-sized plants for the summer beds and borders by the first week in June, when they are planted 6-10 in. apart, according to their size.

Cuttings taken in spring are obtained from plants kept during the winter in a greenhouse, minimum temperature 50 degrees; these plants are from cuttings taken early in August and inserted in a shaded greenhouse or cold frame. The Iresines are tender plants and almost the first to suffer damage from frost, so they must be kept in a greenhouse from October to April. If the plants become so tall as to spoil a flower bed design they may be pinched or even clipped with shears.

Plants with Colored Stems and Leaves. Iresine Herbstii, of southern Brazil, is usually restricted to a height of 12-20 in. by pinching the shoots, but will grow much taller; it has attractive purplish-red stems and leaves. The variety aureo-reticulata has green and red leaves with yellow veins; the variety Wallisii has smaller leaves, bronze-red above and dark red beneath.

I. Lindenii, from Ecuador, has narrow, deep red leaves. As the plants are propagated annually from cuttings and the shoots are pinched, the Iresines seldom produce flowers.

IRIS: FAVORITE GARDEN FLOWERS
The Best Kinds of All Types and How to Grow Them

(I'ris). A large genus of mostly hardy flowering plants most of which have perennial rootstocks or bulbs. Irises grow wild in temperate countries in the Northern Hemisphere. Most which grow from rootstocks have sword-shaped leaves; the bulbous Irises—the English Iris (I. xiphioides) and the Spanish Iris (I. Xiphium)—have narrow leaves. Irises vary in height from dwarf kinds 5-6 in. tall to the tall beardless kinds, 20-48 in. in height. Most Irises bloom in May and June, but in mild climates a representative selection will provide flowers throughout the greater part of the year, commencing with I. unguicularis (stylosa) in January, and concluding with I. alata in late autumn. The Iris belongs to the family Iridaceae. The name is derived from *iris,* the rainbow, and alludes to the beauty and variety of the flowers.

Iris flowers differ in structure from those of most plants. The three outer perianth segments (petals) hang downwards, and are known as the falls; the other three stand erect, and are called standards; in addition, the three styles of the flowers are colored and petal-like in appearance.

Irises are divided into two main sections, those which grow from bulbs and others which have thick rootstocks or rhizomes.

Irises which have thick rhizomes consist of four different types: Tall Bearded, Intermediate Bearded, Dwarf Bearded and Beardless. The Bearded Irises are so called because the outer petals, or falls, have a thick line of fine hairs stretching down the lower half, whereas the falls of the Beardless Irises are hairless.

Bearded Irises. Throughout the length and breadth of the United States there are many gardens where the most important flower is the Bearded Iris. The possible combinations of varieties are endless. For strong garden effect the light colors count more than the dark, which tend to melt into the background and disappear. Too many colors and varieties are often less effective than a few well-chosen ones planted in clumps. A great variety of effect may be had by using different heights and sizes. These Irises can be combined with many plants. The Dwarfs bloom with spring bulbs and rock plants. Some combine well with Daffodils and Hyacinths. The Intermediates come at the same time as Tulips and many of the flowering shrubs, and the Tall Bearded come into bloom when perennials are at their height. Columbines, Lupines, early-flowering shrubs, Oriental Poppies, Sweet William and Anchusa are but a few of those which can

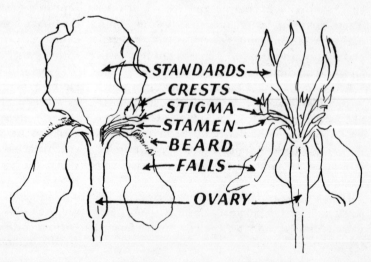

STANDARDS
CRESTS
STIGMA
STAMEN
BEARD
FALLS
OVARY

Parts of the flower of a Bearded Iris (*left*) and a Beardless Iris (*right*).

Tall Bearded Irises make a colorful garden display in late May and June.

make wonderful combinations with Irises.

Bearded Irises have surface rhizomes and broad sword-shaped, evergreen leaves, from 6 to 18 in. in length; the flowers, which appear in May and June, are of varying size, and of various colors. Owing to their gorgeous coloring and their easy cultivation, the Bearded Irises are sometimes called Poor Man's Orchids. The majority are extremely hardy, and will grow in ordinary soil, but good cultivation is necessary to produce the best results. A sunny, well-drained position suits them best, but they will grow and flower in semishade.

Details of Cultivation. The soil should be dug deeply, and a little well-decayed manure worked into the subsoil, and ground limestone and bone meal or lime forked into the top soil. The best time for planting is from July to September, but it may be done even as late as March, although the flowers will be inferior in the first year.

How to Plant. The rhizomes are planted flat and only half-covered. They must not be deeply buried as it is necessary for them to be sun-baked to produce the maximum number of flowers. They are set 6-8 in. apart with the tips of the rhizomes pointing towards the outside of the clumps; if the soil is dry, it must be thoroughly moistened. No further cultivation is required except that an annual top-dressing of leaf mold or well-decayed compost can with advantage be ap-

plied annually in autumn, and lime should be put on the ground every three years. As soon as the flowers have faded the flower stems should be cut off and each fall, after frost, all dead foliage should be cut or pulled off and burned.

When the flowers deteriorate in size and number the plants should be lifted, divided and replanted, preferably on a fresh site or, if they are to occupy the same position, the ground treated

Iris foliage, except that which is green, is cleaned off in the fall and burned.

as recommended for the initial planting. The rhizomes are lifted with a fork, and only the vigorous outside portions selected for replanting. Each piece should have a shoot attached to a few inches of rhizome, and be planted as advised above.

Tall Bearded Irises. The Tall Bearded Irises bloom toward the end of May. They are the most important of all garden Irises. They range in height from 18 to 42 in., sometimes even taller, and have indescribable beauty and range of color. There is much difference in the branching of the stems, some of which may hold ten or more flowers. There is variation, too, in the size, form and texture of the flowers. Terms have been coined to describe the combinations of color. Selfs are of one color throughout; bitones are two shades of one color; bicolors are those of which the standards and falls are of different colors; plicatas are those with feathered markings on the edge of a white or colored ground. The terms blends, veined and shot shades describe themselves. The beards are usually white, tipped with yellow or orange, but in the infinite number of new hybrids there are some with pinkish or bronze beards and others with coral or tangerine tones. The beauty of color combination, of size and form, the time of blooming, the strength of the stem and the hardiness are all matters for consideration. Lists of Bearded Irises are constantly being changed and improved

and yet there remain certain old and proved varieties which are as beautiful if not as rare as the newest introductions. The Bearded Irises of today are the results of many crosses and have a mixed ancestry. Generally speaking, they are hardy if given good drainage and sunshine, but a few of the fine varieties raised in California do not do well in the East.

Consult the catalogues of dealers and specialists for the best varieties.

Intermediate Bearded Irises. A little while after the Dwarf Bearded Irises comes Iris germanica, or Purple Flag, which is seen in so many old gardens. It is about two and one-half feet high, a strong blue-purple, and although the flower is coarsely shaped, it is so well known that many people have a real affection for it. The pale silver-gray Florentina, which comes into bloom a day or so later, is slightly taller, more delicate and much lovelier. The Intermediate Bearded varieties come into bloom at the same time. They are about 12 to 18 in. in height, have a wide range of color and considerable difference in form. For the best and newest available varieties see the catalogues of dealers.

Listed among the Intermediate varieties are some that have a tendency to flower also in September and October and for that reason have been called "fall-blooming" or "autumn-blooming." This term is a little optimistic, for such flowers are not always produced in all climates.

(Left) Iris Wilsonii. (right) Iris Forrestii. Both are natives of China.

Varieties of the dwarf Iris pumila are very satisfactory for planting in rock gardens.

Dwarf Bearded Irises. The earliest Bearded Irises to bloom are the Dwarfs, which, near New York, come into bloom toward the end of April. They range in height from 3 in. to 12 in., and are to be had in white, blue, lavender, purple and yellow.

These plants are valuable for rock gardens and very effective in good-sized clumps in a hardy border. The individual flowers are too small to show unless a considerable number are grouped together. The Dwarf Irises need watching until they are well established to prevent them from being smothered by stronger plants. The best time to transplant is just after they have bloomed. The following are among the best Dwarf Bearded Irises: I. aphylla, 12 in., violet-purple; I. pumila, 10 in., violet-purple; and I. Chamaeiris, 5 in., violet. There are also many varieties in this section and these will be found listed and described in dealers' catalogues.

Beardless Irises. The Beardless Irises are fibrous-rooted, moisture-loving, with narrow, grasslike green leaves. From the gardener's standpoint they are not so important as the Bearded Irises yet they are very valuable both in mixed borders and for naturalizing. Many will grow in apparently dry situations if they have abundant moisture in spring.

In early June come the Siberian Irises. The flat, open flowers are held on tall slender stems and are so prolific that each good-sized clump makes a strong effect. These Irises come in white and various shades of blue and range in height from two to four feet. They do well naturalized near streams or in open meadows, but will grow under ordinary garden conditions. They should be planted in spring and divided when the clumps become too big. The outstanding varieties are: "Snow Queen," "Perry's Blue," "Skylark," "Emperor," "Caesar." Siberian Irises can be grown easily from seed. The Siberian Irises include I. siberica, I. orientalis and varieties and hybrids of these.

In July come the magnificent Japanese Irises (I. Kæmpferi varieties). These have been grown for centuries in Japan and are the results of careful hybridizing. These Irises have very large, gorgeous flowers of white, lavender, deep purple, blue, lavender-pink and every shade between. Japanese Irises like a rich soil that is moist in summer but is not saturated during the winter. Japanese Irises are offered in many named varieties, but there is confusion about them. The best plan is to buy them by sight or grow them from seed, which should be planted as soon as it is ripe.

Two Beardless Irises that grow and bloom along streams or in bogs are I. Pseudacorus, the Yellow Flag of Europe and of Asia, and I.

Siberian Irises planted beside a stream.

versicolor, the blue-purple Iris that grows wild from New Brunswick to Georgia. There is also a cream-yellow form of Pseudacorus, often called white, that is very beautiful. These will also grow in well-drained soils. I. Pseudacorus is naturalized in most of the eastern sections of North America.

Iris spuria varieties are like the Siberians, but far more delicate. They have a wider range of color, but have never been so popular in gardens.

They like rich soil, should be planted in spring and are easily grown from seed. Closely related to I. spuria is ochroleuca, with white and yellow flowers.

The European I. graminea, about 1½ feet high, is not remarkable for its lilac-colored flower, but is worth growing for its fragrance.

Louisiana Iris. A complex of Beardless Irises has become prominent recently under the group name of Louisiana Iris. They represent species,

The flowers of Japanese Irises are broad and flat. The flowers are produced in July by plants that thrive best in moist soil.

and hybrids of these species, both natural and artificial. The species and natural hybrids occur in bogs in Louisiana.

These Irises exhibit an extraordinary color range and succeed under a wide variety of conditions. They thrive much further north than their native range, but, although they live as far north as New York, they do not usually really thrive there. For their best development they

Iris Pseudacorus is a beardless kind that thrives in wet soils.

need soil rich in humus and plenty of water during their spring to fall growing season; drier conditions during the winter seem to be important in the North although in the deep South they persist in wet places. Light shade is advantageous in the South; in the North they grow best in full sunshine.

Many fine named hybrids have been listed, and both they and the species of Louisiana Iris have proved valuable because of their adapta-

bility for gardens in warm climates. Further developments in this group will undoubtedly occur.

I. foliosa and I. fulva are two other species native to the southern United States. The first has blue-lavender flowers that are carried on low stems. The second is a most unusual color, a bright terra cotta. Some of the hybrids made by crossing these two are outstanding plants, the best-known being the beautiful and distinctive "Dorothy K. Williamson," a rich purple borne on angular stems. It blooms late in the month of June.

Other Beardless Irises include I. Bulleyana, 1½ ft., blue-purple and cream; I. Douglasiana, 1½ ft., white to lilac-purple; I. Forrestii, 1½ ft., yellow veined brown-purple; I. innominata, 2½ ft., golden buff veined brown-purple; I. prismatica, 3 ft., blue-violet veined yellow; I. Purdyi, 1 ft., cream veined purple and yellow; I. Wilsonii, 2 ft., with pale yellow veined purple and brown flowers.

I. unguicularis is an Algerian Beardless species that blooms in January or February. It is not hardy north of Washington, D. C., but in the South it is well worth growing. It is about 2 ft. high, and bears fragrant flowers of white or lilac.

Bulbous Irises. Except in a few places on the Pacific Coast, most of these do not flourish in gardens. There are English, Dutch and Spanish types, the names coming from the countries where they were hybridized. They are grown largely by florists and are often very beautiful. In most Eastern gardens, even where apparently hardy, they tend to disappear after a few years of growth. There are, however, a few Bulbous Irises that do grow and increase readily in the East. One of these is the very dwarf I. reticulata, which is deep purple with orange veins. It is very fragrant. It blooms in earliest April and is a delightful plant.

Spanish, English and Dutch Irises. The most popular kinds of bulbous Iris are the Spanish Iris (I. Xiphium); the Dutch Iris, a large-flowered, early hybrid strain; and the English Iris (I. xiphioides). The bulbs are planted in October in groups in the border. Ordinary well-tilled garden soil is suitable, but very heavy or light

Spanish Irises are effective when planted in groups. They grow from bulbs and do not produce much foliage. They are excellent for cutting.

sandy soils are improved by digging in compost or other decayed organic material. The bulbs of Spanish and Dutch Irises are placed 6 in. apart, and 2-3 in. deep; those of the English Iris should be set 3-4 in. deep and 5-6 in. apart. They are best left undisturbed until they show signs of deterioration when they are lifted after the leaves have died down and replanted in freshly prepared soil. (Recommended kinds are mentioned later.)

Bulbous Irises in Pots. The Dutch Irises are excellent plants for growing in pots, flats, or benches in the greenhouse to provide bloom for cutting in winter and early spring. The bulbs are potted in October in a compost of two parts of loam and one part of leaf mold, with sand freely added. Five bulbs are set in a 5-in. pot, the tips just below the surface of the soil. The pots are placed in a frostproof frame until the New Year, when they are removed to a greenhouse, temperature 50 degrees, to make top growth and flower.

Miniature Bulbous Irises. Suitable for the rock garden are: I. Histrio, 6 in., blue and yellow; I. histrioides, blue, 6 in.; I. Danfordiae, yellow; I. persica, 4 in., purple, yellow and green; and I. reticulata, 8 in., purple and orange and its varieties Cantab, Krelagei, etc. Plant them 4 in. apart and 3 in. deep in October, and place a

Dutch Irises are bulbous varieties and are suitable for forcing into early bloom in cool greenhouses.

Iris histrioides, with pale blue, orange-crested flowers, is one of the daintiest of the early-flowering dwarf bulbous Irises. It is suitable for growing in rock gardens and cool greenhouses.

little sand in the bottom of each hole before setting them in position. Dwarf carpeting plants are planted between them and they are not disturbed more often than once in every 3 or 4 years. These Irises are admirable plants for cultivation in pots in a very cool greenhouse.

Kinds of Bulbous Irises. I. xiphioides (English Iris), 18 in., various colors; good varieties are Mont Blanc, white; Queen of the Blues, sky blue; Mauve Queen, rosy-mauve; and La Nuit, ruby-purple.

I. Xiphium (Spanish Iris), 2 ft. The many varieties are useful for cutting and may also be potted in the autumn for greenhouse decoration in the spring. A few of the best are British Queen, white; Sappho, bronze; and Thunderbolt, purple.

In recent years the Dutch Irises have largely superseded the English and Spanish for both greenhouse and garden cultivation. Good varieties include Golden Emperor, the best yellow; Imperator, lavender-purple; Rembrandt, purple-blue; Wedgwood, pale wedgwood-blue; and White Excelsior.

I. alata, blue, 6 in., January (best grown in pots in an unheated greenhouse); I. Histrio, 12 in., porcelain blue, yellow and white, early spring; I. reticulata, 8 in., violet-purple, fragrant, early spring, and varieties Cantab, Cambridge blue, and Krelagei, red-purple; and I. tingitana, 2 ft., blue and yellow, March.

Others are I. histrioides, 8 in., blue; I. buchar-

ica, 12 in., white marked with yellow, spring; I. sindjarensis, 12 in., blue and yellow, spring; and I. Sisyrinchium, 6 in., lavender or purplish-blue, marked with yellow, early summer. I. orchioides, which reaches a height of 18 in., bears handsome yellow flowers, with purplish markings, in spring.

Miscellaneous Irises. Into this group can be put the rarities of some groups and some that do not fit into any other groups. Chief among these are the strange Oncocyclus. These have large flowers usually borne one on a stalk, and appear somewhat top-heavy. They grow from rhizomes, have peculiar veined markings, sometimes almost black. They thrive only in mild climates, but are most important for the part they have played in hybridizing.

The Regelia Iris, closely allied, has crimped and waved petals.

These Irises are rather difficult to grow and require careful treatment. They do best in a sunny, sheltered spot and light, rich soil. During the winter they must be covered with a hand light or frame, to keep off heavy rain. Replanting is not needed each year, but when this becomes necessary the bulbs are lifted when the foliage has died and are stored in sand until planting time.

In this miscellaneous group also may be included the Crested Irises. These are rather dwarf species. I. cristata of the southern United States is but a few inches high. It has blue flowers and a bright yellow crest on each of the lower petals. There is also a rare white form. A related and

The native American Iris cristata.

Iris tectorum, the Japanese Roof Iris, has flowers of clear pale blue, with white crests, on stems 12—18 in. tall.

larger species is I. tectorum, the Roof Iris of Japan, which is blue and also has a white form. It sometimes dies out in Northern gardens but is easily raised from seed. I. cristata thrives in partial shade.

Old clumps of Bearded Iris are dug up and pulled apart immediately after they have flowered.

For propagation purposes the rhizomes are cut into pieces, each having a single fan of leaves.

Propagation of Iris. The rhizomatous Irises are increased by lifting and dividing the clumps, preferably from July–September. Only the strong outside pieces are selected. This method of propagation is necessary to obtain named varieties true to type, but many of the species or wild types can be raised from seeds. The bulbous Irises are increased by removing the offsets during the dormant season and planting them in a nursery bed, or in dealing with the tender sorts, in a cold frame.

The leaves are cut back to a length of 6 to 8 in. and the divisions are planted with the rhizomes barely covered or just showing above the ground surface.

Sowing Seeds. Seeds are sown as soon as they are ripe, in sandy soil, in a cold frame. The seedlings are pricked off and, later are planted in the open ground. The seeds often germinate very irregularly, so that the seed pans should be kept for at least 18 months before being discarded. Most species do not produce flowers until at least 2 years after seed sowing.

IRIS, BLACK. See Ferraria.

IRISH BELLS. A name sometimes applied to Molucella laevis, which see.

IRISH HEATH. See Daboecia.

IRISH IVY. See Hedera.

IRISH JUNIPER. Juniperus, which see.

IRISH YEW. See Taxus.

IRIS, SNAKE'S-HEAD. Hermodactylus, which see.

IRONBARK. Eucalyptus sideroxylon.

IRON CHELATE. Chlorosis, yellowing of foliage caused by an insufficiency of chlorophyll,

[6—2]
Spanish Iris

[6—2a]
Japanese Iris

[6—2b]
Impatiens Sultanii hybrid

[6—2c]
Ixora macrothyrsa

[6—3]
Pfitzer's Juniper
(Juniperus chinensis Pfitzeriana)

[6—3a]
Juniper
(Juniperus communis variety)

is often brought about because plants are unable to absorb sufficient iron for their needs. This may be because the soil is lacking in this element or because the iron present is in a form unavailable to plants.

Iron chelates (marketed under various trade names) have proved exceedingly effective in correcting chlorosis due to iron deficiency, especially if the soil is somewhat acid. They may be applied directly to the soil or as sprays to foliage. The favorable results they bring are quickly observable. These materials should be used strictly according to the manufacturers' directions; if applied in too strong a solution they cause burning of the foliage.

It must be remembered that not all yellowing of foliage is caused by iron deficiency. This result may also be brought about by poor soil drainage, cold, exposure to too strong sunshine, lack of nutrients, and other circumstances.

IRON TREE. Metrosideros, which see.

IRONWEED. Vernonia, which see.

IRONWOOD. Ostrya virginiana, which see.

ISATIS—Woad (Is'atis; Isa'tis). Annual, biennial and perennial plants widely distributed in Europe and temperate Asia, of no great garden value, although the common Woad, Isatis tinctoria, is showy when in bloom, and I. glauca is sometimes planted. The flowers are yellow and produced freely in erect panicles, sometimes 2 ft. long and 7-12 in. through; unfortunately they are very fugitive and are only at their best for ten days or two weeks in late spring. Seeds are sown out of doors in a nursery border in April to yield plants that will bloom the following year; the plants are set 12-18 in. apart.

Woad is the blue dye, obtained from Isatis tinctoria, with which the ancient Britons used to dye their bodies.

Isatis belongs to the Mustard family, Cruciferae, and the name is said to be the ancient Greek for woad.

ISLANDS CHERRY. See Prunus Lyonii.

ISMENE. See Hymenocallis.

ISOCHILUS (Isoch'ilus). Summer-flowering evergreen epiphytic Orchids with slender stems, 12-18 in. high, clothed with narrow alternate leaves. The spikes are terminal and bear numerous small flowers which are usually rose or red.

They grow wild from the West Indies to Brazil. The name is from isos, equal, and cheilos, a lip, and refers to the fact that the lip is approximately equal in size to the sepals and petals.

These Orchids must be grown in a greenhouse with a minimum temperature of 60 degrees in winter. Little water should be given in winter, but during summer the compost must be kept moist. A compost of three parts cut osmunda fiber and two parts sphagnum moss is used; the plants should be repotted about March, when new growths are seen. Large plants should be divided into two or three pieces at that time for they are apt to decay in the centers.

The chief kind is I. linearis, 6-18 in. tall, with deep rose-purple flowers in spring and summer. I. variety major, from Mexico, has taller stems and flowers of similar coloring.

ISOLEPIS GRACILIS. Scirpus cernuus, which see.

ISOLOMA (Isolo'ma). Greenhouse flowering plants from the West Indies and South America which belong to the family Gesneriaceae; they are closely related to Gesneria (Smithiantha and Corytholoma) and Achimenes. Isolomas grow about 1-3 ft. in height, have annual flowering stems, and ovate leaves 1 in. in diameter; the leaves and stems are covered with fine silky hairs.

Isoloma erianthum is a hairy-leaved plant with orange-scarlet flowers. It is suitable for growing in a warm greenhouse.

The flowers, which are produced in the axils of the leaves in summer, are an inch in length, tubular, spreading at the top; they are red, yellow, rose or white, spotted or banded with contrasting colors. Isoloma is derived from *isos*, equal, and *loma*, an edge, and refers to the petals. By some botanists these plants are named Kohleria.

Beautiful Flowering Plants. These plants require a minimum winter temperature of 55 degrees and are potted in a compost of equal parts of light loam and leaf mold or peat moss, with a sprinkling of crushed charcoal and sand.

The rhizomes or roots are laid in a shallow box on a layer of leaf mold or peat moss in February. A little finely sifted compost is sprinkled between them and they are set in a warm greenhouse until the shoots are 1 in. in length. They are then placed in pots, three plants in a 5-in. pot or five plants in a 7-in. pot.

The rhizomes are buried an inch deep and the compost is pressed firmly around them. Water is given very moderately until the pots are well filled with roots; then the soil is kept moist and liquid fertilizer applied once a week.

Summer and Winter Management. Shade must be provided from bright sunlight and the atmosphere kept moist by damping the floor and benches but the foliage ought not to be wet. When the plants are in bloom, less heat and more fresh air are required to prolong the flowering. After the flowers have faded the water supply is gradually reduced; when the leaves have died down, the pots containing the rhizomes are stored under the greenhouse benches during the winter. Propagation is by separating the rhizomes in spring and by seeds.

The principal kinds are I. amabile, dark rose, heavily blotched; I. bogotense, red and yellow; I. erianthum (often misnamed hirsutum), orange-scarlet; I. elegans, purple and yellow; I. triflorum, yellow; and I. digitaliflorum, red or orange-red. These and other species have given rise to the many hybrids now cultivated. All bloom in summer. These plants are sometimes known as Tydaea in gardens.

ISOPLEXIS (Isoplex'is). Tender subshrubs, natives of the Canary Islands, that may be grown in the open in California and other mild climates. They belong to the Figwort family, Scrophulariaceae. The name is derived from *isos*, equal, and *pleko*, to plait, and refers to the equal lengths of certain parts of the corolla.

The culture of Isoplexis presents no particular difficulties. They thrive in any freely drained soil and in full sun and are easily propagated by means of seeds and by cuttings. The kinds most likely to be grown are I. canariensis, a plant of stiff habit that grows to a height of about 4 ft. and flowers in late spring or early summer, and I. Sceptrum, which is similar but larger in all its parts. Both are evergreen and both have orange-yellow flowers more or less netted with tawny veins.

ISOPYRUM THALICTROIDES (Isopy'rum). A hardy dwarf perennial with finely divided leaves and terminal clusters of small, white, anemone-like flowers in April or May. It belongs to the Buttercup family, Ranunculaceae, and is native to Europe. It grows 12 in. in height, and is suitable for planting in the rock garden, near the edge of the herbaceous border, or in the wild garden. It will thrive in ordinary garden soil in a sunny or semishaded position. Planting is done in fall, and propagation is by division of the rootstock at planting time. Plants can also be raised from seed in a cold frame in April.

The name Isopyrum is derived from *isos*, equal, and *pyros*, wheat, because the seeds resemble wheat.

ITALIAN CYPRESS. See Cupressus sempervirens.

ITEA (I'tea; Ite'a). Leaf-losing and evergreen shrubs. One kind, I. virginiana (Virginia Willow, Sweet Spire), is a shrub 3-5 ft. high; a native of the eastern United States, it bears fragrant, creamy-white flowers in dense, racemes in June–July and Handsomely colored foliage in fall. It thrives in well-drained loamy soil, in a sunny position, and may be rather severely pruned in spring, taking care to remove as much as possible of the weaker growth and worn-out wood, leaving vigorous young shoots untouched. Cuttings of short shoots taken in July can be rooted in a close frame, and it can also be propagated by division of its roots. It is hardy as far north as Boston, Massachusetts.

One Kind Rather Tender. I. ilicifolia, the

The Virginia Willow or Sweet Spire, a native of the eastern United States, has drooping racemes of creamy white flowers in early summer.

second kind of Itea, is an evergreen shrub growing 15-18 ft. high in western China, its native country; in mild climates in the United States it grows 8-12 ft. high. It is not hardy in the North. The dark-green, holly-like leaves are ovate in shape, 2-4 in. long, and 1½-2½ in. wide, the margin armed with spiny teeth. The small, greenish-white flowers are in slender pendulous catkins up to 12 in. long, the flowers appearing in July and August. It does not respond so well to drastic pruning as does I. virginiana. Cuttings may be rooted in the same way as those of the latter. I. ilicifolia should be given well-drained, loamy soil.

Itea belongs to the Saxifrage family, Saxifragaceae, and the name is the old Greek name for the Willow.

IVY. Hedera, which see.

IVY ARUM. Scindapsus, which see.

IVY, BOSTON. Parthenocissus tricuspidata, which see.

IVY, ENGLISH. See Hedera.

IVY, GERMAN. Senecio mikanioides, which see.

IVY, GRAPE. Cissus rhombifolia, which see.

IVY, GROUND. Nepeta hederacea, which see.

IVY, JAPANESE. See Parthenocissus.

IVY, KENILWORTH. Cymbalaria muralis, which see.

IVY-LEAVED PELARGONIUM. See Pelargonium.

IVY-LEAVED TOADFLAX. See Cymbalaria.

IVY, POISON. Rhus radicans, which see. Also see Poison Ivy.

IXIA—*Corn Lily* (Ix'ia). Bulbous (really cormous) plants from South Africa, belonging to the Iris family, Iridaceae. They are suitable for growing in pots to decorate the greenhouse in spring and for planting outdoors in favorable localities. The flowers are star-shaped, about 1 in. in diameter, and are borne on slender spikes 12 in. or more in height. The plants grow from corms and have narrow, grasslike foliage. The name Ixia means birdlime; it refers to the sticky juice of some of the species.

When to Pot the Corms. The corms should be potted in September–October in loamy soil with which a little well-decayed manure and coarse sand have been mixed. Five are placed in a 5-in.

The Ixias or Corn Lilies are bulbous plants for the greenhouse and, in mild climates, for the out-of-doors.

pot and covered with compost so that their tops are 1 in. below the surface. The pots are then put in a cold frame and covered with moss or similar material until the shoots appear above the surface of the soil; then they are removed to a greenhouse having a minimum temperature of 40 degrees.

Water must be carefully applied at first, but when the plants are growing freely the soil must be kept moist. When the flowers are over and the leaves begin to change color, less water is given; when the foliage has died, the soil is kept dry until the corms are repotted in the autumn.

Planting Out of Doors. In mild districts Ixias may be grown out of doors, and even as far north as New York City they may succeed in a sheltered, sunny place if well protected with leaves or salt hay over winter. The corms are planted in September–October in light, well-drained soil; they are set 3 in. deep and 3 in. apart. They are lifted and replanted when the leaves have died if the flowers deteriorate in size and quantity.

Propagation. The offsets or small corms which form around the old ones are removed at potting or planting time in the autumn and grown in boxes of soil in the way already described, until they reach flowering size.

The chief kinds are I. viridiflora, 18 in., green and black; I. maculata, orange, spotted with black; and I. paniculata, 18 in., yellow and white. Numerous varieties of rich and showy coloring are described in bulb catalogues.

IXIOLIRION (Ixiolir'ion). Bulbous plants, from Syria, which belong to the Amaryllis family, Amaryllidaceae. They grow 12 in. in height, and produce a tuft of narrow, grasslike leaves. The light blue flowers, which are 1½ in. in length, are produced in clusters of about four on the ends of slender stems 12 in. in length, in June. The name Ixiolirion means the ixia-like Lily.

When to Plant the Bulbs. The bulbs should be planted 3 in. deep and 3 in. apart in fall. They require light, well-drained soil and a sunny sheltered position. In the North they need a winter covering of salt hay or leaves.

Propagation is by offsets or small bulbs which are found around the old bulb.

The principal kind is I. montanum, 12 in., light blue, June.

IXORA—*West Indian Jasmine* (Ixo'ra). Evergreen flowering shrubs which are natives of tropical regions and belong to the family Rubiaceae. They are suitable for outdoor cultivation in the far South. They form bushy shrubs, 3-4 ft. in height, have oval, ovate or oblong leaves 3-6 in. in length, and bear large, terminal clusters of small, white, rose or scarlet flowers in summer. These plants are very ornamental both in flower and foliage. Ixora is named after Isvara, a Malabar deity, to which the flowers were offered.

Ixoras bloom profusely and are very decorative when grown in pots in a warm, moist greenhouse.

Flowering Shrubs for a Hothouse. These shrubs are splendid plants for the greenhouse. They require a minimum winter temperature of 55 degrees. A suitable soil consists of two parts loam, one part peat moss or leaf mold and a sprinkling of crushed charcoal and coarse sand. Repotting is done in March and good drainage is necessary. The plants are pruned into shape in February and frequently sprayed with water until new shoots form; then they are removed from the pots, a little of the old soil is pricked off with a pointed stick, and they are set in slightly larger pots.

Water is applied carefully to the soil until the plants are well rooted in the new compost; then it is given more freely, and liquid manure is applied once a week when flower buds are forming. From September to March the soil is moistened only when it is very nearly dry. In summer the atmosphere is kept moist by damping the floor and benches, and the foliage is frequently syringed, but in winter less damping and syringing are required. Shade from bright sunlight is necessary.

Ixoras are liable to attacks by thrips and mealy bugs, so that it is necessary to sponge or spray the leaves frequently with insecticide to prevent damage by these pests.

Propagation is by inserting cuttings of young shoots in sandy peat in April in a propagating case in a warm greenhouse. The rooted cuttings are potted separately in 3-in. pots and later in larger ones. The tips of the main shoots and the subsequent side branches must be pinched to ensure bushy plants.

The principal kinds are I. acuminata, white; I. coccinea, scarlet, and its variety Fraseri, salmon, tinged with carmine; I. chinensis, light orange, and its variety Prince of Orange, cinnabar-red; I. macrothyrsa, red; and I. lutea, buff-yellow.

J

JABOROSA INTEGRIFOLIA (Jaboro'sa). This low-growing perennial, a native of South America, is in the Nightshade family, Solanaceae. The name is derived from the Arabic *Jabarose*, the Mandrake.

This plant is suitable for mild climates. It needs well-drained, sandy, loamy soil and should be planted in a sheltered, yet sunny, place in March. It bears white flowers in summer, one flower on each stem. Propagation is by lifting and separating the plants into rooted pieces in September or March; or cuttings may be inserted, in July, in pots of sandy soil, in a frame kept closed. If seeds are available, they should be sown in April in a box of light soil in a cold frame.

JACARANDA ACUTIFOLIA (Jacaran'da). An evergreen tree from South America, with ornamental, pinnate leaves and blue flowers in summer; it is suitable chiefly for cultivation out of doors in subtropical regions and, in its young stages, as a pot plant. It belongs to the Bignonia family, Bignoniaceae.

Culture Indoors and Outdoors. In California and Florida this tree is much planted as an ornamental. Even though cut back by frost, it quickly repairs itself after the damaged wood is pruned out, and so it may be grown as a specimen shrub even where it will not attain large tree-size. It thrives in a variety of soils. When cultivated indoors, this tree should be grown in large pots or tubs or planted in a border of prepared soil in the hothouse. The best soil compost consists of peat and loam in equal quantities with a free scattering of sand. During the spring and early summer the atmosphere must be kept warm and moist until growth is complete; no ventilation is needed until the thermometer reaches 70 degrees.

During summer this tree, if grown in pots or tubs, may be placed out of doors to assure that the shoots are well ripened; if it is planted in a border the greenhouse should be ventilated freely in summer. Although it will reach a height of many feet, small specimens grown in 9-in. or 10-in. pots are of decorative value. Little pruning is needed, but the branches may be cut back in March to such an extent as is necessary to keep the trees shapely.

Propagation is by seeds or else by cuttings inserted in a propagating case in July.

JACK FRUIT. Artocarpus integra, which see.

JACK-IN-THE-PULPIT. Arisaema triphyllum, which see.

JACOBEAN LILY. See Sprekelia.

JACOBINIA (Jacobin'ia). Handsome flowering plants for the warm greenhouse and for planting outdoors in frost-free climates; they are natives of South America and belong to the Acanthus family, Acanthaceae.

These plants, some of which bloom in winter, others in summer, are not difficult to manage in a greenhouse in which a minimum winter temperature of 60 degrees can be maintained. During the early summer months they need a warm moist atmosphere, but in July and August more airy conditions suit them best. The plants are repotted in March in a compost of loam, two thirds, and peat moss, one third, with a free addition of sand. It is not necessary to repot the plants every year; if repotting is not done some of the old soil should be removed and replaced with fresh compost. During the summer the soil must be kept always moist but in winter, when the soil naturally dries less quickly, it should not be moistened until it is moderately dry.

Taking Cuttings. Young plants yield the best results, so cuttings should be inserted every year or in alternate years. If these are inserted in

Jacobinia obtusior is an attractive flowering plant for growing in a warm, moist greenhouse. Its flowers are pink.

sand in a propagating case in a greenhouse in July they will form roots; when well-rooted they must be potted separately in small pots, and subsequently into those 5 in. or 6 in. wide, in which they will bloom. If the old plants are grown on from year to year they should be pruned when the flowers have faded to force the development of fresh shoots which will bear next season's blooms.

The showiest kind is Jacobinia chrysostephana, which bears heads or clusters of yellow blooms in winter. J. Ghiesbreghtiana bears red flowers in winter.

The best summer-flowering kinds are J. carnea, J. obtusior and J. velutina. All have heads of pink flowers.

Several of the plants previously grown as Jacobinias are now classed by botanists as Justicia.

JACOB'S-LADDER. Polemonium caeruleum, which see.

JACOB'S-ROD. See Asphodeline.

JACOB'S-STAFF. Fouquieria splendens, which see.

JAMAICA SORREL. See Roselle and Hibiscus Sabdariffa.

JAMESIA AMERICANA (Jame'sia). A hardy leaf-losing shrub 5-7 ft. high, of rather erect and stiff growth, with opposite, gray-green leaves of

Jacobinia chrysostephana bears showy clusters of yellow flowers and is a good winter-blooming plant for the warm greenhouse.

varying size, and white flowers produced in terminal clusters in May. It is a native of western North America, originally discovered in 1820 by Dr. Edwin James, in whose honor it was named. Jamesia belongs to the Saxifrage family, Saxifragaceae.

This shrub requires an open sunny position in well-drained, loamy soil. Cuttings, 4 in. long, taken in July and inserted in coarse sand in a propagating case in frame or greenhouse, form roots in a few weeks' time.

JANKAEA HELDREICHII (Jan'kaea). This rock garden plant belongs to the family Gesneriaceae. It is rare, both in nature and in cultivation, being found only in Thessaly, and there only on a few cliffs and, like its relation Ramonda, in certain exposures only. It is a very beautiful rock plant, exacting in its requirements out of doors, though not at all difficult to grow in a pan in a cool greenhouse where summers are not excessively hot. By some botanists this plant is named Ramonda Heldreichii.

This hardy perennial is in general aspect very like Ramonda; it forms rosettes of ovate leaves, which, however, are thickly coated with a dense, silvery-white, silky down. These rosettes throw off side growths so that a plant eventually will consist of a mass of rosettes. The flowers, borne several on a stem 4-5 in. high in June–July, resemble those of Ramonda, though they are smaller and of shallow, bell-shaped form. They are a delicate lavender color, of an exquisite crystalline, waxlike texture.

For a Shady Crevice in the Rock Garden. Jankaea is a cliff dweller, and is found on limestone formations. It should be planted in a cool, northerly rock crevice, where the roots will be moist during summer, but where the plant is protected from excessive wet about the crown and the silky hairs in winter. The soil should consist of fibrous loam, peat or leaf soil, and sand.

For an Unheated Greenhouse. In the alpine house Jankaea should be planted between stones in a flower pan in the soil compost recommended. The plants should be kept moderately dry, but never parched, during the winter months, and watering should then be done with care. During summer, the growing period, watering may be much more liberal, and even overhead watering at that season is beneficial. The danger of water reaching the leaves has been greatly exaggerated by writers who have had little or no actual experience with Jankaea, with the result that the plant has often been lost through being kept too dry.

Propagation. It may be propagated by seeds sown in spring and carefully shaded—a slow business—by careful division of the rosettes in spring, or by leaf cuttings, i.e., mature leaves pulled off with a heel and inserted in sand in spring, but not in heat.

JAPANESE ANEMONE. See Anemone japonica.

JAPANESE ANGELICA TREE. See Aralia.

JAPANESE CEDAR. Cryptomeria japonica, which see.

JAPANESE DWARF TREES. These are trees that have been systematically dwarfed by being deprived of food material, and by restricting the roots. Trees which are naturally of the largest size are kept to a height of a few inches and those 100 years old may not exceed 2 ft. in height.

The art of growing dwarfed potted trees originated in Japan and has long been popular there.

Jankaea Heldreichii is a charming rock plant for a shady crevice, but is choice enough to deserve cultivation in pots in the alpine house or cool greenhouse. It is related to Ramondia and produces sprays of waxy-textured, lavender-colored flowers in June-July.

A Japanese dwarfed tree of Juniperus horizontalis procumbens, 18 in. high and 60 years old.

Both the trees and the art of cultivating them are called bonzai.

The cultivation of bonzai requires very great patience. At all times the root run must be restricted. The plants are kept in the smallest possible receptacles and highly glazed pots or containers help to restrict growth. Feeding with weak liquid fertilizer occasionally is necessary to keep the plants in good condition.

Perfectly Hardy. Many people make the mistake of regarding these plants as tender: they are perfectly hardy and must be grown under the coolest possible conditions. In the summer months they should be placed out of doors in partial shade. In fact, all the year round, except in severe cold, or when keen winds prevail, these dwarf trees should be put out of doors every day for a few hours; if kept always inside a room window they are certain to lose vigor.

Great care must be taken in watering; the roots must not be allowed to suffer from lack of moisture but the soil should not be watered until it is moderately dry: if overwatered it will become sour and the roots will perish.

Repotting becomes necessary only after several years, and as long as the trees remain healthy it is unwise to disturb them. If repotting should be-come necessary the best compost is fibrous loam with which sand has been mixed.

One secret of success in the management of these dwarf trees is to keep them out of doors as much as possible and especially during warm, moist summer days and nights. They do not suffer from the effects of moderate cold in winter and it is unwise to place them in the middle of a room away from the light or to keep them in a warm room.

Bonzai in America. In recent years considerable interest in bonzai has developed in the United States and Canada and many gardeners, both amateur and professional, train and cultivate dwarfed potted trees. While basing their practices on methods used in Japan, American devotees of this art have tended to simplify procedures to produce more rapid results. The oriental gardener often starts young bonzai that will be cultivated by and give pleasure to his grandchildren; few North Americans plan so long ahead. Fortunately, creditable results can be obtained in much shorter periods. Bonzai developed from seedlings and cuttings may be attractive specimens in 5-10 years; those formed from naturally dwarfed specimens from the wild or from nurseries are decorative immediately.

Collected Specimens. When seeking specimens in nurseries, gardens or from the wild that may be used as bonzai, the grower should attempt to locate stunted, misshapen, irregular and even grotesque ones instead of shapely, vigorous plants such as are preferred for planting in gardens. Specimens chosen should, however, be free of pests and diseases. It is an advantage if they have short, stout trunks of aged appearance and branches arranged in artistic fashion, so that, when established in a small container, the tree or shrub looks like a miniature but old specimen, rather than merely a young one.

Judicious pruning of unwanted branches may add interest to the form of the specimen. If the ground is at all dry it should be thoroughly soaked with water a few hours before the plant is dug. Spring and early fall are the best times for digging specimens to be trained as bonzai. It is important to keep a good ball of soil—one at least 1 ft. in diameter—about the roots. After the plant is dug, it should be carefully replanted in a garden in a lightly shaded place where it is sheltered from strong winds; the soil should be porous and not excessively rich. There the plant should remain for at least 1 year, until it has recovered from the shock of transplanting. Then it may be potted in a suitable container.

Planting Bonzai. Containers for bonzai are usually shallow, not more than 3-4 in. deep inside, and are much wider and longer than they are deep; they resemble trays or shallow dishes rather than flowerpots. They may be made of earthenware, china, stone or other material and be of any shape that pleases the gardener. Holes in the bottom are necessary for drainage.

To prevent loss of soil, the drainage holes are covered with fine wire screening or with a piece of crock placed hollow side down. Next a layer of gravel is placed in the bottom of the container and over it a layer of sand.

Before setting the bonzai in the container, carefully remove from among its roots most (at least two thirds) of the old soil. Do this with a pencil or pointed stick. Be careful not to damage the roots or to allow them to dry. Place the plant in the container, spread out its roots, after first cutting off any that are dead or broken, and work new soil (a porous mixture of loam, coarse sand and peat moss or leaf mold) among them with a slender stick. Press the soil firm. After potting, water thoroughly with a fine spray and protect the newly transplanted specimens from direct sun and wind for two or three weeks.

Established bonzai should be carefully removed from their containers and replanted in fresh soil at intervals; evergreen kinds every 4-5 years, deciduous (leaf-losing) kinds every 1-2 years.

Training. Bonzai are trained to shape by pruning, pinching and wiring. Pruning is done in spring just before new growth begins, and consists of removing with sharp shears unwanted branches. Pinching refers to the nipping back of soft new shoots and the removal of leaves; it reduces vigor and results in the production of smaller leaves. Pinching is done during the season of active growth and, except in the case of Azaleas and other kinds that fail to bloom if the new growths are picked, is done every time the new shoots attain a length of about one inch. Wiring is the practice of bending trunks and branches to desired artistic shapes by pulling them and fixing them in position with guy or anchor wires or wires twisted spirally around their branches. The best time to wire trees is in spring, when the sap is active and the branches are supple.

Suitable Kinds. Almost any trees or shrubs can be grown as bonzai, but the most suitable are those that naturally assume picturesque forms and those that tend to grow slowly. Excellent kinds are Apples, Apricots, Arborvitaes, Azaleas, Bald Cypress, Beeches, Birches, Boxwood, Cedars, Cherries, Cryptomerias, Daphnes, Elms, Flowering Quinces, Ginkgos, Hawthorns, Junipers, Maples, Pines, Plums, Redwood, Spruce, Wisteria.

JAPANESE GARDEN. The art of landscape gardening as developed in Japan differs greatly from that of Western countries. Whether the Japanese garden be large or small it very definitely represents an expanse of natural scenery, usually more or less formalized and of necessity in miniature, and is designed to give satisfaction by providing peace of mind in the contemplation of natural beauty.

Hills, lakes, streams and waterfalls as well as

summer houses, bridges, lanterns, torii (arch-
ways of two uprights and two cross beams, often
beautifully carved and painted) and stones of
distinctive sizes, shapes, colors and textures are
all important features of Japanese gardens and
for correct effects must be developed, selected
and carefully placed according to traditional
symbolism. Expanses of sand and of cultivated
moss are often featured in Japanese gardens.

Before constructing a true Japanese garden the
builder should carefully study one or more of
the excellent illustrated books on the subject.

Pleasing Japanese garden effects may be had
by following tradition less lavishly but by seeking inspiration from Japanese garden design and
restricting the planting to Japanese plants. A
characteristic of Japanese gardens is restraint in
using flowering plants and freedom in planting
evergreens. Care in selecting the kinds of plants
to be used has an important effect in determin-
ing whether or not a Japanese garden made elsewhere than in Japan captures the correct feel-
ing and really looks Japanese.

Kinds to use are large and small trees and
shrubs, herbaceous and alpine plants and plants
for the pool and waterside. Thus the ideal Japanese garden is found on ground varying a good
deal in elevation and kind of soil with, if possible, natural rocks and a stream and pool. With
ground of this description the owner can capture
something of the atmosphere of a real Japanese
garden; there will be rustic bridges across the
stream, a summer house or two whereon vines
can be grown, boggy ground for Irises and Japanese primroses and rocky clefts for dwarf trees.

The Right Soil. The most charming Japanese
garden can only be formed on ground containing little or no lime, for in places where lime is
prevalent shrubs of the Heather family are ruled
out, thereby excluding the very beautiful Kurume Rhododendrons (Azaleas) and others. If
the ground is free from lime it is possible to introduce soil required by special plants, but if the
ground is rich in lime it is very difficult to do
anything to make suitable sites for Rhododendrons and allied shrubs.

In making a selection for a Japanese garden
it will be found that trees, shrubs and woody
climbers play a very important part. Conifers
alone provide many very interesting and attractive kinds. There is the Japanese Cedar, Cryptomeria japonica, a tree of the largest size, and its
low-growing varieties; they are referred to under
Cryptomeria. There are also dwarf varieties of

A bridge in a Japanese garden at the Huntington Botanical Garden, Pasadena, California.

Chamaecyparis obtusa and C. pisifera, which are peculiarly suitable for planting among rocks. The Japanese Larch, Larix leptolepis, is another vigorous tree, as is also Thujopsis dolabrata, a handsome evergreen; its variety nana grows only a few feet high. The Japanese Umbrella Pine, Sciadopitys verticillata, too, is suitable. Pinus densiflora, P. Thunbergii and P. parviflora form quaint little trees when established in rock crevices where there is little soil.

Japanese Cherries. The Japanese Cherries are especially suitable, the flowers varying from white to deep rose or reddish. Some of them have single flowers, others double. They flower with exceptional freedom and never miss a year, the end of April and early May being the usual blossoming time.

There are numerous Crab Apples that are as free-flowering as the Cherries, all worthy of a place in the Japanese garden. Among other leaf-losing trees are various Oaks, Walnuts and Maples, particularly the varieties of Acer palmatum and A. japonicum; these Maples are handsome in spring when coming into leaf and again in autumn before the leaves fall.

The Kurume Rhododendrons, or Azaleas, are among the most brilliant shrubs of the garden, but they are sometimes cut by late frosts and are not suitable for the colder parts of the country. They flower with extraordinary freedom, their flowers being various shades of mauve, red, pink, orange-red, etc. There are many selected varieties of which obtusum variety amoenum, magenta; obtusum variety Arnoldianum, mauve to red; Apple Blossom, pink; Benigiri, crimson; Christmas Cheer, double crimson; Hino-mayo, salmon-pink; and obtusum variety Kirishima, lilac-mauve, are very beautiful.

The Wistarias should always find a place in the Japanese garden, whether they be strictly Japanese kinds or Chinese introduced to Japan. They can either be grown as climbers in the natural way or as stunted bushes. In either way they flower well. Then there are various Vines that are magnificent foliage plants, particularly Vitis Coignetiae, which is vigorous enough to grow over a large tree; the leaves color brilliantly in autumn. Room should be found for the Japanese Quinces.

The hardy Bamboos are particularly good plants for the Japanese garden. They will succeed in moist places near a stream or pond. The Japanese Iris Kaempferi is a very beautiful bog garden plant.

JAPANESE HONEYSUCKLE. Lonicera japonica, which see.

JAPANESE HOP. Humulus japonicus, which see.

JAPANESE IRIS. Iris Kaempferi, which see.

JAPANESE MAPLE. See Acer japonicum and Acer palmatum.

JAPANESE PRIMROSE. See Primula japonica.

JAPANESE QUINCE. See Chaenomeles.

JAPANESE RAISIN TREE. See Hovenia.

JAPANESE ROOF IRIS. Iris tectorum, which see.

JASIONE—*Sheeps Bit Scabious* (Jasio'ne). Hardy annual or herbaceous perennial plants, not exceeding 12 in. in height, which are natives of Europe. They belong to the Bellflower family, Campanulaceae.

For the Rock Garden. These plants are chiefly suitable for the rock garden, where they flourish in well-drained, sandy, loamy soil, in a sunny position. The perennial kinds are propagated by sowing seeds in a flat of light soil placed in a cold frame, or on a prepared bed of fine soil out of doors, in April. The plants may also be lifted and separated into rooted pieces for replanting in October.

The chief perennial kinds are J. Jankae and J. perennis (Sheeps Bit Scabious, Shepherds Scabious); both grow about 12 in. high, and bear light blue flowers in June–July.

Jasione montana, 9-10 in., blue, may be grown as an annual by sowing seeds out of doors in spring, where the plants are to bloom in July, the seedlings being thinned to 4 or 5 in. apart. Or seeds may be sown in a pot of fine soil, in a cold frame, in late July, and the seedlings set in their permanent places in September–October.

JASMINE. See Jasminum, also Jessamine.

JASMINE, CAPE. See Gardenia.

JASMINE, CHILEAN. See Mandevilla.

JASMINE, CONFEDERATE. Trachelospermum jasminoides, which see.

JASMINE, ROCK. Androsace, which see.

JASMINE, STAR. Trachelospermum jasminoides, which see.

JASMINE, WEST INDIAN. See Ixora.

JASMINUM—*Jasmine* (Jasmi'num). Tropical, subtropical and hardy evergreen and leaf-losing climbing plants or shrubs which bear chiefly white or yellow flowers, some being very fragrant. These plants are widely distributed in Asia, but some are found elsewhere. Several are decorative and popular garden plants, particularly those that are fairly hardy. Jasminum belongs to the Olive family, Oleaceae, and the name is said to be derived from the old Persian name for Jasmine.

Hardiness of Jasmines. The hardiest kind is J. nudiflorum, which lives outdoors without protection in southern New York and southern New England. Other kinds that have proved hardy in sheltered locations in southern New York are J. Beesianum, J. fruticans, J. humile and J. stephanense, but none of these is as reliable or vigorous there as in milder climates. Jasminums in general are best suited for planting outdoors in the South.

Cultivation in a Greenhouse. Tender kinds may be grown on trellises or on wires fixed to the roof in a greenhouse heated according to their needs. Cuttings of most of the tender and hardy Jasmines, if taken when about 4 in. long,

in summer, and inserted in a propagating case in a warm greenhouse or a cold frame respectively, soon form roots.

The tender kinds require planting in well-drained loamy soil to which peat moss or leaf mold has been added, with a scattering of sand. If they can be planted in a border, so much the better, but they may be grown in pots. They should be pruned as soon as the flowers are over, the amount of pruning being determined by the available space.

The large yellow-flowered Jasmine Mesnyi (primulinum), a beautiful Jasmine for the cool greenhouse.

Jasmines for a Warm Greenhouse. J. gracillimum, from Borneo, requires a minimum temperature of 55 degrees and bears white fragrant flowers in winter. J. officinale variety grandiflorum, from the Himalayas, bears fragrant white flowers marked with rose, during summer and early autumn. J. Sambac, the Arabian Jasmine, bears fragrant white flowers at almost all times of the year. J. rex, from Siam, is an attractive kind with large, white flowers. All the foregoing are suitable for a greenhouse, with a minimum temperature of 55 degrees.

Yellow Winter Jasmine, Jasminum nudiflorum.

For the greenhouse, the large white-flowered Jasminum rex.

For a Cool Greenhouse. J. Mesnyi (primulinum), from China, has large, often semidouble, yellow flowers during late winter and early spring; it can be grown in a cool sunny greenhouse.

The Winter Jasmine. This favorite climbing plant, Jasminum nudiflorum, thrives in ordinary, well-cultivated garden ground in a sunny position. It is a native of China, and bears yellow, scentless blossoms from November to February, depending upon the climate. In sheltered locations it is hardy as far north as New York City. It is usually trained to a wall, pergola or trellis, or to stakes in the open ground. Although it is one of the easiest of all climbing shrubs to grow, some people fail to get the Winter Jasmine to flower well because they prune it at the wrong time. The shoots should be cut well back as soon as the blooms have faded, and no later pruning should be done.

Summer-flowering Jasmines. A hardy kind with rose-colored flowers in summer is the Chinese J. Beesianum; it is, however, more curious than beautiful, and is unlikely to displace better-known kinds. J. floridum is a yellow-flowered, evergreen bush, native of China; it grows 3 ft. high, flowers in summer, and is nearly hardy. An allied kind with larger leaves and flowers, and of more robust growth, is J. humile variety revolutum, from Afghanistan and the northwest Himalayas. J. fruticans is a tender semi-evergreen shrub bearing yellow flowers during late spring and early summer; it is a native of southern Europe, northern Africa and Asia Minor. J. Parkeri is distinct in that it forms a dwarf evergreen bush about 12 in. high and bears solitary yellow flowers in June. Where hardy, it is a good rock garden shrub.

The White Summer Jasmine, J. officinale, is a vigorous climbing plant from Persia, northwest India and China; it bears white fragrant flowers during summer. In the south of France and other parts of southern Europe a variety of this kind, called affine, is grown in fields and the flowers are used in perfumery. J. stephanense is a hybrid of J. Beesianum and J. officinale. It bears clusters of pink flowers in summer.

JATROPHA (Ja'tropha; Jatro'pha). Mostly tropical, tender trees, shrubs and herbaceous plants, a few of which are cultivated in the greenhouse and for outdoor flower garden use in the deep South. They belong to the family Euphorbiaceae. The name is of Greek origin and refers to the medicinal value possessed by some species.

Jatrophas are easily grown in light, sandy, well-drained soil in sunny locations. They need moderate amounts of water during their season of active growth, comparatively little during the winter season of rest or partial rest. They are readily propagated by means of seeds and may also be increased by cuttings made from firm, young branches.

The favorite decorative kind is J. podagrica, the Tartogo, a native of Central America. It grows to a height of about 18 in. and has a stout, thickened stem and clusters of coral-red flowers.

JEFFERSONIA (Jefferso'nia). Hardy, perennial, spring-blooming plants with two-lobed leaves, which belong to the Barberry family, Berberidaceae. The name commemorates a former President of the United States, Thomas Jefferson.

For the Rock or Woodland Garden. These plants, which grow only 6 in. high, are suitable for cultivation in the rock or woodland garden in partial shade and in soil with which peat or leaf mold and sand have been mixed freely. Planting should be done in early autumn or early spring. Propagation is by lifting and separating the plants in September, or by sowing seeds in sandy peat in a cold frame as soon as they are ripe in summer.

Kinds. J. diphylla (Twinleaf), a native of North America, has white flowers; J. dubia, from China, has lovely blue flowers.

JERUSALEM ARTICHOKE. See Artichoke, also Helianthus tuberosus.

JERUSALEM CHERRY. Solanum Pseudo-Capsicum, which see.

JERUSALEM CHERRY, FALSE. Solanum Capsicastrum, which see.

JERUSALEM CROSS. See Lychnis chalcedonica.

JERUSALEM SAGE. See Phlomis fruticosa.

JERUSALEM THORN. Parkinsonia aculeata, which see; see also Paliurus spina-Christi.

JESSAMINE. See Jasminum.

JESSAMINE, CAROLINA YELLOW. Gelsemium sempervirens, which see.

JESSAMINE, DAY. See Cestrum.

JESSAMINE, WILLOW-LEAVED. See Cestrum.

JETBEAD. Rhodotypos tetrapetala, which see.

JEWBUSH. See Pedilanthus.

JEWELWEED. Impatiens biflora, which see.

JEW'S MALLOW. See Kerria. Corchorus olitorius is also known by this name.

JIMSON WEED. See Datura.

JOB'S-TEARS. See Coix.

JOE-PYE WEED. See Eupatorium.

JOHN INNES SEED AND POTTING COMPOSTS

Standardized Soil Mixtures in Which to Grow Plants Indoors

The research workers of the John Innes Horticultural Institution in England have done amateur as well as professional and commercial gardeners a great service in evolving simple formulas for standard seed and potting composts that suit the majority of plants raised and grown under glass, especially as these composts are quite easy to prepare. These mixtures, or slight modifications of them, are now being used by gardeners in Canada and the United States.

The Ingredients: *Loam.* The three principal soil ingredients are loam, peat and sand. The loam should have come from good pasture land, be slightly greasy to the touch, and should have been stacked for 6 months to become well rotted.

To prepare the loam take a quantity of loam slabs or turves, 4-5 in. thick, in spring, and stack them for 6 months or so. The turves should be stacked grass downwards, with spaces between to allow air to enter, and the quality of the loam will be improved if a 2-in. thickness of strawy manure is spread over every second layer, and the alternate layers are sprinkled with ground limestone.

All gardeners who are seriously interested in growing any quantity of Chrysanthemums, Poinsettias and other plants in pots, should regard a loam stack as very desirable.

Peat. Various types of peat are sold by horticultural dealers under such names as granulated peat, sedge peat, peat moss, and so on, but the important thing, as far as compost-making is concerned, is that it should be of rather coarse texture. Peats to be avoided are the fine and dusty ones and the black or greasy ones.

Leaf Mold. If made from Oak, Beech, Elm or

other small-leaved, deciduous trees, leaf mold is as good as, if not better than, peat as a compost ingredient, but unlike peat it must be sterilized before being used.

Sand. The ideal sand for composts is of coarse texture, free from clay, silt, organic matter, and salt. A good-quality washed builders' sand is generally the most satisfactory and least expensive.

The J.I. Seed Compost. The formula for this is 2 parts by bulk of sterilized loam, 1 part peat, 1 part sand, to each bushel of which are added 1½ oz. superphosphate (18 per cent phosphoric acid) and ¾ oz. ground limestone or chalk.

To prepare the compost, rub the loam through a ⅜-in. sieve. Moisten the peat evenly with a sprinkler. Mix the superphosphate and chalk with some of the sand. Mix the main ingredients, then add the fertilized sand and mix thoroughly so that all are evenly blended.

This compost may be used the next day, and can be stored for any length of time up to 8 weeks after mixing.

Suitable for Most Seeds. This standard compost is recommended by the John Innes Horticultural Institution as suitable for most kinds of seeds sown under glass, including all kinds of bedding plants, Cyclamen, Primulas, Lettuce, Cauliflower and other Brassicas, and Tomatoes.

It is worth noting here that Cyclamen should be pricked out into J.I. seed compost, which should also be used when moving the seedlings into small pots. It should also be noted that the J.I. standard potting compost is recommended for raising Cinerarias, Solanum (Winter Cherry) and Tomatoes from seed.

The J.I. Potting Compost. The basis of this is good loam, peat and sand. The proportions are, by bulk, 7 parts of loam, 3 of peat, and 2 of sand, to each bushel of which are added, for the standard compost, ¾ oz. of ground chalk or limestone and ¼ lb. of a fertilizer compound known as John Innes Base.

The J.I. Base. The formula is: 2 parts (by weight) of hoof and horn (⅛ in. grist; 13 per cent nitrogen), 2 parts superphosphate (18 per cent phosphoric acid), and 1 part sulphate of potash (48 per cent pure potash).

Using the Compost. The compost is prepared in the same way as the seed compost, except that the loam can be used in a coarser state, and, like it, can be used the day after mixing, or can be stored for up to 8 weeks.

Generally, the standard potting compost is used for pricking out seedlings and moving them into small pots, but vigor of plant and season of year must be taken into account to a certain extent, and additional amounts of J.I. Base and chalk may be desirable for some plants.

Thus, for pricking out seedlings of bedding plants and winter Lettuce, a double amount of J.I. Base and limestone is recommended; also for potting in small pots such subjects as rooted Carnation cuttings, Cinerarias, Cucumbers, Solanum, and Tomatoes. This "double-dose" compost is suitable for potting most subjects into larger pots.

Loam Should Be Sterilized. It is useless to produce a compost of good texture and containing a balanced supply of plant foods if the ingredients are contaminated with harmful organisms, either pests or diseases; therefore it is always wise to sterilize, or rather partially sterilize, loam before it is used in John Innes or other composts. This process of sterilization, however, leads to the production of an excess of nitrogen, which may be harmful to the germination of seeds and the growth of young seedlings. It can, however, be counterbalanced by phosphate, hence the reason for including superphosphate in the John Innes formulas.

As most gardeners use the low pressure steam method of sterilization, as for instance in a perforated metal container over water heated from below, a bushel of soil should be sterilized for not less than 1 hour, heating it to a final temperature of 180 degrees F.

The loam should be sterilized in a dry, loose state. If the sand is clean, it will not require sterilizing, nor will the peat. If leaf mold is used, this should be sterilized separately.

JOHNNY-JUMP-UP. Viola tricolor, which see.

JOINT. A term used by gardeners to indicate the node of a stem, i.e., the point from which a leaf is produced.

JONQUIL. See Narcissus.

JOSEPH'S-COAT. See Amaranthus.

JOSHUA TREE. Yucca brevifolia. See Yucca.
JUDAS TREE. See Cercis.
JUGLANS—*Walnut.* Leaf-losing trees, often of considerable size, bearing handsome leaves divided into few or many leaflets, conspicuous catkins of male flowers and very insignificant female flowers that are succeeded by edible and often nourishing nuts enclosed in a thick outer husk. Leaves, sap, and husks contain a good deal of dyeing matter which definitely stains anything with which it comes in contact.

The Black Walnut, Juglans nigra, forms a shapely tree when given room to develop.

The various kinds are found from southeast Europe to the Himalayas, through China to Manchuria and Japan, and in North and South America. Most of the kinds are hardy. They are grown for decorative purposes and some of them for their nuts and timber. See also Walnut.

Juglans is the ancient Latin name for the common Walnut and is said to be derived from the words *Jovis glans,* Jupiter's Acorn. It belongs to the family Juglandaceae.

Raising Walnuts From Seeds. Whenever possible the natural species of Walnut should be raised from seeds. The seeds should be stratified in moist sand for the winter months, to prevent undue drying, and be sown in well-drained, light loamy soil in spring and protected from damage by vermin. Protection is afforded by covering them with wire netting or other appropriate means.

If seeds can be sown in the places where the trees are to grow, it will be an advantage, for root injury at transplanting may cause a serious check to growth. If the seeds are sown in a nursery bed the young plants should be lifted at the end of the first year and the roots carefully trimmed; they should then be replanted. Every second year the plants should be transplanted until they can be planted in permanent places. Varieties and hybrids are increased by grafting.

Planting and Pruning. Walnut trees thrive best in well-drained, loamy soil, although the American Black Walnut gives good results on light land. The trees should be planted in autumn or early spring and given plenty of room for development. Pruning is necessary when trees are young to encourage a single leading shoot, check the undue growth of side branches, and to clear the lower part of the trunk. All such pruning should be done between June and Christmas, for if the trees, whether big or little, are pruned during late winter and spring, they "bleed" profusely, and such "bleeding" is difficult to check.

The Persian Walnut, Juglans regia, is a stately tree of southeastern Europe and Asia Minor that grows 80-100 ft. high and produces the nuts popularly called English Walnuts. There are numerous varieties, varying in hardiness, size of nuts and thickness of the nutshell. They are grown commercially chiefly in the Pacific Coast region, but may be cultivated over a wider area. Certain varieties can survive sub-zero temperatures but late spring frosts can be most injurious to nut production. A good, deep soil is needed for best results. Named varieties are increased by grafting on seedling stocks. Those showing interesting growth variations are J. regia laciniata, with finely cut leaflets; J. regia pendula, with weeping branches; and J. regia praeparturiens, which is a shrubby form that produces thin-shelled nuts at an early age.

The Black Walnut, J. nigra, is a valuable forest tree over much of the eastern half of the United States; it grows to 100 ft. tall in the rich soil of the Mississippi Basin. Numerous varieties with nuts having thinner shells and more meat have been selected and propagated; Huber, Ohio, Stabler, Stambaugh, Snyder, and Thomas are good examples of these superior varieties.

The Butternut, J. cinerea, grows 60-90 ft. high and has a more northerly range than the Black Walnut. Its nut meat is oily and rich. Some varieties of superior quality have been propagated. It is suitable for growing in northern New England.

The Japanese Walnut, J. Sieboldiana, is an ornamental tree that grows to 60 ft. high. It is of distinctive appearance and has very large leaves; its nuts are borne in clusters. It is hardy over most of the Northeast. Heartnut is J. Sieboldiana cordiformis, equally as ornamental as J. Sieboldiana and with nuts of superior quality.

The Chinese Walnut, J. cathayensis, is a vigorous tree with large leaves but its nuts are of little value.

Other Economic Uses. The wood of Black Walnut is highly prized for furniture making, interior finish, and gun stocks. For the latter purpose it is unsurpassed. The nuts retain their flavor after cooking and are widely used in confectionery. Circassian Walnut is the wood of Persian or English Walnut, used in furniture making and for interior finish. Orchards of immense acreage have been planted in California for the production of nuts of superior quality.

JUJUBE. See Zizyphus.

JUNCUS—*Rush* (Jun'cus). Plants which grow in moist ground in various parts of the world; several are wild in North America. They belong to the family Juncaceae. The name is said to be derived from *jungo,* to join, a reference to the use of the stems and narrow leaves for binding purposes.

Very few of the Rushes are sufficiently decorative to be worth planting in gardens, but Juncus effusus spiralis, so named because of the spiral arrangement of the stems, is a useful waterside plant. It thrives in ordinary moist soil and is increased by division in autumn.

JUNEBERRY. See Amelanchier.

JUNIPER. Juniperus, which see.

JUNIPERUS or JUNIPER
Evergreen Trees and Shrubs of Great Diversity and Usefulness

(Junip'erus). These evergreen trees and shrubs are widely distributed in Europe, Asia, North America, the West Indies, the Canary Islands and eastern Africa. Many of them are hardy and form good trees for garden decoration; some are dwarf enough for the rock garden, some are good foundation plants, others grow into trees of moderate size. Some are valuable timber trees in their native countries. They flourish on limestone land and thrive in ordinary soil where there is little lime. Some have variegated foliage.

The Junipers are divided into two groups according to the kind of leaves they bear; the mature trees of one group have very small, closely pressed, scalelike leaves; those of the other group have loosely arranged, needle-like leaves, and are well represented by Juniperus communis. The cones are small, pealike bodies, each containing one or more hard seeds. Juniperus belongs to the Cypress family, Cupressaceae, and the name is the old Latin one for the tree.

Propagation, whenever possible, should be by seeds, but the varieties must be raised by means of cuttings or layers or by grafting. Cuttings of the hardy kinds are taken in late summer or fall and inserted in a propagating case in the greenhouse. The hardy kinds must be grown as sturdily as possible; trees grown from seeds or cuttings in a greenhouse should be removed to a cold frame as soon as they are well rooted.

Young plants, more particularly seedlings, of a number of Junipers which are regarded as hardy are easily injured by cold, and it is wise to provide some protection during very cold weather until they have formed hard wood. Junipers can be safely moved when quite large. Generally, however, it is wise to set the taller kinds in their permanent positions before they become too unwieldy. Planting should be done in early autumn or in early spring.

For rock gardens there are several small, erect kinds that grow very slowly, particularly forms of J. communis; and there are others of prostrate habit that are very effective when growing over rocks. These should be planted from pots while small. The erect-growing kinds require little room, but those with trailing shoots spread over a space of several feet.

Among kinds best suited for rock gardens are selected varieties of J. chinensis, J. communis, J. horizontalis, J. Sabina, J. procumbens and J. squamata.

Juniperus chinensis stricta is often misnamed Juniperus excelsa stricta.

A group of Chinese Junipers, Juniperus chinensis.

Junipers to Grow as Specimens. The following are the best of those which develop into bushes or trees and are suitable for growing out of doors: J. chinensis, a tree up to 60 ft. high; in the variety aurea the young leaves are golden; many branches of the variety japonica bear the awl-shaped or juvenile leaves; japonica aureo-variegata has golden leaves. J. chinensis columnaris is slender and upright; J. chinensis

globosa is a low, dense, rounded plant; J. chinensis mas is conical in shape; J. chinensis plumosa is low and feathery.

Two of the most popular varieties of J. chinensis are J. chinensis Pfizeriana, which forms an attractive broad-spreading plant of a dark gray-green color, and J. chinensis variety Sargentii, which is a more prostrate kind. The variety J. chinensis variegata is a compact form that has white tips on many of its branches.

J. virginiana is one of the commonest kinds in North America. It grows to a maximum height of 100 ft. and is commonly known as Red Cedar. There are many varieties, notably argentea, with silvery leaves; Chamberlaynii, in which most of the leaves are of the juvenile type; compacta, a dwarf dense bush; Kosteri, with silvery leaves; elegantissima, in which the young shoots are tipped with yellow; pendula, with weeping branchlets; Canaertii, of dense, pyramidal shape

and with dark green foliage; glauca, with bluish, glaucous foliage; pyramidalis Hillii, the Dundee Juniper, of narrow, upright outline and with foliage that becomes bluish purple in winter; and Schottii, of very narrow pyramidal outline.

The Common Juniper. J. communis is the common Juniper, found wild in North America, Europe and northern Asia; sometimes it is a bush 3-4 ft. high, at other times it is nearly 20 ft. high; it has awl-shaped leaves. The variety oblongo-pendula has much finer branchlets than

Varieties of the native American Red Cedar, Juniperus virginiana: (a) variety Canaertii, (b) variety glauca, (c) variety pyramidiformis Hillii.

Juniperus squamata prostrata has a ground-hugging kind of neat appearance.

the type and they are pendulous. The varieties hibernica and suecica are of narrow, stiffly erect habit and very slow growing.

Among dwarf varieties of J. communis are: depressa, depressa aurea-spica, compressa, echiniformis, hemisphaerica, saxatalis (nana) and prostrata.

J. drupacea, the Syrian Juniper, is distinct by reason of its narrow, lance-shaped leaves. J.

The slow, compact-growing Juniperus communis compressa is ideal for the rock garden.

excelsa, the Grecian Juniper, grows 80-100 ft. high in Asia Minor. It is of pyramidal outline, distinct and effective, but is recommended for planting in the far South only.

J. **formosana** is one of the less hardy kinds, although it will succeed in southern New England. In China it forms an elegant tree, 40-75 ft. high. J. pachyphlaea, the Alligator Juniper, grows 60 ft. high in Texas, Arizona and Mexico. It is adapted for cultivation in the lower South.

The Graceful Himalayan Juniper. J. recurva is a very handsome tree, 30-40 ft. high, from the Himalayas: the branchlets are pendent and the whole tree is of graceful outline. It may be tried in the far South. Some years ago a tree was received from Upper Burma under the name of Coffin Juniper. This is of very elegant growth and closely related to J. recurva; it is named J. recurva Coxii, and sometimes called J. Coxii.

Juniperus horizontalis, the Creeping Juniper of North America, is a useful kind for planting as a ground cover. In addition to the bluish-green, typical kind, there are many varieties. Among the more important of these are J. horizontalis Douglasii, the Waukegan Juniper, which has steel-blue foliage; J. horizontalis procumbens, a very dwarf form; and J. horizontalis variegata, which has cream-white tips to its branchlets. J.

The Bar Harbor Juniper, Juniperus horizontalis variety Bar Harbor, lower picture, is even more prostrate than Juniperus horizontalis, illustrated above.

horizontalis Bar Harbor has bluish foliage which turns lavender-purple in winter.

Juniperus Sabina, the Savin, is a hardy kind that is a native of Europe and Western Asia. Several horticultural varieties are grown, including J. Sabina tamariscifolia, a low, spreading kind with green foliage, and J. Sabina cupressifolia, which is very prostrate. J. Sabina typically may attain a height of 10 ft.

The Colorado Red Cedar, Juniperus scopulorum, grows to 30 ft. tall and is hardy. Its foliage is yellowish-green or bluish. It provides a number of named varieties, including the columnar J. scopulorum Hillii, which has distinctly bluish foliage.

Juniperus squamata, a hardy native of eastern Asia, is a low, spreading shrub of attractive appearance. Its variety J. squamata Meyeri is of stiff, upright habit and glaucous-blue coloring. J. squamata prostrata is a beautiful, spreading, low-growing variety.

Juniperus occidentalis is not hardy in the North but may be grown in milder climates. A native of the West Coast, it is a gray-green tree or shrub that may attain a height of 40 ft.

Juniperus barbadensis, a native of Bermuda, the Barbados and Antigua, grows to a height of about 40 ft. and is hardy in the United States in the far South only. This kind is commonly known as the Bermuda Cedar; it is the tree most abundant in, and characteristic of, Bermuda.

Economic Uses. The wood of the Junipers is fragrant and very durable. It is often used for fencing, but it is of value for more important purposes. The wood of J. virginiana is sometimes called Pencil Cedar, from the fact that its wood is used for making lead pencils.

In the south of France the wood of J. Oxycedrus is distilled for a medicinal oil it contains. This oil is known as "oil of cade," and it is used in the treatment of skin diseases.

JUPITER'S BEARD. See Anthyllis.

JURINEA (Jurin'ea). Mostly hardy herbaceous perennial subshrubs that are natives of the Mediterranean Region and of central and western Asia. They have thistle-like heads of purple flowers and belong in the Daisy family, the Compositae. The name honors Louis Jurine, a pro-fessor of medicine. These plants are not highly decorative. They are more suitable for use in naturalistic plantings than in formal borders.

Jurineas grow without difficulty in any ordinary well-drained garden soil. They prefer a sunny location and are easily propagated by division of the old clumps in early fall or early spring and by seeds sown in sandy soil in spring.

Kinds most likely to be grown are J. alata, 3-4 ft., Caucasus; J. depressa, 6 in., Caucasus; J. humilis, northern Africa; J. spectabilis, 1 ft., Caucasus.

JUSSIAEA — *Primrose Willow* (Jussiae'a). Aquatic plants that in gardens are usually grown as annuals although they are tender perennials. They belong to the Evening Primrose family, the Onagraceae. The name honors Bernard de Jussieu, an eighteenth-century botanist. The group is mostly American, although a few species occur in the Old World.

Propagation may be effected by seeds sown early in the year indoors, or later outdoors by cuttings taken in summer or fall, and by division. The container in which the seeds are sown should be placed with its soil surface an inch below water level.

The plants should be grown in rich soil kept very wet, or actually submerged an inch or two beneath the water surface. They are suitable for pools, watersides and bog gardens. Those most commonly grown are J. longifolia, 2 ft. tall, flowers yellow, Brazil, and J. repens, trailing, flowers yellow, tropics. J. californica is the Yellow Waterweed, with long stems and floating leaves and yellow flowers.

JUSTICIA (Justic'ia). Tropical plants closely related to Jacobinia, to which genus most of the plants commonly grown under the name of Justicia have now been transferred. Those that remain are of little value. The name commemorates J. Justice, a Scottish gardener, and the genus belongs to the family Acanthaceae. Justicia carnea is synonymous with Jacobinia carnea, and Justicia Ghiesbreghtiana is synonymous with Jacobinia Ghiesbreghtiana.

JUTE. A soft or bast fiber obtained from the stems of Corchorus capsularis and C. olitorius, annual plants extensively grown in India.

K

KADSURA (Kadsu'ra). An uncommon evergreen climbing shrub suitable for planting out of doors in the far South but which elsewhere may be grown in a greenhouse having a minimum temperature of 45 degrees. This shrub belongs to the Magnolia family, Magnoliaceae, and grows wild in Japan. Kadsura is the Japanese name.

The only kind grown in gardens is Kadsura japonica; this will reach a height of 6 or 8 ft. and bears white flowers in July and August. It thrives in ordinary well-drained loamy soil and can be propagated by cuttings made from firm shoots in summer in a frame which is kept close for a few weeks.

In the variety named variegata the leaves are bordered with creamy-white.

KAEMPFERIA (Kaempfer'ia). Tropical plants which have ornamental leaves. They are natives of Borneo, Cochin China and other warm countries and belong to the family Zingiberaceae. The name commemorates a German physician named E. Kaempfer.

Hothouse Plants with Ornamental Leaves. These plants must be grown in a tropical greenhouse having a minimum winter temperature of 65 degrees; during the summer a warm, moist atmosphere must be maintained. The best potting compost consists of peat and loam in equal parts with sand added freely. The leaves die in autumn and during the winter the leafless plants, still in the flowerpots, are kept quite dry.

In February they are taken out of the pots, repotted in fresh compost of the kind advised, and watered carefully until they are growing freely; when in full growth in summer, they need a good deal of water. If an increased stock is required, it is obtained by separating the dormant plants into rooted pieces and repotting them singly in February.

The chief kinds are K. Roscoeana, which has handsome bronze-brown and green leaves; K. ornata, with variegated leaves and yellow flowers, and K. rotunda, which bears fragrant, white flowers tinged with rose or mauve.

KAFFIR BREAD. See Encephalartos.

KAFFIR LILY. See Schizostylis and Haemanthus.

KALANCHOË (Kalan'choë). Tender succulent plants with attractive flowers. They are chiefly natives of tropical and South Africa and belong to the Crassula family, Crassulaceae. Kalanchoë is an ancient Chinese name for one kind.

For a Sunny Greenhouse or Window. These plants must be exposed to the maximum amount of sunlight. A minimum winter temperature of 45 degrees is required. The best compost consists of two parts loam and one part equal quantities of sand and broken brick.

Repotting is done in March, or as soon as new growth commences, and the compost is made firm. After potting, no water is given until the soil becomes dry. No shading is required. During the summer, water must be applied freely; but in winter only sufficient is given to prevent the stems from shriveling.

When to Take Cuttings. Propagation is by cuttings inserted in spring, preferably. Shoots 2-3 in. in length are removed and cut through

A modern variety of Kalanchoë flammea.

below the bottom joint, and a few of the lower leaves are removed. The prepared cuttings are exposed to the air for a few hours to allow a protecting skin to form over the cut portions. The cuttings are then inserted in sand or sandy soil and placed in a light position out of strong sunshine. No water is given until the rooting medium is nearly dry. Rooted plants are first potted in 3-in., and subsequently in 5-in., pots. Kalanchoë can also be raised from seeds sown in pots of sandy soil in spring or summer and by leaf cuttings taken at those same seasons.

The principal kinds are Kalanchoë flammea, orange-scarlet; K. laciniata (carnea), pink; K. Blossfeldiana, orange-red; K. uniflora, a trailing kind with pink flowers; and K. marmorata, white. In addition, a number of garden varieties and hybrids of K. Blossfeldiana and K. flammea have been raised and given varietal names in recent years. All bloom in summer or fall. Other plants that some botanists include in the genus Kalanchoë are in this work treated under Bryophyllum, which see.

KALE. Various sorts of Kale or Borecole are invaluable vegetables which are very easily managed. They are raised from seeds sown in April or early May. The seeds are sown thinly in drills half an inch deep and 8 in. apart.

In July they are planted out finally 2 ft. apart. The Kales thrive in ordinary well-cultivated garden ground which has been enriched with decayed manure and limed well.

If the weather is hot and dry when Kales are planted it is a good plan to dip the roots in a mixture of soil and water before setting them in drills 3 in. deep, and they should be well watered when planting is finished. If the roots are allowed to become dry, growth may be checked so seriously as to render them useless.

The Best Kinds. There are many types and varieties of Kale. The most important are As-

The trailing stems of Kalanchoë uniflora bear fleshy leaves and attractive bell-shaped flowers.

Ornamental Kale, sometimes grown for garden decoration and for use in flower arrangements.

paragus Kale, which, where winters are not severe, produces succulent young shoots in early spring; the Curled or Scotch Kale (Curly Kale), of which there are named varieties or strains having curled or somewhat mosslike leaves; Cottager's Kale; Sprouting Kale, which yields fresh shoots in early spring; Drumhead Kale, with cabbage-like heads; Thousand Headed, which produces a large crop of "greens" in early spring; the Labrador Kale, which yields an abundance of edible leaves; and Hungry Gap, an excep-

tionally hardy kind for late cropping.

Ornamental Kales or varieties with colored leaves are sometimes grown for the sake of their decorative effect in less formal parts of the garden in winter. They are raised from seeds in the way already described; the seeds should be sown in April or May. A packet of mixed seeds will provide plants having leaves of various colors: purplish, reddish, rose, etc., or white with colored markings. The Ornamental Kales are not recommended for eating.

KALMIA: MOUNTAIN LAUREL
How to Grow These Beautiful Flowering Evergreen Shrubs

(Kalm'ia). These evergreen and leaf-losing flowering shrubs are natives of eastern North America and the West Indies and belong to the Heather family, Ericaceae. The name commemorates Peter Kalm, a Swedish botanist.

Shrubs for Lime-free Soil. Kalmias thrive in acid or lime-free loamy soil; leaf mold, peat moss or compost should be dug in the ground freely previous to planting, to provide cool, moist conditions for the roots. A position pro-

tected from midday sun should be chosen, for instance a position facing northwest or one in light shade. An annual mulch of leaf mold, compost, or peat moss should be put on the soil above the roots in spring. Kalmias are very attractive when massed in open woodland and by the waterside.

Planting and Pruning. Planting should be done during October or April. Firm planting is necessary, the roots being thin and very fibrous.

Flowering spray of the Calico Bush or Mountain Laurel, Kalmia latifolia. It thrives in acid soil and is one of the loveliest of evergreen shrubs, bearing dense clusters of blush-pink flowers in late spring.

Little pruning is required, but it may be necessary occasionally to shorten long shoots to keep the bushes shapely: this should be done when the flowers are over, and the faded flowers should be picked off. If, in course of time, the bushes become old and ungainly, they may be cut back close to the ground; they soon renew themselves from the base.

Sowing Seeds and Taking Cuttings. Seeds provide the best means of propagation. They are sown in early spring, in shallow pans or pots filled with fine peaty soil, and placed in a cool greenhouse or in a garden frame. Other methods of propagation are by layering in autumn and taking cuttings in August. Cuttings are difficult to root.

The best-known kind is the Mountain Laurel or Calico Bush, Kalmia latifolia, which forms an attractive shrub that eventually may become 20 ft. or more high, but more usually is from 6-10 ft. tall. It is a native of eastern North America. At a distance a bush when not in flower bears some resemblance to a Rhododendron; the leather-like, rich green leaves are 3-5 in. long and 1-1½ in. wide. The blush-colored flowers are saucer-shaped, ¾-1 in. across, and borne in flattish heads in late spring. There are several varieties, including myrtifolia, a dwarf bush with smaller leaves, and rubra, a variety with deep pink flowers. All are hardy and are splendid garden evergreens.

The Sheep Laurel of eastern North America, Kalmia angustifolia, is a hardy, evergreen shrub, 2-4 ft. high, with oblong leaves 1-2 in. long; the dense clusters of rose-red flowers are borne at the ends of the shoots in June. The varieties include rubra, deep red flowers; pumila or nana, a dwarf form; and rosea, rosy-purple.

K. polifolia (K. glauca) is a small-leaved, hardy, evergreen shrub of rather loose growth, 1½-2 ft. high: the narrow leaves are white on the undersides and the flowers, which open in April, are purplish-rose. It needs a moist, acid soil and is best suited for bog gardens. K. cuneata is a leaf-losing shrub (or partially evergreen in mild districts), a native of North Carolina and South Carolina, 2½-3½ ft. high, with thin leaves and white flowers borne at the ends of the previous year's growth in late spring.

KALOPANAX PICTUS (Kalo'panax; Kalopan'ax). A Japanese tree that is hardy and that is often known as Acanthopanax ricinifolius. It belongs to the Aralia family, Araliaceae. Under favorable conditions it attains a height of 80 ft. and is distinguished by reason of its palmately lobed handsome leaves. Its variety Maximowiczii has more deeply lobed leaves. Propagation is by seeds; cuttings and root cuttings may be tried also.

KALOSANTHES. Rochea coccinea, which see.

KANGAROO PAWS. See Anigozanthos.

KANGAROO VINE. See Cissus.

KANSAS, GARDENING IN. See Regional Gardening.

KANSAS GAY-FEATHER. Liatris pycnostachya, which see.

KATSURA TREE. Cercidiphyllum japonicum, which see.

KAULFUSSIA AMELLOIDES. Charieis heterophylla, which see.

KAURI PINE. Agathis australis. See Agathis.

KEEL. A name given to the somewhat boat-shaped base of the flowers of Sweet Pea and other kinds which belong to the Pea family, Leguminosae.

KENILWORTH IVY. See Cymbalaria muralis.

KENNEDIA—*Australian Bean Flower* (Kenned'ia). Climbing plants from Australia, with attractive flowers, suitable for outdoor cultivation in California and similar climates; elsewhere for greenhouses. They are closely allied to, and resemble, Hardenbergia, and belong to the Pea family, Leguminosae. The woody, twining stems grow 15 ft. in height, have trifoliate evergreen leaves and clusters of pea-shaped, red, reddish-black, white or blue flowers in summer. The name Kennedia commemorates L. Kennedy, an English nurseryman.

Climbing Plants for the Greenhouse. These plants require a minimum winter temperature of 45 degrees. The most suitable compost consists of equal parts of loam, peat, and leaf mold with sand added freely. They are grown in large pots or wooden tubs, or planted out in a bed of soil in the greenhouse, and the shoots are trained to wires or trellis fixed to the wall or roof of the greenhouse. They are kept growing vigorously by top-dressing with fresh compost in spring. Pruning consists of shortening long shoots and removing weak growths in February.

The plants require a semishaded position and abundance of water during the growing season. Throughout the winter the soil is moistened only when it becomes quite dry.

Propagation is by cuttings of side shoots, 3 in. in length, inserted in sand and peat and placed under a bell jar until rooted. They are then potted separately in 3-in. pots and later in 5-in. pots, from which they are set in large pots or tubs, or in a prepared bed of soil.

The chief kinds are K. coccinea, 15 ft., scarlet, and K. prostrata, 3 ft., scarlet. Both flower in summer.

KENTIA (Kent'ia). The Palms commonly grown as Kentias are mostly included in the genus Howea. See Howea.

KENTRANTHUS. Centranthus, which see.

KENTUCKY BLUE GRASS. Poa pratensis, which see.

KENTUCKY COFFEE TREE. See Gymnocladus.

KENTUCKY, GARDENING IN. See Regional Gardening.

KERRIA JAPONICA (Ker'ria). A hardy, leaf-losing shrub which grows 4-5 ft. high and bears single roselike flowers in spring. It is a native of China and belongs to the Rose family, Rosaceae. Kerria commemorates William Kerr, a collector of Chinese plants. He was the first to introduce the double variety in 1804. The single-flowered wild type was not introduced to gardens until 1834. Two or three varieties with variegated leaves are sometimes grown.

Though the Kerria will grow and flower in ordinary garden ground, it is much more satisfactory when planted in deeply dug, loamy soil enriched with decayed manure or compost. It will thrive in the open garden, but is better suited for a lightly shaded position. The double-flowered Kerria makes an effective informal hedge.

Pruning and Propagating. These shrubs are easily propagated by division of the clumps in autumn or in spring. Pruning should be done as soon as flowering has finished, usually during the second half of May. The old branches should

then be cut back to where strong new shoots are seen, and weak, worn-out branches should be cut off near the ground.

Kerria japonica is a bushy shrub with bright green leaves and showy yellow flowers, 1-2 in. across, that are borne freely on arching branches. The double-flowered variety, flore pleno, is commoner in gardens. It is more upright and taller in growth, attaining a height of 6-10 ft.; the yellow, rosette-like flowers are 1½-2 in. across. The double-flowered variety is slightly hardier than the single-flowered kind.

KETELEERIA (Keteleer'ia). Two kinds of evergreen cone-bearing trees from China, K. Davidiana and K. Fortunei, allied to the Fir or Abies, from which they chiefly differ by their cones remaining intact after the seeds ripen and by the different shape of the seeds. They are rare in cultivation and are suitable for the lower South only.

Similar cultivation to that required by the Firs is suitable. (See Abies.) Young plants are decidedly tender, but once hardwood has been formed they withstand a moderate amount of frost. K. Davidiana is a very striking tree with long dark green leaves. Keteleeria belongs to the Pine family, Pinaceae, and the name was given in honor of a French nurseryman, J. B. Keteleer.

KIDNEY VETCH. See Anthyllis.

KIGELIA PINNATA—*Sausage Tree* (Kigel'ia). A tropical African tree belonging to the Bignonia family, Bignoniaceae, that is

This fine Southern Florida specimen of the Sausage Tree produces its curious fruits freely.

occasionally cultivated in the far South as a curiosity. The name Kigelia is derived from a native name.

Kigelia pinnata grows in frost-free climates and attains a height of about 50 ft. It is remarkable for its elongated gourdlike fruits. The Sausage Tree seems to grow without trouble in any reasonably good soil. It is propagated by seeds.

KINGCUP. See Caltha palustris.

KINGFISHER DAISY. See Felicia.

KING PALM. Archontophoenix, which see.

KING'S-SPEAR. Eremurus, which see. See also Asphodeline.

KINNIKINNICK. Arctostaphylos Uva-ursi, which see.

KIRENGESHOMA PALMATA (Kirengesho'-ma). A hardy perennial herbaceous plant, which grows 2 ft. in height, has large, papery, palmate, hairy leaves and bears small terminal clusters of yellow, bell-shaped flowers,· 1½ in. in length, in summer. It is a native of Japan and belongs to the Saxifrage family, Saxifragaceae. The word Kirengeshoma is a Japanese word meaning yellow-flowered. This plant thrives in a semishaded place in ordinary garden soil, preferring that which is fairly light and well drained. It should be planted in spring, and is increased by dividing the rootstock at planting time.

KITAIBELIA VITIFOLIA (Kitaibel'ia). A hardy perennial flowering plant with ornamental foliage. It is a native of eastern Europe and belongs to the Hollyhock family, Malvaceae. The stems, which grow about 8 ft. in height, have large, vinelike leaves; the large pink flowers open in summer. The name Kitaibelia commemorates Paul Kitaibel, of the botanic garden at Pesth.

This plant thrives in a sunny position and is suitable for planting at the back of the herbaceous border. It prefers light, well-drained soil and may be planted in autumn or spring. Propagation is by division of the roots at planting time or by seeds sown out of doors in summer.

KITAMBILLA. See Dovyalis.

KITCHEN GARDEN. That portion of the garden which is devoted chiefly to the cultivation of vegetables; fruit trees are also often planted there.

KITCHINGIA UNIFLORA. The plant sometimes known by this name is treated as Kalanchoë uniflora in this Encyclopedia. See Kalanchoe.

KLEINIA (Klein'ia). Tender, succulent plants, from South Africa, which belong to the Daisy family, Compositae. They have yellow, daisy-like flowers, and are closely allied to the Groundsel (Senecio). The principal kind, K. articulata,

The Golden-Rain Tree, Koelreuteria paniculata, is a good summer-blooming shade tree for sunny locations.

has smooth cylindrical stems from which it derives its common name of Candle Plant. The leaves are hastate (spear-shaped) and 1 in. in length. Kleinias are suitable for planting outdoors in the Southwest and in similar dry, mild climates.

For a Sunny Greenhouse or Window. A minimum winter temperature of 45 degrees is required. The best compost consists of two parts loam and one part sand and crushed brick. Repotting is done in March, or as soon as new growth commences, and the compost is made firm. After potting, no water is applied until the soil becomes quite dry. No shading is required. These plants thrive in a sunny window. During summer, water is applied freely to well-rooted plants, but in the winter sufficient only is given to prevent the stems from shriveling.

When to Take Cuttings. Cuttings are taken at any time from March–August. The shoots are removed and exposed to the air for a few hours to allow the cut surfaces to dry. They are then inserted in sand in the greenhouse. No water is given until the sand becomes nearly dry. Rooted plants are potted first in 3-in. and later in 5-in. pots. Kleinia can also be raised from seeds sown in pots of sandy soil under glass in spring or summer.

The principal kind is K. articulata (Candle Plant), 18 in., yellow. Other kinds in cultivation include K. ficoides, white, creeping; K. fulgens, 2 ft., orange-red; and K. repens, creeping, white.

KNAPWEED. See Centaurea.

KNIPHOFIA—*Torch Lily, Poker Plant* (Kniphof'ia). Herbaceous perennial plants which form large leafy tufts and bear tall, handsome spikes of small, tubular, brilliantly colored flowers chiefly in late summer and early autumn. They belong to the Lily family, Liliaceae, and most of them grow wild in South Africa. They are mostly not reliably hardy in the North. The name Kniphofia commemorates Johann H. Kniphof, a German doctor. In many gardens the Torch Lilies are still grown under the name of Tritoma.

Brilliantly Colored Showy Summer Flowers. These plants make an imposing display when in full bloom. Their tall, erect spikes, on the upper parts of which are the clusters of flowers—chief-

Flowers of the Torch Lily or Poker Plant, Kniphofia.

ly of orange, reddish or yellow coloring—are very striking. The various kinds differ considerably in height and vigor of growth; some of them have long leaves, develop into large clumps and bear flower spikes which reach a height of 5 ft.; others have narrower leaves and the flower spikes are only 2 ft. high. Some bloom in June–July, others in August–September.

The smaller kinds are suitable for planting in the herbaceous border or in beds on the lawn; the more vigorous kinds may be planted in a large herbaceous border and they look well in the less formal parts of the garden, on the edge of, and in open spaces in, woodland, or by the waterside; they are seen to great advantage in open spaces among trees and shrubs where their tall spikes of bright flowers, which have given rise to the popular name of Poker Plant, show perfectly.

Needs Well-drained Soil. Kniphofia thrives best in sandy, loamy soil; clayey ground can be made suitable by adding compost, sand, grit and decayed manure. Very light land is improved by adding compost and manure. In cold localities a sheltered position should be chosen for Kniphofia, but it must also be a sunny one; these plants are not suitable for a shady or even a partially shady place.

Protection in Winter. If there is any doubt as

to whether they are likely to come safely through the winter, the plants should be protected towards the end of the year or they should be dug up each fall and stored over winter in soil in a well-protected cold frame or in a cool cellar. Protection outdoors may be provided by tying the leaves loosely together and surrounding them with salt hay or straw which must be fastened around the leaves to keep them in position. Leaves ought also to be placed on the soil immediately near the plants. If treated in this way, the Kniphofia will come safely through considerable cold weather.

The best time to plant Kniphofia is in spring; the plants will then have the whole summer in which to become established and are much more likely to remain sound during the first winter than if planting is done in autumn. On clayey ground deep planting should be avoided; the roots must not be covered with more than 2 or 3 in. of soil.

If protective materials are used in the way advised, they must be taken off when severe weather seems to be past. Any dead or discolored leaves ought also to be cut off at the same time. If the soil about the plants is then forked up and some fertilizer is put on and turned lightly into the surface of the ground, the plants will soon make progress.

Propagation. It is unwise to disturb Kniphofia plants so long as they continue to flourish. If an increased number is required, the old plants should be lifted in spring and carefully separated into pieces for replanting. If they can be grown in pots in a cold frame for a few months until they are well rooted, it will be an advantage, but they may be planted directly in the places where they are to be grown. Kniphofia can also be grown from seeds, though the seedlings are rather slow growing.

The seeds are sown in a pot of sifted sandy soil in a greenhouse, temperature 50 degrees, in March or April; the seedlings are potted separately in 3-in. pots and kept in a garden frame until the following spring.

The Chief Kinds. There are many species or wild types of Kniphofia, and numerous named varieties, which have been raised by crossbreeding and selection, are sold by nurserymen. The common Poker Plant is Kniphofia Uvaria (alooides), which blooms in August and September; the stems reach a height of nearly 4 ft. and the flowers are orange-red.

Other species are K. Burchellii, 4 ft., deep red and orange-yellow; K. caulescens, 5 ft., which has a short stem (and is thus distinct from other kinds which form tufts of leaves only), grayish leaves and flowers of rose-red; K. Macowanii, 2 ft., light-red; K. Nelsonii, 2½ ft., a beautiful yellow Torch Lily of rather slender growth; K. Northiae, 5 ft., which bears red and pale yellow flowers in June and July; K. rufa, 4 ft., salmon-red, of slender growth; and K. Tuckii, 4 ft., which has large handsome leaves and bears spikes of bright red and yellow flowers.

Of the named varieties these are some of the best: corallina superba, 3 ft., rose-red and deep yellow; Bee's Lemon, 3½ ft.; Goldelse, 2 ft., yellow, of slender growth; Royal Standard, 3-4 ft., a very handsome plant with orange-red flowers; and Sir C. K. Butler, primrose-yellow, 3 ft.

KNOTGRASS. See Polygonum.

KNOTWEED. Polygonum, which see.

KOCHIA SCOPARIA — *Summer Cypress* (Koch'ia). A summer annual, native to the southern countries of Europe, which forms a graceful, symmetrical, leafy bush about 2½ ft. high and is grown for the value of its leaf coloring. The flowers are small and of no decorative value.

A basket containing young plants of Kniphofia rufa in bloom, for sale at a retail nursery.

This plant belongs to the family Chenopodiaceae. During the summer months the leaves of Kochia are light green; at the approach of autumn they become purplish-bronze. Kochia is commonly used for planting in summer flower beds.

When to Sow Seeds. It is usually raised from seeds sown in a greenhouse, temperature 50 degrees, early in March. The seeds are sown in a flat filled with a sifted compost of loam, two thirds, and leaf mold, one third, with a scattering of sand. When the seedlings are 2 in. high, they should be potted singly in 3-in. pots, or set 4 in. apart in flats, 5 in. deep, filled with the soil compost already recommended. It is preferable to grow the seedlings in separate pots; they can then be transplanted without damage to the roots.

It is necessary to take care that the plants do not become dry at the roots, for if their growth is checked they make poor progress and the leaves change color prematurely. The plants are set out of doors in May.

KOELREUTERIA PANICULATA—*Golden-Rain Tree* (Koelreuter'ia). A hardy leaf-losing tree, a native of China, conspicuous by reason of its large, handsome leaves, which are divided into numerous leaflets, and its large terminal

The inflated seed pods of Koelreuteria paniculata turn a warm chocolate brown in fall.

The small bright yellow flowers of the Golden-Rain Tree, Koelreuteria paniculata, are borne in large panicles in summer.

clusters of yellow flowers, which are followed by inflated triangular seed pods, each containing a hard brown seed or seeds. It grows 40-60 ft. high in China, and there are trees 30-40 ft. high in North America. On young vigorous specimens the leaves may be 18 in. long and 9 in. wide but on older trees they rarely exceed 12 in. in length. The flowers appear in summer.

This handsome tree must be given a position exposed to full sun, and planted in well-drained loamy soil. Planting should be done in autumn or spring. It is increased by seeds sown, as soon as ripe, in sandy soil in a cold frame. This tree withstands drought well.

Two other kinds are known, K. bipinnata, from western China, which is not very hardy, and K. apiculata, from central China, which is said to be hardier but is not well known. Koelreuteria belongs to the family Sapindaceae and was named in honor of Joseph G. Koelreuter, a professor of natural history at Karlsruhe in the eighteenth century.

KOENIGA MARITIMA. Lobularia (Alyssum) maritimum, which see.

KOHLERIA. For plants classified by some botanists under this name see Isoloma.

KOHLRABI — *Turnip-stemmed Cabbage* (Kohlra'bi). The botanical name of this vegetable is Brassica caulorapa. It is botanically closely related to the Cabbage, and belongs to the same family, Cruciferae. In appearance, however, Kohlrabi is quite distinct from the Cabbage. It has a large, rounded stem, somewhat similar to

Purple Kohlrabi, an excellent vegetable, is easy to grow.

The Beauty Bush, Kolkwitzia amabilis, has bark which peels away from the stems in large flakes.

that of the Turnip, and leaves develop on its surface.

This vegetable must be grown quickly and used while young, otherwise it becomes tough and develops a strong flavor. It can be grown during hot, dry summer weather when the cultivation of Turnips is difficult. Its chief merit is that it provides a substitute for Turnips during the summer months. It may be grown in the same way as Cabbage except that the plants are spaced 8 in. apart in rows 18 in. apart. Like Turnips, it may also be sowed where the plants are to remain.

KOLKWITZIA AMABILIS — *Beauty Bush* (Kolkwitz'ia). This Chinese leaf-losing shrub belongs to the Honeysuckle family, Caprifoliaceae. It was first introduced to gardens in 1901 by the late Dr. E. H. Wilson, who collected seeds on rocky slopes at 9,000 to 10,000 ft. altitude in Hupeh. It is a vigorous bush 8 or 9 ft. high, of very twiggy growth, with broadly ovate leaves,

The pink-flowered Beauty Bush, Kolkwitzia amabilis.

1-3 in. long, and bell-shaped abelia-like flowers, produced in pairs, pink with yellow throat, in May and June.

This shrub thrives in loamy soil enriched with decayed compost or leaf mold. Propagation is by cuttings inserted in a frame during July or August or by seeds sown in spring. Seedlings vary considerably in color and size of flower. Each year, towards the end of June, the old wood which has recently flowered should be cut out and the bushes trimmed to shape.

The Kolkwitzia is perfectly hardy, and it grows and flowers with remarkable freedom. It is aptly known as the Beauty Bush.

KOREAN CHERRY. The Korean Cherry, Prunus japonica, is a low shrub that grows up to 4 ft. high and bears heavy crops of Cherries about the size of Sour Cherries but much firmer. It is a native of central China and is very hardy. Selected varieties have been segregated by the Minnesota Agricultural Experiment Station and are now available from nurseries.

Seedlings vary greatly in size and quality, most of them being rather acid and astringent, but the best are of fair quality and make good pies.

KRUBI. A name sometimes applied to Amorphophallus titanum, which see.

KUDZU VINE. Pueraria Thunbergiana, which see.

KUMQUAT. See Fortunella.

L

LABEL. Many types of garden labels have been invented but the ideal is yet to be found. The perfect label would be one which was everlasting, easily read yet inconspicuous and cheap. The nearest approaches to the ideal at present are labels of lead or aluminum alloy with raised letters or the names punched into them, and labels of laminated plastic with the letters engraved in them. These kinds are nearly indestructible and can be made in all sizes suitable for the rock garden, herbaceous border, Roses, shrubs and trees.

To letter laminated plastic labels a special, rather costly machine is necessary. This makes the home production of such labels impractical for most amateurs. However, amateurs may be able to have this type of label made for them by commercial producers of plastic signs or by others who possess a suitable engraving machine.

A good type of label for trees and shrubs is the lead label, in which the letters are punched and then filled with white paint. They can be suspended from a branch with a piece of wire, or fixed to an iron stand inserted in the ground. These can be made at home; after the initial expense of the lettered punches the cost of the lead is moderate. Metal labels which have to be written on with special metallic ink are inexpensive, but they are not permanent, as the writing eventually fades.

Celluloid labels enclosed in a glass-covered frame are not costly, but they are rather clumsy. Soft metal labels with the names stamped in are permanent. The advantages of these are that they can be coiled around the branches of shrubs or rose trees. For pot plants plastic labels are popular, especially for Orchids. They can be written on with pen or pencil and are not affected by damp.

The ordinary wooden labels are, however, the

[6—4]
Jacobinia carnea

[6—4a]
Mountain Laurel
(Kalmia latifolia)

[6—4c]
Beautybush
(Kolkwitzia amabilis)

[6—4b]
Kerria japonica pleniflora

[6—5]
Golden Chain (Laburnum)

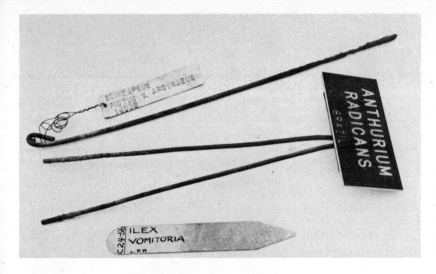

Three types of labels. The upper one is a label made from a strip of aluminum alloy with raised letters punched into it. The center label is made of laminated plastic with letters engraved into it. The bottom label is of zinc, written upon with a special metallic ink.

most popular for pot plants, vegetables, and all temporary crops. They can be purchased ready painted or made at home from spare wood. If it is desired to make them more permanent, the lettering can be varnished over and the lower half soaked in a wood preservative. A preservative such as Cuprinol is satisfactory; under no circumstances should creosote be used, because it is deadly to living plants.

Writing Wooden Labels. Whether wooden labels are to be protected with wood preservative and varnish or not, it pays to take some little care in writing them. If pencil writing is done on bare wood, or even on the surface of labels purchased ready painted, it is very apt to become illegible before the label has served its full pur-

pose; the writing may become unreadable in a matter of a few months or even weeks. By following the simple procedure described below, the life of the label and legibility of the writing on it may be increased several fold.

Rub on the surface that is to be written upon a small amount of white lead and linseed oil paint of somewhat thicker consistency than would normally be used for painting. Wipe the surface nearly dry with a piece of cotton cloth and then, immediately (before the paint begins to dry and become tacky), write on the label with a soft lead pencil. This will make a heavy black mark that will remain readable as long as the label lasts.

LABELLUM. A name used in describing the

Left: Prepare wooden labels by placing a little thick white paint on the wood. *Center:* Rub the paint into the wood with a cloth; remove any excess so that the surface is nearly dry. *Right:* Write with a soft pencil the name of the variety, sowing date, source of seeds, and any other pertinent data.

third or lowest petal of an Orchid flower; this petal (lip or labellum) is usually of different shape from, and much larger than, the two other petals.

LABLAB. Dolichos Lablab, which see.

LABRADOR TEA. See Ledum.

LABURNOCYTISUS ADAMII. This is one of the most interesting trees in cultivation, for it is one of those rarities known as graft hybrids or chimeras. It originated in France, about 1827, after Cytisus purpureus had been grafted on a stock of Laburnum anagyroides. The hybrid grows as large as a Laburnum; its leaves are less silky and smaller than those of the Laburnum, and it bears smaller racemes of purplish-pink flowers, but in addition to this it also produces branches of pure Laburnum, and of pure Cytisus purpureus. As all the flowers are open at once, the tree has a peculiar and interesting appearance. It is increased by grafting on stocks of common Laburnum.

LABURNUM (Labur'num). Handsome, leaf-losing trees which are fairly hardy in the North and have pendent clusters of golden flowers in May and June. There are two principal kinds, L. anagyroides (better known under the name of L. vulgare) and L. alpinum, both natives of Europe; there are numerous varieties and hybrids. There is also a shrubby kind from Greece and Asia Minor, L. caramanicum.

A tree of the common Laburnum, L. anagyroides (vulgare), in full bloom.

Ranking among the most decorative of all spring-flowering deciduous trees are the Laburnums. This flowering spray is Laburnum Vossii, a hybrid with exceptionally long flower racemes.

Laburnums are poisonous in all their parts, and children have died after eating the seeds and shoots. Laburnum belongs to the Pea family, Leguminosae, and the name is the ancient Latin name for the tree.

Propagation and Pruning. Propagation of the commoner kinds is by seeds; named varieties are increased by grafting on stocks of the common Laburnum. Cultivation is of the easiest. Some pruning is necessary while the trees are young in order to encourage height growth, but it is unwise to cut large branches off old trees as the wounds do not heal very well.

Laburnum Lives for 100 Years. Laburnum trees may live 100 or more years. Laburnums are not liable to serious injury by insect pests. The heartwood, very hard, heavy and dark in color, is brown or almost black. In a manufactured state it has the appearance of ebony, more particularly when polished. It is sometimes used in Europe for turnery and cabinetwork.

The Common Laburnum. L. anagyroides (L. vulgare), common Laburnum or Golden Chain, may grow 25 ft. high. The racemes of flowers are 4-6 in. long, but are much longer in the best varieties. A number of varieties have been given distinct names, some being improvements on the type, others not. The best are Alschingeri, with short, nearly upright racemes of flowers; autumnale, which flowers for a second time during late summer; and aureum, which has golden leaves. Bullatum, with curled leaves; pendulum, with pendent branches; and quercifolium, with curiously shaped leaves are only recommended to those who like curious plants.

The Scotch or Alpine Laburnum. L. alpinum is a more vigorous tree than L. anagyroides, and flowers two or three weeks later. It is commonly called the Scotch or Alpine Laburnum and may grow 25-30 ft. high with a trunk 12-18 in. in diameter. The leaves are large and dark green and the inflorescences are much longer than those of L. anagyroides, often 8-9 in. in length.

Of hybrids that have appeared between the Common and Alpine Laburnums, L. Watereri is one of the best. It flowers very freely, bears racemes 9 in. long and grows into a tall tree. Other good hybrids are Parksii and Vossii, the latter having very long racemes of flower.

L. caramanicum is a shrub from Asia Minor and Greece, 6-7 ft. high, with flower racemes 3-6 in. long; it is less hardy than the others and less generally useful.

LACEBUG. See Pests and Diseases.

LACE FERN. Cheilanthes, which see.

LACEFLOWER. Trachymene caerulea, which see.

LACELEAF PLANT. See Aponogeton fenestralis.

LACE VINE. Polygonum Aubertii, which see.

LACHENALIA: CAPE COWSLIP

How to Grow This Group of Beautiful Winter- and Spring-flowering Bulbs

(Lachena'lia). Handsome early spring-flowering bulbs which are suitable for cultivation in a greenhouse in which a minimum temperature of 45 degrees can be maintained, and for planting outdoors in mild climates such as that of southern California. They are natives of South Africa and belong to the Lily family, Liliaceae. The name Lachenalia commemorates a French botanist, M. de la Chenal.

These plants are well suited to cultivation in an amateur's sunny greenhouse where, if the requisite temperature is maintained, they will bloom in February and March. They have strap-shaped leaves, green with brownish markings, and spikes, 8-12 in. high, of small tubular flowers of various colors, chiefly yellow, orange and allied shades.

When to Pot the Bulbs. The bulbs should be potted in August or September; the most suitable potting compost consists of loam, two thirds, and leaf mold and thoroughly decayed manure, one third, with a free scattering of sand. The bulbs should be set about 1½ in. apart, the tops just below the surface of the soil. The soil is thoroughly moistened by means of a watering can having a spray nozzle on the spout, and the pots of bulbs are then placed in a shaded cold frame.

In six or seven weeks the bulbs will be well

The modern large-flowered hybrid Lachenalias, with blooms in rich shades of golden yellow, green and red, makes a lovely spring show in the greenhouse from bulbs potted in August.

This is Lachenalia contaminata, one of the many Cape Cowslips that occur wild in South Africa and are suitable for growing in cool greenhouses.

have turned yellow, the soil should be left quite dry. During the summer months the pots of bulbs should be set in a cold frame in a sunny position; the soil should not be watered. There the bulbs will become well "ripened" or matured, a condition which is essential to their flowering well another year.

Late in August or early in September the bulbs are taken out of the soil, graded into sizes, and repotted in the way already described. The large bulbs should be kept together, and the small ones potted in separate pots. An increased stock is obtained in this way.

Seeds of Lachenalia should be sown in March, in sandy, loamy soil in a greenhouse with a minimum temperature of 45 degrees. Leaf cuttings inserted in sand in early winter afford another means of propagation.

The Chief Kinds. The chief species of Lachenalia are L. tricolor, green, red and yellow, and its variety Nelsonii, yellow; and L. pendula, and its varieties, red flushed with green and purple.

These, however, have now been superseded by the modern named large-flowered varieties which have been raised by crossbreeding and selection. They are chiefly of yellow, orange, orange-red and greenish-yellow coloring. A few handsome ones are Bullfinch, yellow, green and red; Cowslip, yellow; Goldfinch, yellow and red; Greenfinch, greenish-yellow; and San Remo, yellow and red.

LACTIFLORA. A botanical term meaning with milk-white flowers.

LACTUCA—*Lettuce* (Lactu'ca). Hardy annual and perennial plants, natives of various parts of Europe, which belong to the Daisy family, Compositae. The name is derived from *lac*, milk, an allusion to the milky juice which exudes from some kinds. Those of chief value in gardens are the familiar salad vegetables, which are dealt with under the headings of Lettuce and Celtuce.

A few of the hardy perennials are worth planting in a large herbaceous border, but they are scarcely suitable for small gardens. They flourish in ordinary soil in a sunny or partly shaded position and may be planted in autumn and spring. If an increased stock is required the old plants should be lifted and

rooted and should then be placed in a greenhouse in which the thermometer does not fall below 45 degrees in cold weather. A maximum temperature of 55 degrees during the daytime is high enough for the Cape Cowslips; they do not flourish in a hot, moist atmosphere. Care must be taken not to water the soil too freely before the bulbs are well rooted. When the plants are in full growth and the flower spikes are seen, application of weak liquid fertilizer may be given every week with advantage.

During the dull winter months Lachenalias must be kept in as light a position as possible—on a shelf within 18 in. of the glass is a suitable place for them.

Suitable for Planting in Suspended Baskets. These plants are well suited for cultivation in a wire basket suspended from the greenhouse roof. The basket is first lined with moss to prevent the soil from falling out, and the compost already advised is then put in. Some of the bulbs should be set at the side of the basket and others at the top, so that when the plants are in bloom the basket will be well furnished.

When the flowers are over, and the leaves begin to change color, watering must be discontinued gradually, and finally, when the leaves separated into pieces in autumn.

The ornamental kinds chiefly worth growing are L. alpina, 3 ft., purplish-blue; L. Bourgaei, 4 ft., violet-blue; and L. Plumieri, 6-7 ft., purplish-blue. All bloom in July and August. The ornamental Lettuces are sometimes listed under the name of Mulgedium.

LADIES' TRESSES. Spiranthes, which see.

LAD'S-LOVE. Artemisia Abrotanum, which see.

LADY BELL. Adenophora, which see.

LADY FERN. Athyrium Filix-foemina, which see.

LADY OF THE NIGHT. See Brunfelsia.

LADY'S-FINGER. See Anthyllis Vulneraria.

LADY'S-MANTLE. See Alchemilla.

LADY'S-SLIPPER. See Cypripedium.

LADY'S-SMOCK. See Cardamine pratensis.

LAELIA (Lae'lia). A very attractive group of epiphytal Orchids which have evergreen leaves. Great variation exists in the pseudobulbs, leaves and flowers of different kinds. They grow wild chiefly in Central America, Mexico and Brazil. Laelias are closely akin to Cattleya, the only differences being botanical ones. These two Orchids cross-fertilize readily and many beautiful hybrids have been obtained; they are known as Laeliocattleya. A few natural hybrids have also been found. Laelia belongs to the family Orchidaceae.

Laelia anceps, with flowers of lilac-rose in winter, is a beautiful Orchid for the warm greenhouse.

For a Cool Greenhouse. In so varied a group of Orchids as Laelia the temperature and general treatment afforded must also vary. The Mexican kinds can be grown successfully in a greenhouse with a minimum winter temperature of 50-55 degrees: when in full growth they need a warm, moist atmosphere and a temperature of 70-80 degrees. Free ventilation is necessary in hot weather, and the ventilators may then be left open at night with advantage. These Orchids should be managed so that their growth is completed as quickly as possible; when growth is finished, usually after flowering, they should be given cooler and drier conditions and less water at the root.

Orchids for a Tropical Greenhouse. The Laelias from Brazil, with a few exceptions, require a warm, moist atmosphere when growing, and a minimum winter temperature of 55-60 degrees. Those kinds which have hard pseudobulbs should have a decided rest in winter.

The best potting compost consists of osmunda fiber. Those of straggling growth, e.g., L. anceps, may, for convenience, be grown in orchid baskets.

The Chief Kinds. L. purpurata, from Brazil, blooms in May; the flowers, 6-9 in. across, have white or bluish sepals and petals, and crimson or purple lip. There are many varieties: the variety alba has color on the lip; the pure white form is known as Queen Alexandra. All bear several flowers on each spike. L. grandis variety tenebrosa, from Brazil, is of similar habit of growth and has large flowers: the sepals and petals are reddish-brown, and the lip is purple; it flowers about midsummer. L. crispa, from Brazil, often has seven to nine flowers on a spike; they are hardly as large as those of L. purpurata, the sepals and petals being white or blush, and the lip bright purple. It usually flowers in early summer.

L. anceps, from Mexico, the most popular of the Laelias for a cool greenhouse, has short, four-angled pseudobulbs which bear long spikes, each with two to five flowers; the sepals and petals are mauve-red and the lip is crimson. Both this and its numerous white varieties flower at Christmas; so, too, does L. Gouldiana, a Mexican kind similar to L. anceps, but with conical bulbs and bearing from five to eight crimson-red flowers. L. autumnalis, known as the All Saints flower of Mexico, is similar in habit but lighter in floral coloring, and blooms in November.

L. pumila and its varieties praestans and Dayana usually have one flower, seldom two flowers, on a scape or spike. They are of dwarf growth, flower in autumn, and should be grown in a cool, moist greenhouse, minimum temperature 50-55 degrees. L speciosa, the Mexican flower of May, also requires a cool greenhouse. See also Trigonidium and Brassavola.

Typical flowers of Laelio-Cattleya, raised by crossbreeding between Laelia and Cattleya.

LAELIOCATTLEYA. This name is a combination of Laelia and Cattleya and is used for the many beautiful hybrids which have been raised between those orchids. For details of cultivation, see Cattleya.

LAGENARIA SICERARIA—Bottle Gourd (Lagena'ria). An annual trailing plant with ornamental fruits. It is a native of South Africa and belongs to the Cucumber family, Cucurbitaceae. It grows 10-30 ft. in height, has cucumberlike leaves, white flowers and large bottle-shaped fruits, which are ornamental but not edible. The name is derived from lagenos, a flask, from the shape of the fruit.

For Covering an Arbor or Trellis. The seeds are sown where the plants are to grow, or in pots of sandy soil in April in a greenhouse, temperature 55-60 degrees. Seedlings are raised indoors. Early in June they are planted out of doors in rich soil near a trellis or other suitable support to which the shoots cling by their tendrils. Beyond keeping them well supplied with water, no further cultivation is required.

LAGERSTROEMIA — Indian Lilac, Crape Myrtle (Lagerstroe'mia). Small trees and shrubs

with ornamental flowers; they grow wild in Australia and tropical Asia and belong to the family Lythraceae. They have oval leaves about 1 in. in length, and produce terminal or axillary clusters of large, rosy-purple, pink or white flowers with crinkled, crapelike petals in summer. The name Lagerstroemia commemorates M. Lagerstroem, a Swedish botanist.

Popular in the South. The Crape Myrtle is one of the most popular and easily grown shrubs for southern gardens. In sheltered places specimens survive all but the most severe winters even in the vicinity of New York City. They appreciate full sun and thrive in any ordinary well-drained soil. Even if killed back somewhat, removal of the dead wood by pruning in spring will encourage the development of new shoots that will bloom the same season.

In regions where they are not winter-killed, Crape Myrtles may be left unpruned, to develop into small trees, or may be kept shrublike by pruning them hard back and fertilizing them each spring, and thinning out weak and superfluous shoots that develop.

Kinds. L. indica, Crape Myrtle, is the common kind. There are several varieties, including alba, white flowers; purpurea, purple flowers; and rubra, red flowers; double-flowered kinds exist. L. speciosa, Queen Crape Myrtle, is

A fine specimen of Crape Myrtle, Lagerstroemia indica, growing in a southern garden.

planted in southern Florida and southern California.

Propagation is by inserting young shoots outdoors in mild climates in fall as cuttings, or by inserting leafy shoots as cuttings in a close cold frame in summer.

LAGURUS OVATUS—*Hare's-Tail Grass* (Lagu'rus). An ornamental hardy annual Grass which is valuable for cutting during the summer months and, when dried, may be used for vases indoors in winter. It is easily grown in ordinary garden soil in a sunny place and succeeds even on poor light land. The seeds may be sown in early spring, where the plants are to flower, the seedlings being thinned out to about 4 in. apart. Another plan is to sow the seeds in flats of sandy, loamy soil early in September, keep the flats of plants in a cold frame during the winter, and plant them out of doors in April. It is difficult to separate the plants, so several are planted together.

Lagurus belongs to the family Gramineae, and is naturalized in California. The name is derived from *lagos,* a hare, and *oura,* a tail.

LAMARCKIA AUREA (Lamar'ckia; Lamarck'ia). An annual Grass which grows 8-10 in. in height, and has terminal spikes of golden-yellow flowers of silklike texture. It is a native of southern Europe and belongs to the Grass family, Gramineae. The name Lamarckia commemorates J. B. Lamarck, a French naturalist.

When to Sow the Seeds. The seeds are sown outdoors in a sunny position in spring. Ordinary well-drained garden soil is suitable. The seedlings are thinned to 4 in. apart. The flowers are gathered when fully expanded and hung in a cool, airy position to dry for winter decoration. L. aurea is the only kind in cultivation.

LAMBKILL. Kalmia angustifolia, which see.

LAMB'S-EAR. See Stachys lanata.

LAMB'S-LETTUCE. See Corn Salad (Valerianella olitoria).

LAMB'S-QUARTERS. Chenopodium album.

LAMB'S-TONGUE. Stachys lanata, which see.

LAMIUM—*Dead Nettle* (La'mium). Hardy Old World herbaceous perennial plants, some of which are naturalized in North America. L. maculatum has green and white leaves and purplish flowers, and its variety aureum has yellow-ish leaves. They are worth a place in the wild garden. They flourish in ordinary soil and are increased by division in autumn and by summer cuttings. Lamium belongs to the family Labiatae. The name is an old Latin one.

LAMPRANTHUS (Lampran'thus). A group of succulent plants that once were included in Mesembryanthemum but are now segregated as a separate genus. They are shrubby perennials with large, brilliantly colored flowers and are natives of South Africa. They belong in the Carpetweed family, Aizoaceae. Their cultivation is the same as for Mesembryanthemum, which see.

Several different species are grown, of which the ones next described are examples. L. aureus grows to 18 in. tall and has 2-in.-wide golden-yellow flowers. L. coccineus may be 3 ft. tall and has prominently dotted leaves and scarlet flowers. L. glaucus has flattened, rough-dotted leaves and sulphur-yellow flowers; it grows to 2 ft. high. L. reptans is a prostrate plant with dotted, grayish-green leaves and yellow flowers.

LANDSCAPE ARCHITECT. A person, usually possessing a degree in Landscape Architecture, who engages professionally in the art of designing and supervising the laying out of gardens and grounds, both public and private, as well as other areas the planning of which demands a knowledge of plants, their capabilities and needs.

The decline of the large private estates, which once formed a main field of activity for the profession, has been more than compensated for by other and often broader opportunities and activities. Modern home-building trends involve the provision of larger outdoor areas with more sun, and trees and grass adjacent to small homes. This concept has given rise not only to a new type of community planning but to the development of modern apartment house units with important planted areas, the design and development of which require the services of a landscape architect.

Large industrial concerns are becoming increasingly aware of the value of spacious grounds and plantings, and modern factories are planned for suburban areas instead of crowded cities. Big department stores are locating and erecting suburban outlets outside large centers of population. Factories, shopping centers and large stores in suburban areas afford the landscape architect many opportunities to engage in his profession. Town planning, the development of throughways and park systems, airport planning and the design and laying out of modern cemeteries are other branches of planning and design open to the landscape architect.

LANDSCAPING. See Grading: Contouring The Ground; Planning The Garden; Planting: An Important Garden Operation; and Lawn: The Perfect Setting For Garden Flowers.

LANTANA (Lanta'na). Evergreen flowering plants, from tropical America, which belong to the Verbena family, Verbenaceae. They grow 2 to 6 ft. in height, have woody stems, rough, hairy, ovate leaves, 1½ in. in length, and axillary clusters of small, funnel-shaped, lavenderpink, yellow, orange or scarlet flowers in summer. They are used for decorating the greenhouse and for summer bedding where winters are cold, for permanent outdoor planting in the far South. The name Lantana is the old name of the Viburnum.

Cultivation in Pots. These plants thrive in a compost of two parts of loam, one of leaf mold and one part of well-decayed manure and sand. The shoots are pruned hard back in February and the plants are frequently sprayed with wa-

Lantana hybrids, most popular of garden kinds.

ter until they break into growth, when the plants are repotted in larger pots. When they are well rooted, the soil is kept moist, and liquid fertilizer is applied once a week when the plants are in flower. During the winter the soil is moistened only when it becomes dry; at that period a minimum temperature of 50 degrees is suitable.

As Basket Plants. The trailing Lantana montevidensis, which is often known in gardens as L. delicatissima, is excellent for growing in hanging wire baskets. Several young plants may be set around the sides and in the top of a large basket in spring or early summer. Before planting, the basket should be lined with sheet moss and be partly filled with soil; additional sheet moss and soil are placed in position as the plants are set around the sides. The surface soil is finished off nearly level with the top of the basket but with a slight depression in its center to hold water.

Established baskets should have the shoots of the Lantanas they contain pruned fairly hard back in February or March, should then be topdressed with rich soil and should be placed in a warm, sunny greenhouse and be kept syringed freely to induce new growth. Plants that have filled the available soil in the baskets with healthy roots benefit greatly from being fed with dilute liquid fertilizer twice a week from spring through fall.

Lantana montevidiensis has trailing stems and is useful for covering walls and for planting in hanging baskets.

Trained as Standards. Lantanas lend themselves particularly well to training as standards (specimens grown in "tree form," each having a single stem to a height of 2-3 ft. and a bushy top). To grow standard Lantanas, young plants are selected in late winter or spring, as soon as they are established in their first pots. All side shoots are pinched off promptly when they appear but the main central stem is not pinched. As soon as the first pots are filled with roots the plants are transferred to larger ones. Repotting is repeated as often as root growth makes it necessary until July, when the last potting for the season may be done.

At the time of the second potting a straight cane or stake is inserted in the soil and the plant is kept tied to this. When the single stem (which is to form the trunk of the tree) reaches the height at which the grower wants the head of the specimen to begin to form, its tip is pinched out to induce branching. Side branches that develop are pinched occasionally to encourage the development of a bushy head. Lantana standards live for many years and under good care increase in size and beauty annually.

For Summer Bedding. For this purpose cuttings are taken in February or March and inserted in a propagating case in a greenhouse, in a 60-70 degree temperature. When rooted, they are potted in 3-in. pots and the main shoots are pinched to make the plants branch. Eventually they are hardened off and planted out in the flower beds in June.

In the autumn a few of the plants are lifted, potted, and kept in the greenhouse to provide cuttings in the following spring.

The chief kinds are L. Camara, 6 ft., orange, and its variety nivea, 3 ft., white; L. trifolia, 3 ft., red; L. hybrida, 2 ft., yellow and red; L. montevidensis (Sellowiana or delicatissima), trailing, lavender-pink. All bloom in summer. There are also a number of named garden varieties.

LAPAGERIA (Lapage'ria). Tender climbing plants with attractive flowers. They are found wild in Chile and belong to the Lily family, Liliaceae. The name honors the Empress Josephine, born Marie Josèphe Rose Tascher de la Pagerie. They have wiry, twining stems, dark green, ovate, leathery leaves, and large, bell-shaped, pink, white or red flowers in summer.

A Climbing Plant. Lapageria rosea is the only species. It requires a shady moist position in a greenhouse with a minimum temperature of 40 degrees; in mild climates it may be grown outdoors. The plants are set in large pots or tubs or in a specially prepared border of soil in the greenhouse and the shoots are trained to wires. The best compost consists of three parts fibrous peat, one part loam and one part sand and crushed charcoal. Perfect drainage is essential. From April to September, water is applied liberally to the soil and the atmosphere is kept cool and moist. During the winter the soil is watered only when it becomes quite dry, and less atmospheric moisture is required.

When grown out of doors in mild climates, they require a well-drained bed of soil, as advised for plants grown under glass, and a shaded location.

Propagation is by layering strong shoots in pots of sandy peat in early autumn. Plants may also be raised from seeds and from cuttings.

The chief kind is L. rosea, pink, and popular varieties of it are albiflora, white, and superba, red. See illustration on page 976.

LAPEYROUSIA (Lapeyrou'sia). Hardy bulb plants, suitable for the rock garden and well-drained, sunny border in mild climates, and as pot plants. They are natives of the Cape of Good Hope, and belong to the Iris family, Iridaceae. These plants grow about 9 in. in height, have narrow grasslike leaves 6 in. in length, and

A dainty bulbous plant, the red-flowered Lapeyrousia cruenta.

Lapageria rosea, a climbing plant for a cool greenhouse. It produces its pink flowers of waxlike appearance in summer.

bear small spikes of scarlet flowers in summer. The name Lapeyrousia commemorates Jean François de la Peyrouse, a French botanist.

When to Plant the Bulbs. The bulbs are planted 3 in. deep and 4 in. apart in October. They require a sunny position and light, well-drained soil, and should not be disturbed until they show signs of deterioration. A top-dressing of leaf mold or compost is beneficial in spring.

For the Cool Greenhouse. They may also be grown in pots in a greenhouse or frame. The bulbs are potted, several in a 5-in. pot, in Octo-ber, and the pots are plunged in a frostproof cold frame until the shoots appear; they then are placed in a light, well-ventilated greenhouse and carefully watered. After flowering, less water is given, and they are gradually dried off as the leaves die down.

The chief kinds are: L. (Anomatheca) cruenta, red, 9 in., summer; L. grandiflora, red with yellow eye; and L. juncea, rose-pink, 12-18 in.

LARCH. See Larix.

LARCH, GOLDEN. Pseudolarix amabilis, which see.

LARDIZABALA BITERNATA (Lardizaba'-la). A vigorous evergreen climbing plant suitable for planting in the warmer parts of the United States. The leaves are divided into three, six, or nine leaflets, which are dark green and leathery in texture. Male and female organs are found in separate flowers, the male flowers being borne several together, the female flowers singly. The flowers are purple and white and borne in May, but are not very conspicuous among the leaves. The fruits are 2-3 in. long and sausage-shaped. Lardizabala thrives in ordinary garden soil in a sunny position, and is propagated by cuttings placed in a cold frame in summer. It is a native of Chile and belongs to the family Lardizabalaceae; the name was given in honor of M. Lardizabaly, a Spanish patron of natural history.

LARIX: THE LARCH

Cone-Bearing Trees of Grace and Beauty

(Lar'ix). Leaf-losing trees found wild in northerly regions, or at a considerable elevation in the mountainous parts of temperate countries; they are widely distributed in central Europe, the Himalayas, China, Korea, Siberia and Japan, and in North America. They are among the most beautiful of leaf-losing trees in spring, by reason of the delicate green of the young leaves and the beauty of the female flowers which are often pink. In autumn they are again very striking when the leaves turn pale golden-yellow.

The Larches are easily distinguished among Conifers or cone-bearing trees by their leaves, which are arranged as in the Cedar of Lebanon; those on terminal shoots, leaders and branches surround the shoot, whilst the side growths bear rosettes of leaves. These side shoots grow very slowly, a fraction of an inch a year, but the fresh annual growth at the ends of the branches may be 2 ft., and the leading or central shoot or stem may grow 4 ft. or more. The seeds are small and winged and are produced in cones which are usually brown when ripe. Larix is the old Latin name for the Larch; this tree belongs to the Pine family, Pinaceae.

Cone-bearing branch of the Japanese Larch, Larix leptolepis.

The European Larch, Larix decidua.

Culture. Larches are widely grown as timber trees. They thrive on hillside plantations and do well in most soils where drainage is good. The American Larch, however, is found in swampy places and is suitable for planting in boggy soil and by watersides. When Larches are grown as ornamental specimens some pruning may be necessary in their early years in order to develop a single leading stem to each tree. Later, the prompt removal of poor branches is conducive to a clean appearance.

American Larches. Larix laricina, commonly known as Tamarack and Hackmatack, grows over a wide range in North America; it grows to 60 ft. high and has a narrow, pyramidal head. The cones are less than 1 in. long, smaller than those of other Larches. L. occidentalis, Western Larch, grows to 150 ft. tall in its native range, which is from British Columbia to Oregon. It is hardy in Massachusetts.

The European Larch is L. decidua, a valuable tree that grows up to 150 ft. high under natural conditions. It has been widely planted in eastern North America. Distinctive forms are L. decidua pendula, with weeping branches, and L. de-

cidua pyramidalis, which is of compact upright form.

The Japanese Larch is L. leptolepis, formerly L. Kaempferi. It is the fastest growing and most ornamental of the Larches and grows to 90 ft. tall. It is hardy in Massachusetts.

The Chinese Larch is L. Potaninii, a more recent introduction, and not yet widely grown. L. Gmelinii, Dahurian Larch, is likely to be better represented in cultivation by its variety japonica, the Kurile Larch, and its variety Principis-Rupprechtii, the Prince Ruppert Larch. Both are growing well in Massachusetts.

Economic Uses. Larch timber is of good quality and is variously used for building purposes. Being very durable in contact with soil and water, it makes excellent posts and has been widely used in the building of small boats. Tamarack turpentine was used by the early settlers to take the ache out of wounds.

Propagation. Except in the case of a few named varieties, propagation is by seeds. Seeds of all the better-known kinds are sown in a bed of well-drained soil in spring. The ground should be dug and cleared of weeds. The time of sowing differs by a few weeks according to the local climate. As a rule seedlings appear about six weeks from the time of sowing and it is unwise to sow so early that the tiny seedlings are exposed to late frosts. From the beginning to the middle of April is a good time for sowing, but if the ground is very wet it is better to delay the work rather than attempt to sow at a given date.

Seedbeds should upon no account be made on a site subject to flooding after heavy storms; where late frosts are experienced, provision should be made for sheltering the plants at night. During hot sunshine in spring a little shade is also an advantage.

The seed should be sown thinly and covered with 1/4 in. of coarse sand. Before being sown, the seeds should be mixed with red lead. Seeds of rare kinds ought to be sown in flats or pots in a frame. The few named varieties are grafted on stocks of their respective types, previously established in pots.

LARKSPUR, ANNUAL. Delphinium Ajacis, which see.

LARVA. The immature or grub stage of an

insect. It is the stage in which the greatest amount of feeding usually takes place; hence larval stages are more often than not responsible for the bulk of the damage in the case of insects which are pests. The larval stages of some insects are sometimes referred to as nymphs, particularly when these larval stages resemble their parents to a marked degree, e.g., capsid bugs. The larval stages of butterflies, moths and sawflies are usually referred to as caterpillars. The plural of larva is larvae.

LASIANDRA. Tibouchina, which see.

LASTHENIA GLABRATA (Lasthe′nia). A dwarf, hardy, annual flowering plant of California, which belongs to the Daisy family, Compositae. It grows 12 in. in height, has lance-shaped leaves, 4 in. in length, and bears yellow flowers, 1 in. in diameter, in summer. The name Lasthenia commemorates a Greek girl who was a pupil of Plato.

When to Sow the Seeds. The seeds of this annual are sown ¼ in. deep out of doors in spring. They require light, well-drained soil and a sunny position in the rock garden, or near the edge of the flower border. The seedlings must be thinned out to 6 in. apart.

The chief kind is L. glabrata, 12 in., bright yellow, summer.

LASTREA. A large group of Ferns now referred chiefly to Dryopteris and to Polystichum, which see.

LATANIA (Lata′nia). Palms, from Mauritius, which grow about 40 ft. tall, have large, fan-shaped, bright green leaves, and are useful for cultivation in pots in a warm greenhouse or for planting outdoors in south Florida. The name is from an East Indian one.

For a Warm Greenhouse. These Palms are easily managed in a greenhouse with a minimum winter temperature of 55 degrees. During the summer a tropical atmosphere must be maintained, with a temperature of from 80-90 degrees, and the air must be kept moist by damping down and syringing. The best compost consists of half fibrous· loam and half peat, with sand added freely.

Repotting, when necessary, should be done in March. During the summer months the soil in the pots must be kept moist; in winter less mois-

ture is needed, but the soil must not be allowed to become dry.

Propagation is by seeds, which are sown in pots of sandy peat and loam, in spring; the seed pots are plunged in a propagating case to ensure a bottom heat of 75-80 degrees.

The chief kinds are L. Commersonii, and L. Verschaffeltii. The Bourbon Palm, previously named L. borbonica, is now Livistona chinensis, which see.

LATERAL. A term used by gardeners to indicate the side shoots which develop on the main branches of a tree, shrub, or other plant.

LATH HOUSE. A structure, usually flat-roofed, made of wood or metal slats, or builders' laths fastened to a framework of lumber, piping or other suitable supports, with spaces between the laths to permit the free passage of air and admit sufficient light and, at the same time, to provide shade from the sun.

Such structures are used for the growing of young Azaleas, Rhododendrons, and other plants that are benefited by protection from the sun. They are also used in the propagation of these and other plants. In warm regions the lath house is used for growing Palms, Ferns, Camellias and for the propagation of many leafy plants.

Recently the lath house has assumed a new

An interior view of a lath house.

role. It has become an important piece of equipment in the modern retail nursery for the housing of all manner of plants during the sales and planting season. Here, protected from the sun, and with their roots buried in sawdust, peat or humus, plants that are dug and are awaiting sale require less watering and care and retain their fresh condition longer; moreover, there is less risk, when they are finally planted, than with plants that have been stored in the open.

Lath houses designed for this purpose are usually completely open on the side facing north. Sometimes the lath, instead of being fixed to the framework, is formed into movable shades so that a section can be rolled up or down as required. Laths made of aluminum are now often used in place of the wood lath, and are popular because of their lightness and greater durability.

LATHYRUS—*Sweet Pea, Perennial Pea* (Lath′-yrus). Hardy annual and herbaceous plants which are natives of southern and eastern Europe chiefly, and belong to the family Leguminosae. The name is one used by the Greek author Theophrastus.

The most popular member of this genus is Lathyrus odoratus, the Sweet Pea. For full details of cultivation see Sweet Peas.

Perennial Peas. The Perennial, or Everlasting Peas as they are often called, are easily grown and attractive flowering plants. They flourish in ordinary well-cultivated garden soil; as they are of climbing growth, they must be supported by a trellis, or by sticks. They look attractive towards the back of a large herbaceous border, where, if provided with support, they will add to the color display in July.

The perennial Peas should be planted in a sunny position in autumn or in spring; they can be increased by division in October, though it is better to leave them undisturbed, and to raise a fresh stock by sowing seeds singly in 3-in. pots filled with sandy, loamy soil, in March or April; the seedlings, when well rooted, should be planted out of doors in the place where they are to remain.

The common perennial Pea is Lathyrus latifolius, 6 or 7 ft. high, which bears purplish-rose flowers in July and August; a variety named White Pearl, which has large white flowers, is more attractive, and Rose Queen is also worth planting.

.Other kinds worth noting include L. magellanicus (Lord Anson's Pea), 6 ft., purplish-blue, July–August; L. pubescens, 4 ft., lavender-blue, July–August; and L. rotundifolius, 5 ft., carmine-rose, June–July.

LATTICELEAF. Aponogeton, which see.

LAUREL. See Laurus.

LAUREL, ALEXANDRIAN. See Danaë racemosa.

LAUREL, CALIFORNIA. Umbellularia californica, which see.

LAUREL, CHERRY. Prunus Laurocerasus, which see.

LAUREL, MOUNTAIN. Kalmia latifolia, which see.

LAUREL OAK. Quercus laurifolia, which see.

LAUREL, OREGON. See Arbutus.

LAUREL, PORTUGAL. Prunus lusitanica, which see.

LAUREL, SHEEP. See Kalmia angustifolia.

LAUREL, SPOTTED. The popular name of an evergreen shrub, Aucuba, which see. It is also called Japanese Laurel.

LAUREL, SPURGE. See Daphne Laureola.

LAURESTINUS. Viburnum Tinus, which see.

LAURUS NOBILIS—*Laurel, Sweet Bay* (Laur′-us). An evergreen tree, often grown as a shrub; a native of the Mediterranean region, it is not hardy in the North. It has classic associations, for its dark green, fragrant leaves were twined into wreaths by the ancient Greeks and Romans, who used them to crown the victors in their sports and wars.

This tree may grow 40 or more ft. high in the United States, with many branches and a wide-spreading head, and under the best conditions in southern Europe it reaches a height of 60 ft. It thrives in well-drained loamy soil. Cuttings of young shoots, inserted in a frame in July, will form roots in a few weeks if the frame is kept close.

Suitable for Cultivation in Tubs. It is very often grown in large tubs and clipped into pyramid form or into a round head surmounting a stem of several feet. Such plants are often used out of doors in summer and for conservatory decoration in winter. They require one or more annual clippings, an occasional washing with the garden hose to clean the leaves, and feeding to keep them in good condition. Male and female flowers are on different trees, and the latter are followed by black berries.

The leaves contain an essential oil which is sometimes used in perfumery, and whole leaves are used for flavoring and other culinary purposes. Laurus gives its name to the family Lauraceae and the name is the old Latin one for the Sweet Bay tree. There is a variety, angustifolia, with smaller leaves than the type.

LAVANDULA—*Lavender* (Lavan'dula). About twenty kinds are known; they grow wild chiefly in the Mediterranean region. The name Lavandula is supposed by some to be from the Latin *lavare,* to wash, a reference to its use in the preparation of lavender water. Lavender belongs to the Mint family, Labiatae. Some kinds are perennial herbs, others are shrubs.

The Most Suitable Soil. Lavender thrives best in a sunny, sheltered position. The most suitable soil is light, well drained, sandy loam in which compost or decayed manure has been mixed. In such soil the plants are much less liable to damage by frosts than when grown in heavy, wet ground. The Lavender makes an admirable informal, low hedge.

When to Take Cuttings. Propagation of the

A bed of Lavender, Lavandula officinalis, in full bloom. Several distinct varieties are grown; one, alba, has white flowers.

shrubby Lavenders is by cuttings made of the side shoots during August or early September. These should be 3 or 4 in. long; they are inserted in sandy soil out of doors, where the winters are mild, and covered with a bell jar. In harsher climates the cuttings should be placed in a close cold frame. The following spring the rooted cuttings should be planted in a nursery border. The tops must be pinched to make the plants branch, and in October, or the following spring, the young plants should be set in their permanent positions.

Propagation by Division. In climates that are moderately mild, Lavender plants, especially the dwarf varieties, are propagated by pulling the old plants to pieces (division) in early October and planting them in a cold frame or where they are to remain.

Most of the Lavenders can also be grown from seeds sown in flats of sandy soil in a cold frame or greenhouse in spring.

Planting and Pruning. The best time to plant Lavender is during October or April. Pruning or trimming should be done each year as soon as the blooms have faded, so that the bushes have time to make a little new growth before winter. Hard pruning is sometimes done in April, but this means the loss of a season's flowers. When Lavender bushes become old and straggling it is better to start again with young bushes rather

The Lavender, Lavandula officinalis, is attractive in foliage as well as bloom.

than to try to recondition them by hard pruning.

Considerable difference of opinion has existed among botanists as to whether two distinct species are grown as the common Lavender; most now classify all varieties of common Lavender under one species, Lavendula officinalis.

Old English Lavender. Lavandula officinalis (L. Spica), the English Lavender, grows 3-4 ft. high; it is said to have been first introduced to British gardens from southern Europe in 1568. There are several varieties: alba, white; Grappenhall Variety, a strong-growing and late-flowering Lavender; nana, sometimes called Dwarf French Lavender, 9 in. high; Munstead Dwarf, 18 in., an early-flowering variety with dark lavender-blue flowers; Folgate Variety, late-flowering and dwarf; and Twickel Purple, a compact variety with rich purple flowers.

Lavandula dentata is an attractive shrub, 1-2 ft. high from southeastern Europe; it has hoary or pubescent leaves and bears dark purple flowers in summer. It is less hardy than the English Lavender.

L. Stoechas is another tender, hoary-leaved Lavender, 1-1½ ft. high, from the Mediterranean region; it has dark purple flowers. L. multifida (pinnatifida) is a cut-leaved kind from the Canary Islands, 2 ft. tall and hardy in mild climates only.

Economic Uses. The Lavender (Lavandula officinalis) is a valuable plant for the sake of its sweet-smelling flowers. The flowers are rich in essential oil which is obtained by distillation and used very extensively in perfumery. There is also a good demand for the dried flowers, which are used for filling sachets and for placing among linen. The best quality of Lavender oil is produced in England, although a good deal is obtained from the south of Europe.

LAVATERA—*Rose Mallow, Tree Mallow* (Lava'tera; Lavate'ra). Shrubs, perennials and annuals, of great value in the garden; they belong to the Mallow family, Malvaceae, and grow wild in southern Europe, California, the Himalayas and other places. Lavatera commemorates the Swiss botanists, MM. Lavater.

The Annual Rose Mallow. The most popular kind is the annual Rose Mallow (Lavatera trimestris), from southern Europe, which grows 2-3 ft. high, and bears large, rose-colored flowers. It is raised from seeds sown outdoors in spring where the plants are to bloom. It is necessary to sow the seeds thinly, for the seedlings must be thinned out until they are 10 or 12 in. apart, to enable them to reach their full development. If the formation of seed pods is prevented by removing the faded blooms, the plants will flower, where summers are not excessively hot, throughout many weeks. Ordinary well-cultivated garden soil is suitable and a sunny position must be chosen.

Beautiful Varieties. There are several beautiful named varieties which are finer than the original species or wild type, and they should be grown in preference to the latter. Among them are Sunset, Loveliness, and splendens, all with large flowers of rich coloring. There is also a white variety, alba.

These annuals provide a magnificent display in the flower border during July and August, and even in September, if they are well grown by sowing seeds in rich deeply dug ground and preventing seed formation.

Greenhouse Culture. Improved varieties of the annual Lavatera trimestris are excellent for growing in cool greenhouses, both as decorative pot plants and to supply cut flowers. Their blooming season is late winter and spring. Seeds should be sown from September to January in porous soil in well-drained pots or flats. As soon as the seedlings are large enough to handle, they should be lifted and set 2 in. apart in flats, or individually in 2½-in. pots. They are kept growing in a sunny location where the night temperature is about 50 degrees F. and the temperature on sunny days is 5-10 degrees higher. Care should be taken not to keep the soil constantly saturated; it should be allowed to become nearly dry before water is applied, then enough should be given to soak it thoroughly.

When the plants begin to crowd each other in the flats or are well rooted in the pots, they are potted in 4- or 5-in. pots in a coarse, rich porous soil or are planted in benches of similar soil and are spaced 8-9 in. apart; if potted, they are later repotted into 6-8-in. pots, in which they will flower.

When the final pots or the soil in the benches

[6–6]

Lantana Camara varieties

[6—7]
Poker Plant
(Kniphofia)

[6—7a]
Crape Myrtle
(Lagerstroemia indica)

[6—7b]
Crape Myrtle
(Lagerstroemia indica alba)

[6—7c]
Golden Privet
(Ligustrum ovalifolium aureomarginatur

The Rose Mallow, Lavatera trimestris, is one of the loveliest of annuals. Its flowers are pink.

is well filled with roots, weekly applications of dilute liquid fertilizer are beneficial. The plants should be staked and tied neatly.

Tree Mallows. Lavatera Olbia is the best of the Tree Mallows. It is a vigorous plant, 5-6 ft. high, has woody stems and bears flowers of carmine-rose color in summer. It flourishes in ordinary, well-drained garden soil in a sunny position, and may be pruned in March by shortening the shoots of the past summer's growth to within 9 or 10 in. of the base. Under this treatment it will remain shapely, annually producing fresh, strong shoots. Such pruning is not, however, nec-

essary unless, as sometimes happens, the branches are damaged by frost in winter; they must then be cut back in March to such an extent as is necessary to leave only sound, undamaged growth.

This kind, like the next mentioned (L. arborea), is not reliably hardy where winters are much colder than those of Washington, D. C.

Lavatera arborea, from southern Europe, is still more vigorous, reaching a height of from 6-10 ft. It has attractive leaves and bears purplish flowers in summer. A variety which has variegated, green and pale-yellow leaves is sometimes used for planting in summer flower beds; it is then treated as an annual, and raised from seeds sown in a greenhouse in February or March. After having been potted separately in 3-in. and then in 5-in. pots, the plants are hardened off in a cold frame and planted out of doors in June.

Lavatera assurgentiflora, a native of the islands off the coast of southern California, is hardy in mild climates only. It grows to a height of 6-10 ft. and bears rose-purple flowers that are veined with darker purple. This kind is a shrub that attains a height of 5-6 ft. and blooms the first year from seed. It is very resistant to drought and in California is often planted as a windbreak.

Lavatera insularis, a native of the Coronado Islands and Lower California, is more rarely cultivated than L. assurgentiflora. It is hardy only in mild climates and forms a low shrub that bears yellowish-white flowers that are striped and tipped with purple.

Propagation. The best way to propagate the Tree Mallows is by sowing seeds singly in 3-in. pots of sandy loamy soil placed in a frame, in April. The seedlings are planted out of doors when they have filled the pots with roots. It is wise to choose fairly sheltered, though sunny, positions for the Tree Mallows, for they are liable to be damaged in severe weather.

LAVENDER. See Lavendula.

LAVENDER COTTON. Santolina Chamaecyparissus, which see.

LAVENDER, SEA. Limonium, which see.

LAWN: THE PERFECT SETTING FOR GARDEN FLOWERS
Full Instructions on How to Make and Maintain Good Lawns

A well-kept lawn adds immeasurably to the charm and beauty of a garden. Attractive in itself, it affords the perfect setting for flowers, shrubs, ornamental plants and many garden features. See Planning the Garden, Planting the Garden.

The perfect lawn cannot be made or maintained without some effort. Inattention as much as mismanagement can lead to deterioration. The lawn is ever open to weed invasion, and the perennial upkeep of an even, velvety sward of grasses calls for intelligent and regular care.

Lawns are made by sowing seeds, laying turf, planting plugs (small pieces of turf), planting sprigs (rooted shoots) and by planting stolons (fragments of creeping stem). Whichever method is used, the site must first be very thoroughly prepared. This may involve draining and grading, and most surely will necessitate loosening the ground deeply and incorporating with it decayed organic matter, fertilizer and possibly lime and other conditioners. Every effort must be made to have a planting bed free of weeds and weed seeds.

Where a sufficient depth of reasonably good topsoil does not exist, that which is there must be improved to a depth of 6-8 in., or additional good soil must be brought in. Improvement of comparatively infertile soil can be effected by following a program of growing successive crops of green manures or cover crops (see Fertilizers) for a period of a year or two and turning them under as soon as they are 6-8 in. tall. The ground should be fertilized before each green manure

Steep, short grass banks such as these are not too difficult to manage, but long, steep banks planted with lawn are not practicable.

A well-kept lawn forms a perfect setting for the home.

crop is sown. Adequate soil preparation is the basis of good lawn making.

An open, sunny location is best for a lawn, but good results may be had in partial shade provided the grass receives sun for 4-6 hours each day or dappled sunshine for a longer period. Shade from buildings is usually less detrimental than that from trees because, where these latter are, the grass has to compete with them for moisture and nutrients as well as get along with reduced light. Trees which mass their roots near the ground surface, as do Maples, Beeches and Planes, are especially difficult to grow a good lawn under, and often it is quite impossible to maintain turf under old specimens of these trees. In such places other ground covers, such as Pachysandra and Euonymus Fortunei coloratus, must be substituted or, in extreme cases, some form of paving.

Lawns on steep banks present special problems of making and maintenance, and thought should be given before making them if the grade is steeper than one in four (a 1-ft. drop for each 4 ft. horizontal). It is quite possible to keep a bank with a grade as steep as one in one covered with good turf but this necessitates constant and special care in fertilizing, watering and other chores of upkeep. Mowing steep, long banks is difficult; where such exist it is usually advisable to plant them with a ground-cover plant other than grass. See Banks.

Good drainage is highly important, being essential to the welfare of the finer lawn grasses and the exclusion of moss and certain weeds. To test the drainage, dig a hole 24 in. deep in winter. If the water rises to within 9 in. or less of the top, and the soil is heavy, drainage is necessary.

The most permanent and efficient drainage is given by agricultural drain tiles. These are laid 12-15 in. deep, in a grid or herringbone pattern. The grid system consists of a main drain of 4-in. diameter at the lower end of the lawn area, fed by subsidiary 3-in. drains at 12-18 ft.

intervals. The herringbone pattern has a central main drain with subsidiary drains running into it alternately on either side. The subsidiary drains are set to fall slightly, 1 in 200, to the main drain, and the main drain empties into any convenient ditch or outlet, or, at worst, a soakaway sump or dry well consisting of a 2-3 ft. square, 4-ft.-deep hole, filled with stones, rubble and clinkers. This latter device will only work if the subsoil is fairly porous.

An alternative plan for small lawns on poorly drained soils is to put a 6-in. layer of rough ashes or clinkers under the top 4-6 in. of soil and incorporate material such as sifted ashes, coarse sand or burnt earth with this topsoil. Where the subsoil is reasonably free-draining, but the topsoil inclined to be heavy, it is sufficient to work in ashes or sand.

Preparing the Site

The major part of the soil preparation—all except fertilizing and final raking of the surface to produce a fine sowing or planting bed—should be completed several weeks ahead of planting time. This allows the soil to settle and gives time for weed seeds to germinate and be destroyed by cultivation or chemical sprays.

Where contours have to be changed considerably the topsoil should be first stripped off and piled in conveniently located heaps, for replacing later.

Grading. Do all grading as early as possible. Where much is needed, the topsoil should be stripped off and placed in convenient piles on areas that will not be disturbed by the grading operations. When this has been done, the undersoil may be contoured as desired, and you may improve it by mixing with it organic matter, fertilizer and—if it is very clayey—coarse cinders or sand. After this, the topsoil may be replaced and it, in turn, improved by adding organic matter such as peat moss, sedge peat, compost, rotted manure or leaf mold. See Grading.

Turning the Soil. In preparation for lawn making, the soil should be turned to a minimum depth of 6 in.—8-10 in. is even better. This may be done with a spade, spading fork, plow or rotary tiller. If the soil below a depth of 6 in. is poor, do not dig or plow so deeply that much of it is brought to the surface or is mixed with the topsoil; grass cannot be expected to thrive in infertile subsoil.

Heavy soils, those containing much clay, can be greatly improved and lightened by the addition of fine coal cinders (not dustlike ashes, but gritty particles) or by the addition of coarse sand as well as generous amounts of decayed organic material such as compost, leaf mold, well-rotted manure, sedge peat and peat moss. All these materials should be thoroughly mixed with the upper six inches. Liming often is of great benefit to clayey soils.

Light soils, those that are sandy or gravelly, benefit greatly from the liberal addition of decayed organic matter; these soils are also benefited if you incorporate clay soil or clay in them. The latter may be spread to about a depth of 1 in. over the surface and be mixed with the upper three inches of soil.

When to Prepare the Soil. If at all possible, the basic preparation for a lawn that is to be made in spring should be completed in fall; if this is not practicable, it should be done just as early in spring as it is possible to work on the land.

Preparations for lawns that are to be made in fall (the preferred time) should be well under way in July, and before the end of that month all basic work should be done. From then until sowing or planting time every effort should be made to destroy all weeds that appear, so that a

(1) The first step in making a lawn is spading and incorporating manure, peat moss or other organic material with the soil. (2) The second is fertilizing and then raking to loosen the clods. (3) The third step is sowing the seed broadcast. (4) The fourth step is rolling, to consolidate the surface and to prevent the seed from being washed out.

clean planting or sowing bed is available later.

Liming is not necessary for lawns unless the soil is excessively acid. Most grasses prefer a slightly acid soil, one that tests pH 6.0-6.5. Bent Grasses and Fescues tolerate an even greater acidity, pH 4.5-5.5. To determine whether or not the soil needs lime and, if so, how much is needed, it is advisable to have a soil test made.

Fertilizing should be done about 2-3 weeks before sowing, planting, turfing or sprigging. A good general fertilizer is one of 4 parts by weight superphosphate, 2 parts sulphate of ammonia, and 1 part sulphate of potash, at 1½ to 2 oz. per sq. yd.; the heavier (2 oz.) dosage is for light soils or soils in partial shade or under trees. A complete commercial fertilizer such as a 5-10-5 or, preferably, one prepared especially for lawns, may be substituted, using 4-5 lbs. of the 5-10-5 to each 100 sq. ft. or an equivalent amount of another fertilizer.

The final preparation of the seedbed should be done about two weeks before sowing. Rake the soil thoroughly and roll it lightly, when it is nonsticky and dryish, in two opposite directions, to give firmness. Then rake to provide the fine crumbly condition ready for sowing.

Sowing

It is generally held that late summer or early fall is best for sowing a lawn, since the soil is then warm and conducive to good germination, and autumn weather favors growth, being coolish and moist as a rule. However, early spring sowings succeed, provided there is no serious drought in late spring or summer. Even this risk can be minimized by careful preparation of the soil; a deep, fertile seed bed encourages the young grass plants to root deeply, and deep-rooted plants are better able to withstand dry weather than shallow-rooted ones.

When spring sowings are made, it is best to sow the grass as soon as the soil is dry enough to be worked into a nice, crumbly condition; however, it is inadvisable to sow seed or attempt to make the seed bed if the soil is so sticky that it clings tenaciously to tools and shoes. This is particularly true of clayey soils.

Selecting the Proper Grass. For the South,

Stones and builders' debris may clutter the ground around a new home. Before spreading new topsoil or turning over old topsoil, remove all rubbish.

If the lawn area is fairly extensive, the soil may be loosened and turned over with a garden tractor (above) or with a rototiller.

grasses requiring very sandy soil, sun and low fertility are Carpet, Bahia and Centipede Grasses. Bermuda Grass can grow under the same conditions, except that it requires a high degree of fertility. For shady areas, St. Augustine and Manila Grass (Zoysia matrella) make the best lawns. Bermuda, Manila and Carpet Grasses also grow in heavy soils but only Carpet Grass can be depended upon to thrive in moist soils.

For northern lawns, mixtures of more than one kind of grass are usually preferable to those made of one grass only, although for special purposes, such as golf putting greens, special strains of Bent Grass are often maintained as pure stands and Zoysia japonica and its variety known as Meyer Zoysia are used alone.

The most important grasses for northern lawns —that is, for lawns in the cooler and more humid regions of North America as opposed to the more subtropical areas of the South—are Bluegrasses, Fescues, Bents, Zoysia japonica and its variety and a group of temporary grasses used as nurse grasses to hold the soil and discourage weeds until the permanent grasses are well established.

Kentucky Bluegrass and its improved variety Merion Bluegrass are the most important permanent grasses for sunny areas. They form pleasing turf and wear well. In very hot weather they are partially dormant; they make their chief growth in spring and fall. In most northern lawns these should form at least 50 per cent of seed mixtures.

Rough-stalked Bluegrass is a kind of special

A spreader may be used to distribute fertilizer evenly over the ground surface.

A harrow dragged over the ground mixes in the fertilizer and levels the surface.

A final raking brings the surface into fine condition for seed sowing.

When seeding, the spreader should be pushed back and forth in overlapping strips to distribute half the required amount of seed, and then at right angles to these strips to distribute the other half.

value for shaded places. The turf it forms is lighter in color and looser than that of Kentucky Bluegrass and it is less tolerant of dryness.

Chewings Fescue stands dryness well and tolerates less fertile soil than the Bluegrasses. It forms a hard-wearing turf, but, as it does not spread by creeping, injuries suffered by the turf do not heal rapidly. This grass needs frequent mowing. Illahee Fescue and Trinity Fescue are similar and require the same conditions. They are of more creeping habit.

Creeping Bent is propagated by stolons and forms a magnificent dense, close turf. It requires a great deal of attention to keep it in good condition, and it must be grown in full sun in a rich, moist, slightly acid soil. A number of named varieties of Creeping Bent are available; two of the best are Washington and Metropolitan. Very similar to Creeping Bent, but not quite as uniform in appearance, is Seaside Bent; this kind can be grown from seeds. Velvet Bent is the dwarfest, and the finest of lawn grasses. It forms an emerald-green turf and can be used in seed mixtures. It grows in sun or partial shade and stands close mowing. Special strains of this grass are Raritan and Emerald.

Rhode Island or Colonial Bent, which is also known as Highland Bent, Astoria Bent, New Zealand Bent, Prince Edward Island Bent and Browntop, is an excellent grass to use in mixture with Bluegrass and other grasses or to use alone for special purposes. It requires full sun

After the seed is sown the area is rolled with a light roller. This large one has been drained of water ballast to lighten it.

The first mowing should be done with a sharp machine when the grass is about 2½ in. high.

and requires moist, fertile soil. It does not creep, and thus a turf made of it does not heal quickly if injured. It is raised from seeds.

Zoysia japonica and its variety Meyer Zoysia are propagated by plugs or sprigs. They are well suited for sandy soils and areas near the sea. Unfortunately they turn light brown in fall and remain that way until late spring. They are not suitable for regions of very cold winters but survive as far north as southern New York and southern New England.

Quick-growing temporary grasses that are used in mixtures as nurse grasses are Redtop, Meadow Fescue (useful as a nurse grass in shade), Perennial Ryegras and Italian Ryegrass. Domestic Ryegrass is a mixture of Perennial and Italian Ryegrasses.

Clover is sometimes added to lawn grass mixtures in the proportion of not more than 5 per cent. It stands dry weather well but does not wear as well as grasses do and so does not stand walking upon as well.

For an Attractive Lawn. The type of maintenance, the level of fertility, the quantity and frequency of irrigation, and the soil reaction (acid or alkaline) determine, more than the kind of seed that is sown, what kind of lawn develops. There is a fine Bluegrass lawn on a Pennsylvania farm that was started with straight Timothy. No Bluegrass was ever sown. Annual generous feeding with superphosphate and chicken manure together with high mowing (2 in.) produced a Bluegrass lawn where none was planted! This resulted from the high fertility and from Bluegrass seeds that were introduced accidentally from plants growing in the immediate vicinity.

A useful seed mixture that produces results under most conditions and that can be used where doubt exists as to what species is best adapted is:

Kentucky Bluegrass	50 per cent
Chewings Fescue	30 per cent
Rough-stalked Meadow Grass	5 per cent
Rhode Island Bent	5 per cent
Redtop	10 per cent

Kentucky Bluegrass will predominate if the soil is well drained and fertile, and if the lawn mower is set to cut at 1½ in.

Fescue will prevail under high mowing if the soil is low in fertility and dry. Heavy irrigation will destroy it. Shaded areas will be mostly Fescue if the soil is dry.

Bentgrass will be dominant under close mowing and frequent watering.

Rough-stalked Meadow Grass will be prevalent in the shade where moisture is abundant. It can tolerate very close mowing.

Redtop may last a year or several years. It thrives on moist soils and tolerates acidity and low fertility.

This mixture has much to recommend it to the gardener who is not sure about grasses. Clover, if desired, may be seeded in the early spring as a separate operation, at the rate of about a half pound for 4,000 sq. ft.

Good mixtures to suit various soils and environmental conditions are offered by all good seedsmen.

The selection of the grass for lawns in the more arid regions of the country depends largely upon the irrigation. Lawns that rely upon natural rainfall are limited to Buffalo Grass, Grama Grass and Crested Wheat Grass as the principal species. Under irrigation, most of the northern grasses, with the exception of Fescue, can be grown. In the hot, arid regions, Bermuda is best for irrigated lawns, and in the cool, arid area, a Kentucky Bluegrass mixture is best.

In cool, arid regions, under irrigation, Kentucky Bluegrass predominates. Bermuda Grass-Carpet Grass mixtures sometimes are used in the South where conditions vary from wet to dry. Mixtures are neither popular nor so necessary where strong creeping grasses predominate. Either one alone will be satisfactory in most cases, and will look better too.

Ryegrass often is used in low-cost mixtures to produce quick results. Ryegrass has a significant place in producing good lawns, but only when it is used "out of season." Its greatest use in the North is when it is seeded heavily by itself in the spring to provide a temporary lawn, to keep summer weeds to a minimum and to build the soil. In the fall the Ryegrass should be dug in and the permanent mixture seeded. In the South Ryegrass can be used as a temporary winter cover in preparation for spring planting, but complete destruction of the Ryegrass is essential before planting summer grasses. It also is used to a great extent for winter turf on Bermuda Grass sod, seeded directly into the existing turf in October.

Rate of Sowing. Where economy must be practiced, a lawn can be made by sowing at 1 oz. per sq. yd., provided the soil is clean, the soil surface fine, and turf is not required too quickly. To get a good sward reasonably quickly, however, a rate of 1½-2 oz. per sq. yd. should be used. To achieve even distribution, it is wise to divide the seed into two equal portions, one half to be sown lengthwise and the other half across the direction of the first sowing. It is also helpful to mark the lawn area off into 2- to 4-yd. squares. Then divide the two half-portions of the seed separately into the number of squares and sow one square at a time. If you use a seed distributor, this marking-off is unnecessary. If the seed seems very fine, it can be bulked by mixing with it a little sand to facilitate still further even sowing.

Sowing should be done in calm, dullish weather, and when the soil is dry enough not to stick to the shoes, as mentioned earlier. After sowing, cover the seed thinly with a sifting of good topsoil or rake carefully in. It should not be buried more than about ⅛-inch deep. Light to medium soils may then be lightly rolled or patted flat with the back of a spade, but on heavy soils it is better not to roll, owing to the tendency of the soil to cake.

Protection from Birds. Small areas can be protected from birds by a network of crisscrossing black cotton thread on sticks about 4 in. above the soil. Or the seed may be dressed with an organic-mercury seed dressing (1-2 oz. per bushel of seed) which makes it distasteful to birds and less likely to be attacked by parasitic soil fungi. (Birds are unlikely to seriously disturb large areas of newly sown grass.)

Managing the New Lawn. Given good germinating weather the seedlings should appear in from 5-14 days and make quick growth. When about 2½ in. high, the grass is ready for cutting, preferably with a reel-type mower, with sharp blades, set to cut at 1½ in. Most annual or biennial weeds from seeds blown on to the soil since it was prepared will die under the mower and can be ignored.

Lawns from Turf

These lawns are most costly, but more quickly made. The site and soil should be prepared, cultivated and fertilized as for sowing. Good turf is expensive and not too common. Care should be paid to the species of grass present, rather than to the weeds.

Normally, the pieces of turf are cut 1 ft. wide, by 1, 2 or 3 ft. long, and preferably 1½-2 in. thick, since thin turf gives a better root system than thick. Before laying, each slab of turf should be inspected and any rosette weeds or coarse grasses pulled or pushed out.

When to Lay Turf. Turf can be laid at almost any time of the year if there are adequate watering facilities available. In practice, the best time is late summer and early spring.

Turfing should begin at one side or corner, and laying is done facing the prepared soil, the gardener standing or kneeling on a board to avoid indenting the newly laid turf. The turfs are laid with joints alternating, like brickwork, but packed closely together. It should not be necessary to beat the turf down if the soil surface has been properly prepared. After laying, a top-dressing of sand or sandy loam is applied and brushed well into the joints, and the turf rolled. A top-dressing of fine sifted compost or lawn peat may then be applied with advantage.

Watering will be needed in dry weather, and if the turf is inclined to crack, top-dressings of sand and peat in equal proportions should be applied. When the grass begins to grow away, regular mowing should begin.

Sprigging or Plugging. A popular method of making lawns, particularly in the warmer parts of the country, is by planting, a few inches apart, sprigs (rooted shoots) or plugs (small pieces of established turf) of certain grasses that spread quickly and soon mat together and form a turf over the whole area. Zoysia Grass and Bermuda Grass are examples of kinds that are planted in this way.

Stolons. Choice strains of Bent Grasses, such as Washington and Metropolitan, are increased by

Turfs for lawn making may be cut to even thickness by inverting them in a shallow three-sided box and slicing the surplus soil from their bottoms with a scythe blade or sharp knife.

Each sod is laid on a level surface and is patted down so that it makes firm contact with the soil beneath.

The box containing the turf that has been cut to an even thickness is inverted to release the piece of sod.

With the face of a spade the turfs are butted together to minimize the size of the crevices between them.

Turfs are laid with the joints alternating like those of bricks in a wall.

After the sod is laid, sand or sandy soil is sprinkled over it and is brushed in to fill the crevices.

means of stolons. This is the method used to establish many golf greens. The stolons, stems growing on or just beneath the soil surface, are cut into pieces about ½ in. long and are scattered like seed over a well-prepared soil surface. After they are sown, they should lie about ½ in. apart. They are then covered to a depth of ½ in. with rich, sifted soil and the area is lightly rolled.

Bent Grass lawns made in this way are extremely uniform in appearance but their upkeep is very costly. They need constant attention in such matters as watering, fertilizing and mowing and are very susceptible to disease. They are distinctly special-purpose lawns and are not generally practicable for home owners.

Lawn Management

The plant population of a lawn is ever subject to change. Weeds invade, and even the predominating grass species may vary according to how the lawn is managed. The maintenance of a

Here plugs of grass are being taken from an established lawn to be used for planting a new lawn.

pleasing good sward of grasses calls for regular care and understanding attention.

Mowing. The height of the cut is extremely important. Too close mowing weakens the grasses, encourages moss and weeds—especially Crab Grass—and excessively depresses soil fertility. With the exception of lawns made of Bent Grass, northern lawns should be cut not lower than 1½ in., and in hot summer weather it is better to cut at a height of 2 in. Bent Grass lawns may be cut at a height of 1 in. or even lower. Southern lawns made of such grasses as Bermuda, St. Augustine and Centipede may be mown at a height of 1 in. Southern winter lawns made of Rye Grass should be cut to a height of 1¼ in.

When the cut is light and the weather is dry the clippings may be left on the lawn. However, if a heavy growth is cut off and it is likely to lie so thickly on the turf that it will smother the grass beneath it, the clippings should be caught in a catcher attached to the mower or they should be raked up afterwards.

It is better to mow often and take a little off each time than to let the grass grow excessively tall and then take a heavy cut. With most grasses the best plan is to cut as soon as the grass is 1 in. higher than the height at which it is to be kept. With Bent Grass, not more than half an inch of growth should be allowed before cutting, and less is better. This means that ordinary lawns will need cutting once a week in summer and twice or even three times a week through spring and fall, if the weather is moist or the lawns are kept well watered. Bent Grass lawns will need attention even more frequently.

It is a mistake to mow too early in spring; if the grass is permitted to make some obvious growth before the first mowing it will have a better chance to develop good root growth, which will stand it in good stead throughout the season. It is a mistake, too, to mow too late in the fall; the grass may be allowed to go into the winter ½ in. longer than its regular cutting height.

Mowing should be done when the grass is dry, as wet grass clogs and the clippings tend to cling together. It should not be done during cold, drying winds. Mowing should be done in parallel strips; the direction of the cutting may be varied at each mowing so that it is at right angles to that used at the previous mowing. Mowing in the same direction each time may tend to produce corrugations and ribbing, and allows coarse grasses to become established.

Lawn Mowers. Lawn mowers may be power driven or hand operated. The latter are useful for cutting in confined spaces and for areas up to 2,000 or 2,500 sq. ft. For larger lawns it usually pays to use a power machine. Gasoline

Hand lawn mowers are suitable for cutting areas of limited size.

mowers may be used on smaller plots but the extra work of bringing them from and returning them to storage, of keeping the engine in running condition, of cleaning and watching fuel needs, etc., scarcely makes them worthwhile if an able-bodied person is available to use a hand mower. If hand mowing is beyond the physical capacity of whoever keeps a small plot of grass, an electric rotary mower may be the answer. This machine is powered by plugging a cord into an outlet, just the way a vacuum cleaner is. No messy handling of gasoline and oil is involved, the mowers are lightweight, they run quietly.

Hand mowers cut with a revolving reel of several curved knives that scissor against a stationary horizontal bed knife. They come with from four to nine knives. For ordinary lawns five are best; for Creeping Bent lawns seven. Hand mowers may be had with rubber-tired or plain metal wheels. Those with ball bearings run easiest.

Power mowers are of two main types, those that cut with a revolving reel of knives like hand mowers, and rotary types that cut by the knife action of a propeller-like blade which revolves horizontally close to the ground, inside a metal housing. Reel types can be adjusted to cut more closely and give a cleaner, neater cut than rotaries; moreover, they can be fitted with grass catchers. Rotaries have advantages, too. They cut closer to trees, fences, walls, etc., and so reduce the need for trimming; they are able to cut high grass and weeds; they cut whether going forwards or backwards. They are less delicately adjusted

A reel-type power mower.

A small motor-driven lawn mower with an attachment in the rear for catching the clippings.

than reel types and generally stand rougher usage.

A third power mower is the hammer-knife type with small, free-swinging blades mounted on a horizontal revolving shaft. These move out by centrifugal force and slice the grass neatly. If they hit an obstruction, they fold back. Hammer-knife mowers appear promising but are not as time-tested as reels and rotaries.

Whichever mower you buy, get a good one. See that it has a strong frame and bearings, clutches, pins and drives of high quality. Make

A rotary-type power mower.

Clippings caught in the grass-catcher attachment are collected and placed on the compost pile or used for mulching shrubs and flowers.

sure that reel mowers have five or more securely fastened blades of high-quality steel, thick enough to wear well and stand many grindings. The bed knife, particularly, should be of high-quality steel, very sturdy and arranged for easy adjustment.

The motor is important in power mowers. It should be powerful enough for the work it is likely to be called upon to do. Cheaper models, especially among rotaries, often have motors adequate for ideal conditions but liable to fail when the going gets difficult. Note that some rotaries are propelled by the motor; with others the cutting blade is power driven but the machine must be pushed by hand. This is easy because the pusher does not supply energy for shearing grass as with a hand-operated reel machine; he simply trundles the mower along. With rotaries up to 21-in. size there is little or no advantage in self-propulsion. Usually in such sizes both self-propelled and push models have motors of the same horsepower. An advantage of the push model is that all the power is available for cutting; when the going is rough, this model performs better than the type in which some of the power is used for propelling the mower.

If you are unfamiliar with power mowers, consult a thoroughly reliable dealer. Have him demonstrate various types and be sure you understand the capabilities, limitations and operation of both motor and machine before you buy.

Care of mowers during the operating season, and especially before winter storage, is of great importance. Keep the mower clean. After each use, free it of grass clippings, wipe its blades with an oily rag and, if it is wet, put it where it will dry quickly. Make sure that it is oiled occasionally.

Winterize your mower at the end of the season by having it sharpened and, if necessary, repaired. Clean it by scraping, brushing and washing, and then coat all unpainted metal, such as knives, with heavy oil. Oil all bearings and moving parts, revolving or working them up and down a few times to spread the oil.

Drain old oil out of power mowers, flush with gasoline, then fill with regular oil (not the thin winter type). Drain the gas tank and rinse it with clean gas. Do the same with the sediment bowl if the engine has one. Remove the spark plug, squirt a little motor oil into the head of the cylinder and give the engine a few turns to cover the walls and moving parts with it.

Store mowers in a dry place. Take care that oil is not spilled on rubber tires or on the floors with which tires come in contact.

For best efficiency, clean the lawn mower and wipe its blades with an oily rag after each mowing.

Trimming the Edges. The margins of lawns have an untidy appearance unless they are trimmed regularly and neatly. Special machines are available for doing this. Trimming may also be done with shears, preferably long-handled ones. It is, however, wise to keep lawn edges to a minimum and avoid cutting up the lawn area with flower beds. Another solution is to line the

This rotary cutter is used to trim the edges of lawns.

Long-handled edging shears may be used to trim grass margins.

edges with metal strips or beveled concrete edging to stop the outward growth of the grass.

Rolling. The chief purpose of rolling is to consolidate the root systems of the grasses. Heavy rolling must be avoided. Rolling is more beneficial on sandy than on heavy soils. The turf should be switched or brushed before being rolled, especially in spring. For most purposes, a 200-lb. roller is ample. Light rolling puts a "face" on turf; heavy rolling may cause a hard, caked layer. The roller should only be used when the surface is dry. An occasional rolling after frosty weather is helpful in reconsolidating the turf. Newly sown turf only needs a light rolling before mowing. Hollows should be filled in before rolling, do not use the roller to compress lumpiness. The direction of the rolling should be varied for successive rollings.

Raking and Harrowing. Raking is useful to check weeds like clover and chickweed by severing the runners; to remove dead foliage and to admit air, moisture and fertilizers to plant roots. A fine spring-toothed rake is most useful. Harrowing or dragging with stiff brushes or small har-

rows is useful in working in top-dressings, etc.

Switching. This is done with a long, 15-20-ft. flexible bamboo cane to scatter worm casts and to work in dressings, particularly on fine lawns.

Spiking and Forking. These operations are beneficial to aerate matted or overconsolidated turf, and to permit the ready penetration of top-dressings, fertilizers, and so forth, to the roots. Spiking can be done with a spiking roller or with special tubular forks, removing small cores of

In small areas ordinary sheep shears (grass shears) may be used to keep the edges of lawns neat and trim.

To prevent too great consolidation of the surface, lawns may be spiked with a fork or with a machine made especially for this purpose.

of well-rotted organic matter, such as garden compost, leaf mold, decayed manure, spent hotbed or mushroom-bed compost and peat: (2) sharp sand; (3) loam; and (4) wood ashes, if available. All top-dressings are best sifted through a $\frac{3}{16}$-in. sieve.

The composition of a top-dressing depends on the nature of the soil. For most soils of average texture, a mixture of equal parts by bulk of sifted rotted organic material and good loam, applied at rates of 1-2 lb. per sq. yd., is suitable. On heavy soils, the loam should be replaced by sand. Such a top-dressing should be applied in late autumn or early winter after spiking or forking, or in early spring.

Sand is helpful since it dries the lawn surface, encourages increasing tillers (side shoots) from the grass plants, and develops good drainage, particularly on heavy soils. It should not be overdone, however. It should be applied in winter or early spring and raked, harrowed or brushed in.

soil, or it may be done with a garden fork, inserted 4 in., wiggled, withdrawn and reinserted at 6-in. distances. Most lawns benefit from spiking and forking at least once a year.

Top-dressings. Top-dressing of the garden lawn is as important to its maintenance as proper mowing. The materials used are: (1) some form

Fertilizing. Leaching and removal of clippings gradually impoverishes the soil, and this loss of fertility must be made good. The time to apply fertilizers is in spring before the season of active growth, and in early fall. Lawns need fertilizers specially compounded for them, and many man-

Top-dressing the lawn each year with well-decayed organic matter and good topsoil is very beneficial.

To encourage a healthy growth of grass, lawns should be fertilized each spring and early fall.

ufacturers put out fertilizers blended to suit lawn grasses. These grasses need phosphates, nitrogen and potash in proper balance.

A good mixture for lawns on ordinary soils is: 3 parts sulphate of ammonia, 3 parts dried blood, 8 parts fine bone meal, 5 parts superphosphate, 1 part sulphate of potash, 1 part sulphate of iron, all by weight. This is applied at 2-3 oz. per sq. yd., and may be repeated at 1-oz. per sq. yd. 4 weeks later.

As growth increases, the need for nitrogen grows, and a popular treatment for intensively managed turf is the regular application of sulphate of ammonia at rates of ¼ to ½ oz. per sq. yd. at 3-4-week intervals throughout the growing season, applied in showery weather, or watered in. This gives excellent results on all soils except heavy, acid clay, where the dressing should be alternated with calcium nitrate at the same rate. Under such treatment, however, regular top-dressing in autumn and a balanced fertilization in spring are equally essential.

Excellent brands of ready-mixed proprietary lawn fertilizers are on the market and can be used with advantage, especially by the amateur who is unskilled in mixing fertilizers. Always follow the manufacturers' directions closely.

Watering. Not only do grasses consist of some 80 per cent water, but the loss of soil moisture

Specially installed underground sprinkler systems make it possible to keep the lawn watered with minimum trouble.

by transpiration and evaporation from a lawn is very high on a hot summer day. The ability of a lawn to withstand drought depends partly on the water-holding capacity of the soil, and partly upon the density of the sward. Soils rich with decayed organic matter hold water better than thin, sandy soils. Dense turf gives more shade against hot sun.

In dry weather, it is better to water to saturate the soil once than to give several light sprinkles. The water must penetrate and soak the soil to a depth of several inches to do any good. It is advisable to water before the effects of drought become apparent in seared and yellowing foliage. At least 2, preferably more, gallons of water should be applied per square yard. If the soil is at all packed, it helps to spike or prick the turf before application to assist penetration. The frequency of watering depends upon the intensity of the drought and the water-retentiveness of the soil. Application can be made by hose or by sprinkler. A thorough soaking every 5-7 days in dry weather is usually enough.

Earthworm Control. Although earthworms help soil drainage by their tunneling and increase soil fertility somewhat, their presence is undesired in lawn soils because of their unsightly casts in autumn-to-spring months; the casts often become weed traps and stifle grass growth. The time to carry out earthworm eradication is in autumn or spring, during mild weather, when the worms are active in the topsoil and casting. Various materials can be used.

Mowrah meal, applied at 6-8 oz. per sq. yd., and copiously watered in, froths as it dissolves and then causes the worms to come rapidly to the surface, where they usually die. Turf remains worm-free for about 2 years. Mowrah meal is toxic to fish and should not be used near ponds.

Lead arsenate powder, applied at 1½-2 oz. per sq. yd., does not need to be watered in, but, as it is *poisonous* to animals and humans, it must be used with due care. It acts rather slowly, killing the worms in the soil, but is effective for at least 5-6 years, often longer. Once rain has fallen, any danger to animals is removed.

Rotenone powder, applied at ½ oz. per sq. yd., watered in with 1 gallon of water, gives results equivalent to those obtained with Mowrah meal, though, like it, rotenone is toxic to fish and should not be used near fish ponds.

Potassium permanganate at ½ oz. per gallon of water per sq. yd. brings the worms to the surface, from which they can be swept up and disposed of.

Lawn Weed Control. The most effective deterrent of weeds in lawns is good culture on the lines already described, whereby the grasses can hold their own in competition. Weed control in lawns has been revolutionized by the recent advent of selective weed killers based on growth-regulating substances or synthetic hormones. These substances are absorbed by the plants and act internally, so stimulating and distorting growth processes that the plants are exhausted and die. Broadly, monocotyledon plants (such as grasses) are not affected, but many dicotyledon plants, which include many lawn weeds, are susceptible. Thus the weed killers have selective action.

Selective weed killers useful on lawns are sold under various brand names. Those based on 2,4D are extremely effective against most broad-leaved weeds, including Broad-leaved Plantain, Buckhorn Plantain, Hieraceum, Creeping Buttercup, Creeping Thistle, Dandelion, Dock and English Daisy. Chickweed and some others are much more resistant to 2,4D.

Great care must be taken when using 2,4D not to let the spray drift onto garden plants such as trees, shrubs, perennials, annuals and vegetables; it will cause distortion and kill most of these just as it does most broad-leaved weeds.

Chemical control of Crab Grass is based on the use of potassium cyanate, phenyl mercuric acetate or di-sodium methyl arsonate. These materials are included in the various name-brand Crab Grass sprays and dusts that are sold by dealers in horticultural supplies. They should always be used strictly according to the manufacturers' directions. Not always are results as good as expected, and desirable grasses may be harmed, at least temporarily, by the use of these chemicals.

The control of Crab Grass must be effected by good lawn management practices, such as watering, feeding when needed, and hand weeding, as well as by chemical means.

Chickweed, Clover, Knotweed, Selfheal (Prunella) and some other lawn weeds are killed or seriously injured by di-sodium methyl arsonate.

Hand weeding still remains an important chore in the proper maintenance of lawns. A great step forward can be made in keeping the lawn weed-free if weeds are pulled out promptly while they are small and before they have opportunity to set seeds.

LAWN, ALPINE. The garden feature known as an alpine lawn is a special rock-garden planting that simulates as closely as possible the flowering meadows of the Alps and other high mountainous regions. Alpine lawns are little known in North American gardens, but in Europe, especially in Great Britain, they have attained popu-

A knife with a curved blade, such as a grapefruit knife, is a handy tool with which to remove weeds from lawns.

The fragrant-leaved creeping Thyme, Thymus Serpyllum, is a favorite plant for alpine lawns.

larity among rock-garden enthusiasts. It does not seem probable that alpine lawns will thrive in American and Canadian gardens except in the Pacific Northwest. Hot, dry summers are definitely unfavorable to their establishment.

Alpine lawns are composed of many low, creeping and matting plants such as Thymes, Antennarias, and low Veronicas intermixed and interplanted with spring-flowering bulbs such as Crocuses, Narcissi and Scillas, and exquisite flowering alpines such as Gentians, Anemones and Campanulas. The plants mat together to form a springy, short turf that will stand a certain amount of walking upon.

LAWN, CHAMOMILE. In dry positions where grass will not flourish, the establishment of a lawn of fragrant Chamomile (Anthemis nobilis, which see) is worth considering. Drought has no effect on its greenness; it can be cut in exactly the same way as grass, and when freshly mown emits a delightful perfume. Unfortunately seeds of Chamomile are rather expensive.

One way to make a lawn of Chamomile is to sow a mixture of lawn grass and Chamomile seeds. The Chamomile, being the stronger grower, will eventually smother the other lawn grasses.

Another method is to sow the seeds of Chamomile in spring, in a nursery bed out of doors. In early autumn the seedlings are planted 6 in. apart on the area to be formed into lawn. There are single and double-flowered forms of Chamomile, but the former only is employed for making a Chamomile lawn.

LAWN LEAF. See Dichondra.

LAWSONIA (Lawson'ia). A native northern African and southwestern Asiatic plant that was named in honor of Dr. Isaac Lawson, a botanical traveler. L. inermis, known as Mignonette Tree and Henna Tree, is the only kind. It is a tree or shrub belonging to the Loosestrife family, Lythraceae, and attains a height up to 20 ft. It bears many-flowered panicles of fragrant flowers, white, rose or cinnabar-red. Its varieties alba and rubra bear white and red flowers respectively. This plant is grown in the warmer parts of the United States as a decorative item. It is propagated by seeds and cuttings and grows without difficulty. It is the source of henna dye.

LAWSON'S CYPRESS. See Chamaecyparis Lawsoniana.

LAYERING: A METHOD OF PLANT PROPAGATION

Details of How to Raise Plants by This Easy Means

Layering is one of the easiest methods of propagating trees and shrubs; many kinds that are difficult to increase by other means can be successfully dealt with in this way.

Briefly, layering consists of inducing a branch to form roots while still attached to the plant on which it grows, then to cut it off and establish it as a new and separate plant either by potting or planting it in suitable soil. Layers, in a sense, are cuttings which are rooted before they are removed from their parent plants. Because layers have roots before they are called upon to function on their own, they are easier to re-establish than cuttings which have no such advantage.

In conventional layering the parts of the stems from which roots develop are covered with soil. To make this convenient to do, the shoots are either bent to the ground or the plant that is to provide shoots for layering is cut down close to the ground to induce the development of new shoots, the bases of which may be covered by hilling soil around them without bending the shoots down. Shoots used for layering are usually one year old but in many cases older wood can be induced to form roots. Plants kept chiefly for the purpose of producing shoots for layering are called stools or stock plants.

In a modification of conventional layering, shoots are caused to root into sphagnum moss, soil or other suitable medium, held in containers or wrapped in polyethylene film. This technique is called air-layering. See Air-Layering, also Ringing.

Layering is a particularly useful method for adoption by the inexperienced and by those who have not the convenience of a propagating greenhouse or frame. Moreover, it is a very convenient means of raising an extra plant or two of a specimen of which the owner is very fond, when he would experience difficulty in raising them in any other way.

But layering is much wider in scope than this. It is employed for raising many kinds of fruit tree stocks required for budding and grafting, such as the Malling stocks for dwarf Apple trees and Quince and Pear stocks for Pear trees. It is sometimes practiced in order to obtain, as quickly as possible, strongly rooted bushes or trees of such fruits as Gooseberries, Currants, Figs, Mulberries, etc. Blackberries and Loganberries are commonly propagated by layering the tips of ripened canes, a process which is called tip layering.

Fruit Tree Stocks. Many kinds of fruits are readily propagated by layering. Usually a layer is a branch or strong young growth bent over and covered, at the point of contact with the earth, with two or three inches of soil. Often it is advisable to make a small notch or tongue in the underside of the buried portion of the shoot or branch, thus impeding the flow of sap and accelerating rooting from around that point. When sufficiently rooted, at the end of the season, the layered part is lifted, detached from the parent and treated as a separate plant or tree.

For raising fruit-tree stocks by layering, two

Here may be seen shoots and roots developing from a Rambler Rose branch that layered itself.

methods are in commonly accepted practice.

Mound or Stool Layering. The oldest method is to layer the new shoots from "stool" plants. This is called mound layering or stool layering. Maiden or one-year-old trees of the type of stock required are planted in spring or fall about 2 ft. 6 in. or 3 ft. apart, with 3 ft. between the rows. They are allowed to grow for one year. Then, in late winter, before growth begins, they are cut back close to ground level. When they have produced several short young shoots, fine soil is drawn up around the base of the growths. As the season advances, they are earthed up with more soil until the base of each young growth is surrounded by fine soil to a depth of 6 in. or more.

With these stocks, it is rarely necessary to make any notch or cut in the shoots layered; roots are produced from the lower part of the buried growths quite freely without any further assistance on the part of the gardener. No harm, however, is done by notching the shoots.

After the leaves have dropped in autumn, the soil is removed from around the stocks and each well-rooted shoot is stripped off or cut off with 4 in. or more of rooted base. These rooted growths are planted in nursery rows and, if they are to be budded or grafted, they are budded during the next summer or are grafted after being a year in the nursery rows.

When stripping the stools of rooted growths in autumn, one or two sturdy shoots and all unrooted growths should be left to each stool; these are cut hard back in late winter so that they will send up new shoots for the next season's layering. Stools, with careful management, will

(Left) Slitting the branch of a shrub ready for layering. (Top) The slit branch is pegged down. (Right) When rooted, the layered portion of the branch is severed from the parent and replanted in a nursery bed or in its permanent location.

remain fully productive for very many years.

Filberts and varieties of Quince may be propagated by stool layers in this manner, the rooted growths being cut off and planted in fall and trained to form trees or bushes with a clean stem, without budding or grafting.

Trench layering is widely practiced. Stocks of selected types are planted in rows during autumn, 3 ft. apart in the rows, with 3-4 ft. between the rows, each stock being planted not upright, but at an angle of 30-40 degrees from the horizontal and pointing straight along the row, so that it can easily be bent down to the ground for layering. The trees are then allowed to grow for one season with ordinary care. Late the following winter or spring, a shallow trench or furrow is opened up along the row and, after being cut back part way, each stock is bent down so that the top of one is close against the base of the next in the row and its main stem is in the trench. Each stock is secured in place with one or two stout pegs driven into the soil to hold it flat against the earth.

As young shoots grow from the layered stocks in spring, more fine soil is drawn up around the base of the shoots. This is continued until late summer, by which time the base of each lateral shoot has been covered with 6 in. or more of soil. In dealing with the stocks for stone fruit trees, such as Cherries and Plums, the layered stock should be covered with 1 in. of soil before any growth is made in spring; if the bases of the young shoots become at all hard and woody, as they will with exposure to light, they do not root freely later on. It is best if no soil is drawn up to the layered Apple and Pear stocks until the new growth is 2 or 3 in. high in early spring.

The underground portions of the growths send out roots freely, or moderately so, according to the variety or type. In autumn, the soil is drawn away from the rows, the stocks are uncovered and the rooted growths are cut off almost at their point of origin. They are at once planted 1 ft. apart with 2 ft. 6 in. between the rows, in a nursery bed, to be ready for budding the next summer or grafting in the spring following.

When the rooted growths are removed from the layered stock, one strong shoot should be left close to the base of each old stock, so that it can be bent over and layered the next spring alongside the older piece which was layered the previous year. If this is done, the stock bed is rejuvenated each spring, the older stubs are cut away entirely every few years.

A selected grade of standard type of stock for each kind of fruit should be obtained when it is desired to establish a stool or stock bed, for some types are vastly superior to others both in rooting and in the performance of the trees ultimately budded or grafted on to them.

When setting aside definite plants to form shoots for layering, healthy young trees and shrubs are planted in good ground and, when well established, after one or two years, they are cut down to the ground line. Young shoots appear which, in the course of a season, may grow 4-5 ft. long. These are the shoots layered. At first there may only be a few shoots, but as time goes on and the stools become vigorous a large number is produced. Then the best are selected for layering and the others cut out.

One defect in layered trees is that they are more liable to produce suckers than trees raised from seeds, and it is a good plan, when removing them from the parent stool, to cut out any basal growth buds that may be found. It may sometimes happen that trees raised from layers do not form a very good leader. This can often be rectified by allowing the rooted layer to grow for twelve months and then cut it down to the ground; a vigorous growth will start from a dormant bud and grow into a fine tree in less time than if the old shoots were kept.

Some of the dwarf kinds of Prunus, such as P. nana and P. japonica flore-pleno, give much better results from layers than from cuttings. If layered in spring, well-rooted plants can be taken up in October. Wisteria and the ornamental Vines can be increased by pegging down long branches in summer.

Layering Older Branches. In mound layering and trench layering, the rooted portions are young, current year's shoots. In many cases it is quite practicable to induce much older branches to form roots from portions not too far removed from their extremities. To do this, the branches or shoots are bent down and pegged into position, the points being kept erect. The shoots may be notched or tongued at the buried point, they may be slightly twisted, or they may be simply pegged down without being wounded in any way.

As a rule shoots that are tongued or slit root more quickly than those that are not, though, given time, many untongued branches will form roots. Elms, Planes, Maples, Magnolias, Ashes, fancy varieties of Beech and many others can be raised in this way. Oaks are very difficult and rarely respond. European Beech, however, roots very well and it is not unusual to find quite large branches rooted by natural layering at the base of an old tree, and such natural layers are capable of growing into full-sized trees. Many shrubs such as Rhododendrons, Forsythias, Lilacs, etc., are easily propagated in this way.

Serpentine Layering. Long shoots of viny plants such as Clematis may be induced to form roots and new plants at several places along one stem by a process known as continuous layering or serpentine layering. The shoot is laid along the ground in "snake" fashion, alternately covered with soil and exposed. On the underside, at each node that is covered, it may be cut to form a slight tongue. The shoot is pegged down at each place that it is covered with soil.

In due time roots develop from the buried portions and new shoots from the aboveground sections of the stem. When they have grown for a season and are well established, the stems are severed to form separate plants. Serpentine layering is usually done in spring, and the separating of the layers in the fall of the same year, or in the fall of the following year if the young plants do not have satisfactory root systems at the end of the first season.

Quite naturally those plants that produce branches from near the ground are most easily layered. It is possible also to layer branches at some distance from the ground (see Air Layering). Do not, on any account, try to layer branches into hard, unworked soil. They may root but they do very much better if good soil is provided for them.

A modification of the ordinary method of layering is sometimes practiced in raising various kinds of fruit tree stocks and some kinds of trees. Young trees are planted on an incline so that the branches are in contact with the soil. They are then spread out, pegged into position if necessary, and covered with soil. Burying causes etiolation (absence of green coloring) of the buds and they gradually form roots and shoots.

Layering Conifers. Branches of some Conifers root well from natural layers, particularly various kinds of Spruce (Picea), Thuja and Cupressus, although it is not usual to propagate them by this means. An interesting instance of reafforestation (renewal of tree growth) by the natural layering of the lower branches of the European Spruce goes on continuously on some of the mountains of Sweden. It is too cold for the seed to ripen and a particular form of Spruce perpetuates itself by the natural layering of its branches.

Various kinds of shrubs can be conveniently raised from layers, notably some of the harder-wooded Spiraeas, such as S. arguta and S. Thunbergii, that are rather difficult to grow from cuttings. Branches layered in spring are ready to cut away from the parent plant in autumn of the same year. Many layered branches or shoots root well enough during the first summer for removal from the stool, but some have to be left two years. Magnolias increased by means of layers should be left undisturbed for two years; so, too, should Rhododendrons.

Layering Rhododendrons. When the large-leaved Rhododendrons and the deciduous kinds (Azaleas) are layered (into sandy soil containing peat) they may be notched before they are set in position, and given two years to become really well rooted before cutting them free. Plants rooted from layers have a great advantage over grafted plants, for there is no danger of suckers growing from the understock and spoiling the named kind; if suckers do appear they are from the named kind and are left.

Layering Hardy Heathers. A simple way to increase hardy Heathers is by opening out bushy plants, placing sandy peat among the shoots and weighting down the latter with stones. Propagated in this way, the plants should not be broken up for two years. Quite large branches of Aucuba japonica, if layered in spring, can often be removed as rooted plants the following autumn.

Not all plants, however, are successful when increased by layers although the layers may root well. Eucryphia glutinosa, a very beautiful July- and August-flowering shrub, is a case in point.

In this instance, plants raised from layers rarely grow well after removal from the parent plant and there are many deaths among the young plants. This plant should be increased by seeds. Brooms are not suitable plants for layering, particularly the more vigorous kinds; but, as many of them are easily increased by seeds, there is no reason for layering.

Currant and Gooseberry bushes are easily increased by layering. A shoot or young branch is bent down to the ground in summer, pegged in position and covered with 2 in. or so of soil. A notch or tongue cut halfway through the buried portion, from the underside upwards, promotes quick rooting, but is not essential. If kept moist, the buried part roots strongly and by the end of winter may be dug up, the rooted part severed from the parent bush and planted in another part of the garden. The tip of branches, if bent over in summer and covered with soil, root readily; they are lifted, cut off and transplanted in winter.

Propagation of Currants and Gooseberries by layering is to be recommended, however, only when it is desired to raise strong, young bushes very quickly; for all garden purposes, propagation by cuttings planted in autumn provides the best and most fruitful bushes.

Mulberries may be increased by bending down a healthy branch to the ground and covering it with soil in late summer, a notch being cut in the part of the branch to be buried to encourage quicker rooting than would naturally result. Alternatively, a fruiting branch may be layered in a large tub or pot filled with light, loamy soil and a ring of bark removed at the point where the branch runs through the soil. If the soil is kept moist, roots will be produced freely about the "ringed" part. In autumn the rooted branch may be severed from the parent tree, for transplanting to the garden, before growth commences in spring.

Fig trees to be propagated this way should be layered before growth commences in spring. A strong branch with several young shoots of the previous year's growth should be bent over to the ground and the young shoots covered with soil to within a few inches of their tops. With some varieties, it is advisable to make a tongue or upward cut about halfway through the wood immediately below each young shoot or joint, to assist rooting; this cut serves to arrest the flow of sap and excites rapid root action. In most soils the shoots produce strong roots from the part below ground and by the end of the season make sturdy young plants which may then be severed from the old branch and planted elsewhere—in pots, or, if required, in the greenhouse border, or against a sunny wall in the garden. If the soil is heavy, sand and peat moss or leaf mold should be added to the ground where the branch is to be layered.

Tip-layering the new growths of a Loganberry. The tip, after it has rooted, is severed in early spring (below) and the growth tied back into position for fruiting.

Loganberries, Black Raspberries and Blackberries take root readily when the tip of a stout cane is buried in the soil. The cane tip should be bent over to the ground and layered in late summer, the top three inches or so being buried in loosened soil, or in a small pot filled with loam and sunk to the rim in the ground. The top leaves should just protrude above the soil, the layer being held in place with a stout peg driven in just behind the end. If kept moist during early autumn, the buried tip will root readily and by the end of the following year may be dug up, severed from the cane and planted in the permanent position prepared for it.

Strawberries are propagated by layering the runners in summer, this being the natural method of increase for a true runner plant. The runners produced in June and July are prostrate stems which take their nourishment from the parent plant until the buds or tiny plants along the runner stem have rooted in the soil. The runner stem will produce two or three small plants; the growing point elongates and forms another small plant at the next joint that is sufficiently vigorous. In practice, however, it is advisable to pinch off the growing point of the runner stalk after the first plantlet is formed on the runner; only one plant on each runner—the first one that develops—is layered.

The best results will be obtained if the number of runners produced by one plant is limited to five. The runners may be layered in the open ground close to the old plant or in small pots filled with loamy soil and plunged to their rims in the ground among the plants. The selected plantlets on the runner are held in close contact with the soil by placing a large stone over the runner, or by using a small peg. The ground at the spot where each runner plant is to be layered should be loosened slightly with the fork and fine soil drawn up around the base of the pegged-down plant.

If you are layering in small pots, the runner stalk immediately behind the plantlet should be covered with soil and pegged securely in position. It is important to nip out the growing point of the runner immediately beyond each layer to prevent further extension. Within a few weeks the layered plants will have rooted and can then be severed by cutting through the connecting runner stalk; they should be lifted and planted in the permanent bed.

It is most important to propagate only from healthy, strong-growing and heavy-bearing plants of a good strain.

Layering Border Carnations. Although Border Carnations can be propagated by cuttings, far better plants are obtained by layering. The best time for this work is early in July. Several shoots are selected on each plant, the lowest leaves are stripped off and a slit is made in the side of the stem and continued up the middle so that it passes through a joint. The slit shoot is secured in the soil by means of a hairpin or small wire peg, so placed that it keeps the end of the shoot upright. Before layering, leaf mold and sand are added to the soil.

LAYIA (Lay'ia). Beautiful hardy annuals which grow up to 18 in. tall and bloom in summer. They belong to the Daisy family, Compositae, and grow wild in western North America. The name commemorates G. T. Lay, a naturalist.

These plants should be grown in well-drained or rather light soil, in a sunny spot; they are not suitable for heavy, clayey soil, unless this has

Strawberry plants can be increased very quickly by means of layering shortly after the fruit is harvested. The best method is to peg down the layers singly in small pots of sandy loamy soil.

Layia elegans is an attractive annual up to 18 in. tall, which thrives in sun and in well-drained, moderately light soil. The flowers are yellow, edged with white.

been made friable by mixing in compost and sand freely. The seeds are sown out of doors early in spring, where the plants are to bloom in July and August; the seedlings should be thinned out until finally they are 4-5 in. apart. Layias are chiefly suitable for sowing near the front of the flower border. They thrive best where summers are moderately cool.

The most popular kind is Layia elegans (Tidytips), which grows 12 in. high and bears rather large blooms, yellow with white margin. Other kinds are L. Calliglossa, 12 in., yellow; L. glandulosa, 18 in., white and yellow, and L. platyglossa, 9-10 in., yellow.

LEADER. A term used by gardeners to indicate the terminal shoot which extends the branch of a tree or shrub.

LEAD PLANT. See Amorpha canescens.

LEADWORT. Plumbago, which see.

LEAF. Foliage leaves of plants exhibit great variety both in size and shape. A typical leaf may have three distinct parts: the leaf blade, the leaf

stalk or petiole, and stipules. The blade is usually thin, flat and green; it is in reference to the leaf blade that the word leaf is usually employed. The petiole or leaf stalk is sometimes absent, the leaf blade being borne directly on the main stem; the leaf is then said to be sessile. When the leaf stalk is attached to the lower surface of the leaf rather than at the margin, the leaf is described as peltate.

Stipules are usually small leaflike parts which occur in pairs at the base of the leaf stalk at the point of its attachment to the main stem.

Simple Leaves. When the leaf consists of a single blade it is said to be simple and if the

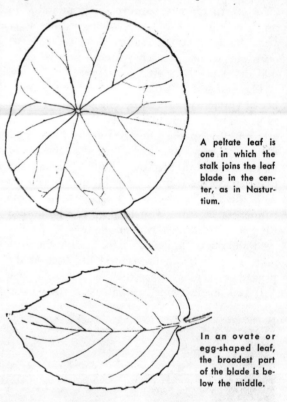

A peltate leaf is one in which the stalk joins the leaf blade in the center, as in Nasturtium.

In an ovate or egg-shaped leaf, the broadest part of the blade is below the middle.

margin is not indented we speak of a simple, entire leaf. Frequently, however, the margin is indented in some manner or another. In a ciliate leaf the margin may be bordered with thick hairs, or with fine, hairlike teeth. When the teeth are larger and regular, rather like the teeth of a saw, the leaf edge is said to be serrate. If the teeth, instead of being sharp or pointed, are blunt and rounded, we have a crenate leaf. If

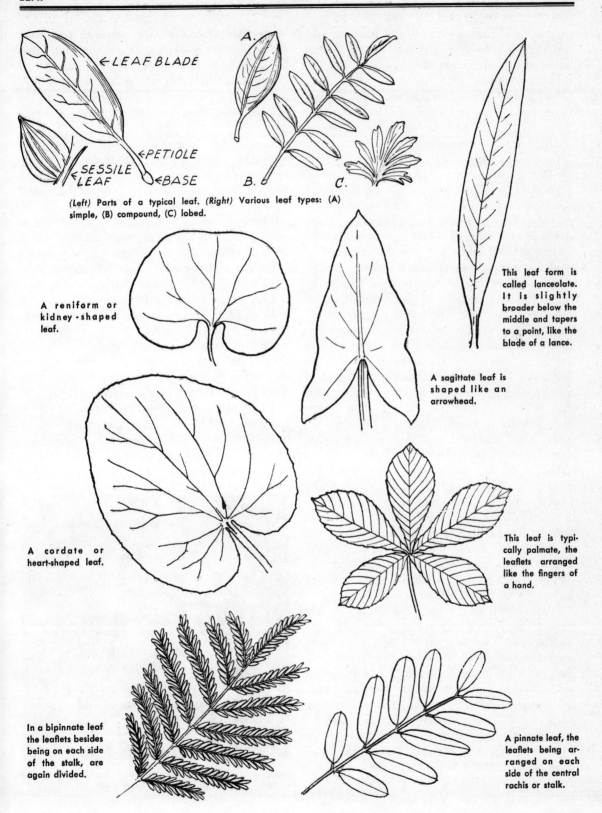

(Left) Parts of a typical leaf. (Right) Various leaf types: (A) simple, (B) compound, (C) lobed.

A reniform or kidney-shaped leaf.

A cordate or heart-shaped leaf.

A sagittate leaf is shaped like an arrowhead.

This leaf form is called lanceolate. It is slightly broader below the middle and tapers to a point, like the blade of a lance.

This leaf is typically palmate, the leaflets arranged like the fingers of a hand.

In a bipinnate leaf the leaflets besides being on each side of the stalk, are again divided.

A pinnate leaf, the leaflets being arranged on each side of the central rachis or stalk.

these indentations are broad and irregular, the leaf edge is sinuate; if the edges are not only indented but also wavy instead of flat the leaf becomes undulate.

In a lobed leaf the indentations of the leaf are larger but do not reach the midrib. When incisions reach the midrib the leaf is said to be dissected, divided or compound.

Compound Leaves. In divided or compound leaves each division or segment is quite separate from other segments but all are attached to a common mid-rib or petiole. Each separate segment is called a leaflet. The divisions of a dissected or of a compound leaf may themselves be further divided, and their margins may be indented as may be those of simple leaves.

When the leaflets or segments of a leaf are arranged on the two sides of the midrib, like the branches of a feather, the leaf is pinnate. If the leaflets are again divided the leaf is bipinnate. In a compound palmate leaf the leaflets all join the stalk at the same point so that they appear to resemble a hand with the fingers outstretched. If a compound palmate leaf has three leaflets it is said to be tripalmate or ternate; when it has four leaflets, it is quadripalmate, and so on, while a palmate leaf with five leaflets is frequently spoken of as digitate.

Besides the differences in shape which are due to serrations or indentations of the leaf edge, or to division of the leaf into leaflets, the leaves of different plants vary much in their general shape, different types of leaves being characteristic of different plants.

The cone-bearing trees such as the Pine, Cedar, Fir and Spruce, all have narrow leaves which are needle-shaped or acicular.

Leaves which are flat and long and narrow are termed linear or, if they are broadest below the middle and taper to a point like a lance, they are lanceolate. Ovate leaves are egg-shaped with the broadest part below the middle, while similar shaped leaves, but with the broadest part near the apex, are termed obovate. Oval and oblong leaves are, of course, leaves which, in shape, resemble either an oval or an oblong figure.

Other common leaf shapes include the reniform, shaped like a kidney; the cordate, like a heart; and the sagittate, like an arrowhead.

Modified Leaves. Finally, we must remember that either the whole leaf or a single leaflet may be modified to form spines. It must not be supposed, however, that all spines are modified leaves. The thorns of the Hawthorn and the prickles of a Rose are of an entirely different nature.

In climbing plants a leaf or leaflet is frequently replaced by a tendril. The Sweet Pea climbs by means of tendrils which have replaced the topmost leaflet of each of the pinnate compound leaves.

The leaves of some plants may be reduced to small scales which are only with difficulty recognized as leaves. This is so in the Butcher's Broom —the flat leafy body is really a flattened stem.

LEAF CUTTINGS. See Cuttings.

LEAF HOPPER. See Pests and Diseases.

LEAFLET. One of the divisions or segments of a compound leaf. See Leaf.

LEAF-LOSING. As used in this work, this term is the same as deciduous. It refers to plants that naturally lose their foliage annually and are without leaves for a part of each year.

LEAF MINER. See Pests and Diseases.

LEAF MOLD. This material, which consists of decayed leaves, is of great value in gardening. It forms an important ingredient of soil composts used in the cultivation of plants in pots

Leaves of deciduous trees and shrubs piled together and allowed to decay form a valuable source of leaf mold.

Pockets of natural leaf mold may be found in low places in woods and forests.

Leaf mold that has sufficiently decayed for use may be rubbed through a coarse sieve.

and, if mixed with heavy clayey soil, helps to make it more easily cultivated. Leaf mold is an admirable mulch or soil covering for Rhododendron, Azalea and other shrubs which need to be kept cool and moist at the roots in dry weather. It is a desirable ingredient of the soil when hardy Ferns, hardy Primulas and many other plants which delight in a humus-rich soil and what gardeners call a "cool, moist, root-run," are planted.

The best leaf mold is flaky and crumbly, sufficiently rotted to be susceptible of being rubbed without difficulty through a sieve having a half-inch mesh, but not so decayed that the veins and structure of the leaves cannot be easily seen.

Leaf mold is made by heaping together leaves of deciduous trees and shrubs (in general, evergreens do not make good leaf mold) and allowing them to decay. When the leaf-mold pile is made, the leaves should be wet and the heap should be trodden firm. It should be turned over every six months or so, the outer portions being placed on the inside of the new heap and the inner portions on the outside. Ordinarily it takes from a year and a half to two years for the leaves to rot sufficiently to be good leaf mold.

The leaf-mold pile should be made in an out-of-the-way corner of the garden, in partial shade, and protected, if possible, from sweeping winds. It should not be in a low-lying place where water collects. Leaves of any kinds of deciduous trees and shrubs may be used; contrary to popular belief, Oak leaves make splendid leaf mold

and, after they are well decayed, are not excessively acid.

If leaves are stored under cover, and kept dry, they can be used either alone, or mixed with fresh manure for the purpose of forming hotbeds. When the hotbeds have served their purpose the spent material is invaluable for digging into the ground.

Leaf mold is of particular value for use as a mulch on light land which dries out quickly in hot weather. If sifted leaf mold is put on the lawn in early spring, it benefits the soil and promotes the growth of the finer grasses. Leaf mold adds to the store of humus or decayed vegetable matter in the soil, and may be regarded as a

The sifted leaf mold, a light, loose, flaky material is splendid organic matter for mixing with potting soil.

useful substitute for farmyard manure in that respect.

The proportion of leaf mold generally used in potting composts is one third of the whole. A mixture of loam (old turf), two thirds, and leaf mold, one third, with a free scattering of sand, is a compost which suits numerous plants which are cultivated in pots. As an excess of leaf mold encourages the development of soft, sappy growth, it must not be used too freely, especially in the cultivation of plants which bloom freely only when the shoots or branches are well ripened, that is to say which become hard and firm at the end of the season of growth. Chrysanthemum and Fuchsia are examples.

Leaves should be gathered as they fall; if this work is deferred until all the leaves are down, many of them will have become mixed with the soil, trodden into paths or the lawn grass, and it will be difficult to remove them.

Substitutes for Leaf Mold. When leaf mold cannot be readily obtained, peat moss, sedge peat or commercial humus may be substituted for it in the preparation of seed soils and potting soils and for other garden purposes.

LEAF ROLLER. See Pests and Diseases.

LEAF SCALD. See Scalding.

LEAF SCORCH. This term is used to describe a condition of foliage that causes it to appear dried as though it had been killed by heat. It may be caused by high temperatures, dryness, disease organisms or lack of certain elements in the soil, as, for instance, potash. See Physiological Diseases, under Pests and Diseases.

LEAF SKELETONIZER. See Pests and Diseases.

LEAF SOIL. A term sometimes used for leaf mold, which see.

LEAF TIER. See Pests and Diseases.

LEATHERLEAF. Chamaedaphne calyculata, which see.

LEATHERWOOD. See Cyrilla.

LEBANON CANDYTUFT. Aethionema, which see.

LEDUM—*Labrador Tea* (Le'dum). Evergreen shrubs which are widely distributed in cold regions in the Northern Hemisphere, and are also found wild on mountains in more southerly places. They often grow in wet, peaty soil. Le-

dum belongs to the Heather family, Ericaceae; the name is derived from *ledon*, a Greek name for Cistus.

For Peat or Lime-free Soil. These shrubs flourish under the same conditions as the hardy Heather. They should be planted in a sunny place, in early autumn or in spring, in peat soil or in loamy soil that is acid in its reaction. They are propagated chiefly by cuttings in July–August in a cold frame which is kept close for a few weeks. Seeds may be sown in a cold frame in autumn or spring, or shoots may be layered by weighting or pegging them in the soil in September.

The Chief Kinds. Ledum palustre, a bush 1-4 ft. high, with small green leaves covered beneath by rust-colored felt, is native of very northerly regions of Europe, Asia and North America. There are several varieties, of which nanum, of very dwarf growth, is most distinct.

Ledum groenlandicum (latifolium), called Labrador Tea because the leaves are used for a tealike beverage, grows 2-3 ft. high and, like the other kind, bears dense round heads of white flowers in spring. The variety compactum is of dwarf and compact growth. It is found in Arctic regions of North America and in Greenland.

LEEA (Lee'a). This group of plants, named after James Lee, an English nurseryman, belongs to the Grape family, Vitaceae. It contains a number of shrubs and small trees that are natives of tropical Asia and Africa. They are usually grown as foliage plants in greenhouses and succeed best in a rich, peaty loam soil. In the far South they may be grown outdoors. They are easily propagated by cuttings which root readily in a warm propagating case in spring. When grown in the greenhouse, they appreciate a moist atmosphere and light shade from strong sunshine. Well-rooted plants should be fed regularly with dilute liquid fertilizers from spring through fall.

Two species and one variety of Leea are sometimes cultivated. L. amabilis has bronzy-green foliage with white veins and white stripes, and its variety, L. amabilis splendens, has red stems and its leaves variegated with bright red. L. sambucina has bronze-tinged leaves with rosy veins.

LEEK. This vegetable belongs to the same

Young Leeks growing vigorously. Each is in the hole made by the dibber at planting time.

family (Liliaceae) as the Onion, and is of value in the autumn and winter months, when it provides a most acceptable dish. Its botanical name is Allium Porrum. The Leek is considered by botanists to be a form or variety, developed under cultivation, of Allium Ampeloprasum, which grows wild in southern Europe.

A Very Hardy Vegetable. The Leek is a very hardy vegetable and can be recommended to those whose gardens are in cold climates or in exposed, cold locations.

Planting seedling Leeks with a dibber.

Sowing Leeks Out of Doors. A supply of Leeks for ordinary kitchen use can be grown with little trouble. The plants must, however, be set in deeply dug soil enriched with manure or rich compost.

Seeds are sown on a small bed raked down to a fine surface. Spring or early summer is the best time to sow the seeds out of doors, and they should be set in drills ½ in. deep and 8 in. apart. When the seedlings are up, the ground between the rows should be hoed frequently to keep down weeds.

Leek Cultivation. If the seedlings come up thickly, it will be necessary to thin them out to some extent to prevent overcrowding, and to give the plants every chance to develop strongly. It is not necessary to transplant them until June; they will be ready to be planted out finally. It is the usual practice to plant them in holes

Leeks—the harvest.

about 6 in. deep made with a dibber. The Leek plant is set with its roots at the bottom of the hole, and water is then poured in. This will wash in enough soil to anchor the roots—there is no need to fill the hole with soil.

When Leeks are grown to produce blanched stems of moderate length, they should be set 6 in. apart. Further earthing up will be necessary if blanched stems of a greater length than 6 or 8 in. are required. As the Leek is perfectly hardy, it is left in the ground to be dug as required for use, but in late winter it is sound practice to lift the Leeks that remain, and heel them in in a shady east- or north-facing border to delay their going to seed. However, they may also be planted closely together in a root cellar.

The Leek is singularly free from damage by plant pests and diseases and that is another reason for recommending its extended cultivation. It gives less trouble than most vegetables if care is taken to prepare the ground correctly and to plant out the seedlings in their final positions as early in the summer as possible. Failure to produce good Leeks is generally due to sowing the seeds too late and planting on poor land where the plants suffer from lack of moisture in dry weather. Good Leeks cannot be expected unless the plants are so treated that they will make free and uninterrupted growth.

LEGGY. A term used by gardeners to describe plants of which the stems have lost their lowest leaves and have thus become bare or "leggy."

LEGUMINOUS. A term used in reference to plants which belong to the Pea family, Leguminosae.

LEIOPHYLLUM—*Sand Myrtle* (Leiophyl'-lum). Low, hardy, compact-growing, small-leaved evergreen shrubs which are covered with small blush-white or white flowers in May and June. They grow as natives in eastern North America and belong to the Heather family, Ericaceae. The name is from *leios,* smooth, and *phyllon,* a leaf, and refers to the leaves' being quite smooth.

The Sand Myrtles thrive in peaty soil and in acid, sandy loam; decayed leaf mold or peat should be added generously to ordinary garden soil when preparing it for planting. Leiophyllums are useful shrubs for the front of a shrubbery border, and L. Lyonii (sometimes called L. buxifolium variety prostratum) is very satisfactory for rock gardens and for use as a ground cover.

The best times for planting are early October and the spring. Little or no pruning is required. When the bushes become old and begin to get straggly, replace them with young plants. The best method of propagation is by cuttings, 1-1½ in. long, made from the ends of the shoots, and inserted in peat moss and sand in a cold frame during August, or in a propagating bench in a greenhouse in fall. They may also be raised from

seeds sown in sandy, peaty soil in fall or spring.

The common Sand Myrtle, L. buxifolium, grows 1-2 ft. high. It occurs naturally from New Jersey to Florida in sandy soil. L. Hugeri grows to 3 ft. tall and is found wild in North Carolina and South Carolina. L. Lyonii, sometimes called the Allegheny Sand Myrtle, grows 6-9 in. tall, is very compact and prostrate and is a native of the mountains of North Carolina and Tennessee.

LEMAIREOCEREUS (Lemaireocer'eus). A group of large, shrublike Cacti that are mostly of columnar habit. They belong to the botanical family Cactaceae and are natives of warm regions in North, South and Central America and in Cuba. Their propagation and culture are dealt with under Cacti, which see. They were once known as Cereus.

Many different kinds are grown by specialists. L. marginatus, the Organ-Pipe Cactus, and L. pruinosus are among those that are best known. Other kinds include L. Beneckei, L. griseus, L. Thurberi, and L. Weberi.

LEMNA—*Duckweed* (Lem'na). The Duckweed, which is an aquatic annual, is a familiar sight on pools and ponds and especially where there is no flow of water. Duckweed spreads very quickly and should be raked off the water surface when present in only small quantities or it will prove a nuisance during the summer months. Fish and waterfowl, particularly ducks, feed on it and provide the best means of getting rid of it. Duckweed belongs to the family Lemnaceae.

LEMON. See Citrus.

LEMON GRASS. See Cymbopogon.

LEMON MINT. Monarda pectinata, which see.

LEMON-SCENTED GERANIUM. See Pelargonium.

LEMON THYME. See Thymus Serpyllum.

LEMON VERBENA. See Lippia citriodora.

LENTEN ROSE. Helleborus orientalis, which see.

LENTIL. The common name given to one of the pulses, Lens esculenta. It is a small annual plant, and is grown in many temperate countries for its orange-colored, pealike seeds, which have from ancient times been an important article of food. Although Lentils are grown in various European countries, they are not culti-vated as an important crop in the United States.

LEONOTIS—*Lion's-Ear* (Leono'tis). Evergreen flowering shrubs, from South Africa, which be-long to the Nettle family, Labiatae. They grow about 5 ft. in height and have narrow ovate or lanceolate leaves, 2 in. in length, toothed at the margin. They bear successive whorls of orange-scarlet flowers in autumn, which are in the form of compact tufts on the end of a long stalk, whence their common name, Lion's-Ear. The name Leonotis is derived from *leon,* a lion, and *ous,* an ear, and refers to the shape of the flow-ers.

Summer and Winter Management. These plants are suitable for planting outdoors in Cal-ifornia and in other mild climates, and as green-house plants. When grown indoors, they require a minimum winter temperature of 45 degrees. The best soil consists of equal parts of loam, leaf mold and peat, with sand added freely. They should be repotted in March. The branches of the old plants should be shortened by one third: if they are well syringed they will soon break into fresh growth; when that happens they should be set in larger pots. Water is carefully applied until roots are formed in the new soil, but it must be given freely for the remainder of

Leonotis Leonurus is a free-flowering South African plant that bears showy spikes of bright orange flowers in fall.

the summer. During the winter the soil is mois-tened only when it becomes quite dry.

Propagation is by inserting shoots, 3 in. in length, in sandy peat in April. The cuttings are covered with a bell jar until roots have formed, when they are potted in 3-in. pots and subse-quently in 7-in. pots, in which they will flower in late summer. The tips of the main shoots are pinched off and the subsequent side shoots are similarly treated to ensure bushy plants. When well rooted, these plants require an abundance of fresh air, and should only be shaded from the fiercest rays of the sun. Seeds may also be sown in pots of sandy soil in spring and the seedlings treated as advised for cuttings.

The chief kind is L. Leonurus, 5 ft., orange, autumn.

LEONTICE—*Lion's-Leaf* (Leonti'ce). Dwarf, perennial flowering plants, which are suitable for a sunny, sheltered place in the rock garden. They grow 18 in. in height and have tuberous roots; the leaves are pinnate and in a tuft close to the soil; the flowers, which are produced in a raceme (loose spike), are yellow, 1 in. in di-ameter. These plants are found wild in Turke-stan and the Caucasus, and belong to the Bar-berry family, Berberidaceae. The name Leontice is derived from *leon,* a lion, because of the re-semblance of the leaf of one kind, L. Leonto-petalum, to the impression of a lion's foot.

For the Rock Garden. The tuberous roots should be planted in October in a sunny, shel-tered place in the rock garden. The bases of the tubers only are buried and the soil should be light and well drained. A thick layer of ashes is spread over them during the winter. This is re-moved in spring and replaced with leaf mold. Propagation is by division of the tuberous roots at planting time.

The chief kinds are L. Albertii, 8 in., yellow, April; L. Leontopetalum, 12 in., yellow, April.

**LEONTOPODIUM — ***Edelweiss* (Leontopo'-dium). A small group of rock garden plants of which only two kinds are in general cultivation; they are natives of the Alps of Europe and the Himalayas, and belong to the Daisy family Com-positae. The name is derived from the Greek *leon,* a lion, and *pous,* a foot, from a supposed resemblance of the flower head to a lion's foot.

The Edelweiss, Leontopodium alpinum, from the Swiss Alps. This quaint though not outstandingly attractive alpine is quite easy to raise from seed and can be grown successfully in a well-drained, sunny position in the rock garden.

Edelweiss is a dwarf perennial herb found abundantly in many parts of the Alps, though it has become scarce in the popular tourist centers, owing to a certain superstition that it is rare and grows only in "difficult" places; this has prompted tourists to pick it as a trophy.

It is of tufted habit with narrow leaves and the whole plant has a silver-white appearance. It produces a number of erect flower stems, 4-6 in. high, each carrying a star-shaped "flower" composed of a number of white leafy bracts, in the center of which are the inconspicuous clusters of true flowers. The plant is more interesting than beautiful, yet it is worth growing in the rock garden if only for its quaintness and on account of the legend and romance which attach to it.

Planting and Propagation. It should be given a light, poor soil, in a sunny position, and perfect drainage. The scree or moraine (see Moraine) suits it perfectly. The flowering time is June. Propagation is most satisfactory by seeds sown in spring in pots of sandy soil in a frame, but the plant may also be increased by careful division in September.

Leontopodium alpinum, the true Edelweiss of the European Alps, is the best kind to grow, being dwarfer, neater, more silvery white, than the others. The lighter and poorer the soil and the sunnier the position, the more typically silvery it will be. It is said, moreover, that lime in the soil enhances the silvery color of the leaves.

The Lemon-scented Edelweiss. Leontopodium haplophylloides (aloysiodorum) is an interesting plant which was introduced from Tibet by Reginald Farrer. It bears a general superficial resemblance to the European Edelweiss, though the flower heads are subdivided, and are less starlike. The whole plant is fragrant, giving off a strong scent of lemon. This curious plant is quite hardy, easy to grow under the same conditions as L. alpinum, and may be increased by division in spring. It can also be raised from seeds.

LEOPARD FLOWER. Belamcanda chinensis, which see.

LEOPARD LILY. Lilium pardalinum, which see.

LEOPARD PLANT. Ligularia Kaempferi aureo-maculata, which see.

LEOPARD'S-BANE. See Doronicum.

LEPACHYS—*Coneflower* (Lep'achys). Hardy perennial and annual flowering plants. They are natives of North America and belong to the Daisy family, Compositae. They grow 3-5 ft. tall, have divided leaves and yellow flowers with an elongated disc in the center. The name is from *lepis,* scale, and *pachys,* thick, and refers to the thickened involucre scales.

When to Sow Seeds. Although some kinds are perennial, they are often treated as annuals. The perennial kinds may be raised in the greenhouse by sowing seeds in pans of sandy soil in February; the seedlings are gradually hardened off and in May are planted out of doors, where they will flower the same season. Alternatively, the seeds of perennials may be sown outdoors in May to produce plants that will flower the following year. The annual kinds are sown out of doors in April where they are to flower; the seedlings

[6—8]

A lawn framed with trees, shrubs and flowers

[6—9]
Summer Snowflake
(Leucojum aestivum)

[6—9a]
Leucothöe Catesbaei

are thinned out to 12 in. apart. They require a sunny position and light well-drained soil.

The best kinds are L. pinnata, 4-5 ft., yellow; L. columnifera, 3 ft., yellow, and its variety pulcherrima, yellow and brown, both good plants for providing flowers for cutting.

LEPIDIUM—*Cress, Peppergrass* (Lepid'ium). Hardy perennial and annual plants which grow wild in certain areas with temperate climates, including North America. They belong to the Mustard family, Cruciferae, and are not of sufficient attraction to be cultivated for their flowers. L. sativum (Cress) is grown as a salad (see Cress). The name Lepidium is derived from *lepis,* a scale, and alludes to the shape of the pods.

LEPTINELLA. Included in Cotula, which see.

LEPTOCEREUS (Leptocer'eus). Cacti, of variable habits, of the West Indies. They have prominent, ribbed joints, slender spines and small flowers with short tubes. Their culture is the same as for Cereus, which see. See also Cacti.

Leptocereus Leonii is a branched shrub growing 15-18 ft. tall; its stems have spines over 3 in. long and bear pink flowers. L. quadricostatus attains a height of some 12 ft. and has many branches. The flowers of this Puerto Rican kind are greenish-white or yellowish-white.

LEPTOPTERIS (Lepto'pteris). Beautiful tender Ferns with fronds of filmy texture. They require rather special treatment and are rarely cultivated. They are found wild in New Zealand, Australia and the Pacific Islands. The name is from *leptos,* slender, and *pteris,* fern. At one time these Ferns were called Todea.

L. superba, the best-known kind, is a beautiful Fern with very finely divided fronds, 2-4 ft. in length. L. Fraseri is also a very attractive kind, with finely divided fronds, but dwarfer in stature, the fronds averaging 2 ft. in length. L. Moorei is another dwarf kind, having finely divided fronds, 18 in. in length. L. hymenophylloides has tripinnate (three times divided) fronds, 1-2 ft. in length, and 8-12 in. broad.

Dense Shade and Moist Atmosphere Needed. These Ferns are easily grown if they are given suitable conditions. They require dense shade and a very moist atmosphere. A greenhouse with a north aspect is best, but, where this cannot be

provided, the glass must be heavily shaded in sunny weather. The atmosphere must be kept very moist by damping the floor, walls and benches at all times of the year. No syringing is required. A minimum winter temperature of 40 degrees is suitable.

For a Rockery in the Greenhouse. These Ferns may be grown in large flowerpots or pans, but they are most successful when planted out in a prepared bed or rockery in the greenhouse. The mound of soil is made up on the floor with a gentle slope towards the front, and the compost should consist of equal parts of fibrous, sandy loam, peat and leaf mold, to which a liberal amount of coarse sand is added, also a small quantity of crushed charcoal.

To complete the rockery effect and to assist in keeping the roots cool, a few large lumps of sandstone are arranged on the surface. The Ferns are then planted from small pots, and the soil is kept constantly moist.

L. superba and L. hymenophylloides may be planted outdoors in mild localities. They should be planted in sheltered shady nooks and covered with large hand lights or a cold frame to provide a moist atmosphere.

Propagation. New plants may be obtained by separating small side growths when these are available, and potting or planting them as advised. Spores may also be sown to increase the stock. Mature fronds are gathered, and kept in a paper bag for a few hours, by which time the fertile spores will have fallen to the bottom of the bag. Seed pans are then prepared, and filled with finely sifted compost which is well moistened. The spores are sown on the surface, and the pan is placed in a saucer of water with a pane of glass as a covering to maintain a moist atmosphere.

When the spores germinate they form small, flat, heart-shaped structures, prothallia, upon which the male and female organs are formed. As soon as fertilization has taken place, the small Fern plants commence to develop, and when the first fronds appear, the prothallia are lifted in tiny clumps and pricked out, 1 in. apart, in a pan of finely sifted compost. They are put in a propagating case, the atmosphere of which is kept moist, and when they have sufficiently developed they are potted separately in small pots and grown in the case until they are large enough to be planted out.

LEPTOSIPHON. Gilia, which see.

LEPTOSPERMUM (Leptosper'mum). Evergreen flowering shrubs, from New Zealand and Australia, which belong to the family Myrtaceae. They bear small flowers of various colors, chiefly in early summer. The name is derived from *leptos,* slender, and *sperma,* a seed.

These shrubs are not hardy; they are suitable for planting out of doors in light, well-drained soils in California and similar mild climates. They need a sunny location.

Cultivation in Pots. They are suitable for cultivation in large flowerpots in a cool greenhouse. If grown in this way, they should be placed out of doors during the summer months; before frost comes they should again be placed under glass.

Suitable Soil. Well-drained, loamy soil, with which peat and sand have been mixed freely, provides the most suitable compost for Leptospermum. Planting should be done in spring.

A double-flowered variety of Leptospermum scoparium.

Very little pruning is needed, but if it should be necessary to shorten unduly long branches, or to thin out weak, useless shoots, the work should be done as soon as the flowers have faded.

Taking Cuttings. Leptospermum is propagated by means of cuttings made from "half-ripe" or moderately firm shoots; the cuttings, 4 in. or so long, are taken in summer and are set in sandy peat; the cuttings must be planted firmly. Care must be taken not to overwater the cuttings.

The frame in which the cuttings are placed must be kept close for a few weeks, or the cuttings must be covered with a hand light or bell jar.

The chief kind is Leptospermum scoparium, which will grow 5-10 ft. in height, according to the location in which it is planted and the climatic conditions; it bears small, white flowers in June–July. There are several attractive varieties of this shrub; the favorite is Nichollsii, which bears deep rose-red flowers. Others are Chapmannii, bright red; pubescens, white flowers and silver-white leaves; and bullatum, which has light reddish blooms in early spring. Of these the hardiest is L. scoparium Chapmannii.

A very beautiful variety is Leptospermum scoparium Boscawenii, which bears pale pink flowers; it is, however, one of the least hardy. Leptospermum stellatum, an Australian shrub which bears white flowers, is very rare in cultivation. Others are L. laevigatum (Australian Tea Tree) and L. pubescens, both of which bear white flowers.

LEPTOSYNE. See Coreopsis.

LEPTOTES BICOLOR (Lep'totes; Lepto'tes). A winter-flowering Orchid from Brazil, which can be cultivated in a hothouse having a minimum winter temperature of 55 degrees. It has short stems, each stem with one leaf, and needs much the same treatment as Cattleya. The flowers, which open chiefly in winter, have white sepals and petals and purple lips. The plant is sometimes called Tetramicra.

LESCHENAULTIA (Leschenaul'tia). Evergreen flowering shrubs from Australia, which belong to the family Goodeniaceae. These shrubs, which grow about 1-3 ft. in height, have heathlike leaves and bear racemes of small, tubular blue or scarlet flowers in summer. They may be grown outdoors in California and similar mild climates and in greenhouses.

When cultivated under glass, these shrubs require a minimum winter temperature of 45 degrees and a compost of three parts of fibrous peat and one part sand. Repotting is done in March, and the soil must be made firm. Pruning, which consists of removing the tips of the shoots only, is carried out after the flowers have faded. Watering must be done carefully at all times of the year; the soil should never be allowed to become really dry, although less water is required in winter than in summer. Very little shading is needed, and the greenhouse must be ventilated very freely.

Propagation is by inserting cuttings in sand and peat moss in a propagating greenhouse in April.

The chief kinds are L. biloba, 3 ft., blue, summer; L. formosa, 12 in., scarlet, summer; and L. linarioides, 4 ft., greenish-yellow and reddish, summer.

LESPEDEZA—*Bush Clover* (Lespede'za). Herbaceous plants, subshrubs, and shrubs, few of which are sufficiently attractive to warrant general cultivation. Those cultivated are hardy and are of value in that they bloom from late summer onwards. Lespedeza belongs to the Pea family, Leguminosae; the name was given in commemoration of a Spanish governor of Florida named Lespedez.

The Lespedezas require a sunny position and should be planted in well-drained, loamy soil. Propagation is by seeds sown in light soil in

Branches of rosy-purple-flowered Lespedeza Thunbergii arranged in a vase.

March or by cuttings in summer. The previous year's shoots should be cut down in February.

The best kind is L. Thunbergii (L. formosa), a native of China and Japan. It grows into a large shrub, and in late August and September bears large inflorescences of small, rosy-purple, pea-shaped flowers. The variety albiflora has white flowers.

The next most ornamental kind is L. bicolor, a native of northern China, Manchuria and Japan. This also attains a height of about 10 ft. It has rosy-purple flowers in July–August.

LETTUCE: A FAVORITE SALAD CROP
How to Maintain a Supply of Quality Produce

No other salad crop is grown and used throughout the year in such large quantities as Lettuce. Commercial vegetable growers consider it one of their best-paying crops.

The varieties of Lettuce are grouped into three main classes, Cabbage, Romaine or Cos, and Leaf. The first has round or flattened heads; the heads of the Romaine or Cos are usually tall and elongated in shape; those of the Leaf Lettuce are of loose, open habit. There are also va-rieties intermediate between these types. The Cabbage and Cos Lettuce are invaluable salad vegetables in early spring, while the Leaf types are more serviceable in the summer. All the varieties are by no means amenable to one kind of treatment; some are best when sown in spring, others in autumn; some are suitable for growing under glass, and others are not.

Lactuca sativa, from which the present-day Lettuce has been derived, belongs to the Daisy

Two rows of Romaine or Cos Lettuce are here growing beside a row of Leaf Lettuce.

botanical family that is called the Compositae.

The origin of the cultivated Lettuce is somewhat obscure, as also is the date of its introduction into Europe.

Preparing the Soil. Lettuce will grow in any rich, fairly moist, but well-drained soil that has a sunny exposure. A medium loam or sandy loam is preferred. Heavy clay soil should be aerated by digging in liberal quantities of sand, ashes, rough compost or strawy manure. Cool weather and ample supplies of water often make success possible even though soil conditions are not of the best; this is especially true if the soil is cultivated frequently and if varieties adapted to the time of year are chosen. Lettuce will not thrive in dry soil.

When preparing the soil, dig in a generous amount of well-rotted manure, compost, or other decayed organic material as well as superphosphate at the rate of 2-3 lb. to each 100 sq. ft. If the soil is more than slightly acid, a dressing of lime, raked into the surface a week or two before the seeds are sown or before young plants are set out, will prove beneficial. At this time, too, rake in a dressing of a complete vegetable garden fertilizer such as a 5-10-5.

Sowing Early Indoors. In the North early crops can be harvested by sowing seeds in a greenhouse or other environment where there is good light and where a temperature of 55° F. can be maintained some 8-10 weeks before weather conditions will permit the resulting young plants to be set outdoors. As soon as the plants are large enough to handle, they are transplanted 2 in. apart in flats or in a hotbed. When the young plants begin to touch each other, they should gradually be given more ventilation and thus be hardened preparatory to planting outdoors. Set the young plants 10-12 in. apart in rows and allow 12-15 in. between the rows.

The first outdoor sowing should be made as early in spring as possible, as soon as the soil is friable and dry enough to work. At this early date the seeds should be covered as lightly as possible so that they are in close contact with the warmer upper soil; this ensures quick germination and reduces the danger of rotting. However, lettuce seeds and young plants tolerate considerable frost. At this first outdoor sowing it is a good plan to seed a short row with the intention of transplanting the seedlings, when about 2 in. high, to their final growing quarters. Never allow the baby plants to become crowded; this will seriously weaken them.

To maintain a steady supply of Lettuce, sow at monthly intervals until about August 15 in the lower and middle North and upper South and all the year round in the far South. In the upper North, choose a last sowing date that will enable the crop to be harvested before killing

These young Cabbage Lettuce plants will develop into solid heads as they mature.

Oak Leaf is a popular variety of Leaf Lettuce for summer use.

frost. Always select varieties suitable for the season; in particular, choose hot-weather types (they are listed in seedsmen's catalogues) for summer use. Varieties that mature well in late spring do not thrive in hot summer days.

Some gardeners prefer to sow in rows where the plants are to complete their development, rather than to sow in short rows and transplant. Plants raised from seeds sown where the crop is to complete its growth must be thinned early. The early thinnings may be transplanted to other rows, the later ones used for salads. The transplanted seedlings will mature ten days later than the plants left in the rows. All sowings made after the weather begins to get warm (in the North after mid-May) should be made where the plants are intended to mature. Early thinning, to 4 in. apart, followed by a later thinning that leaves the plants 1 ft. apart, gives better results.

Water. The best lettuce is harvested from soil that is rich in organic matter and that is supplied at all times with plenty of water. This ensures rapid growth and the consequent crispness that is so desirable in this salad vegetable. It is important that ample water be provided by irrigation during hot, dry weather.

Cultivation. Shallow cultivation between the rows should be done every week to control weeds and stimulate rapid growth.

Lettuce in Greenhouses and Frames. Lettuce is plentiful in food stores at all seasons and few gardeners feel that greenhouse space or even frame space is warranted for this crop. However, varieties such as Bibb, May King, Grand Rapids and Romaine Paris White are easily grown under glass and may be sown any time from October to January and grown in a bench in a well-ventilated, sunny greenhouse where the temperature is 40-50 degrees at night. The soil should be rich in organic matter and well drained.

A cold frame is also suitable to grow out-of-season Lettuce in, provided it is well protected from severe frost. From such a frame both extra-early and extra-late crops may be had. It is important that frames be amply ventilated whenever the weather is favorable. This prevents rot and ensures the leaves' being crisper.

A cold frame is very useful for protecting late crops of Lettuce from fall and early winter frosts. Even in the North, Lettuce from cold frames may be cut almost or quite until Christmas if the frame is well covered at night; in many parts of the South, Lettuce may be harvested throughout the winter from cold frames when open garden produce may not be had. A heated frame or hotbed makes possible the production of Lettuce over even a longer season.

Varieties. *Leaf kinds for early or spring sowings:* Black Seeded Simpson, Early Curled Simpson, Grand Rapids and Early Prizehead.

Cabbage kinds for early or spring sowings: Bibb and May King.

Leaf kinds for early summer sowings: Salad Bowl, Oak Leaf and Bronze Beauty.

Cabbage kinds for early summer sowings: Slobolt, Imperial No. 44, Great Lakes, Iceberg, Big Boston and Wayahead.

Romaine or Cos: Paris White, Express Cos, and Dark Green.

Leaf kinds for late summer sowings: Greenhart and Grand Rapids.

Cabbage kinds for late summer sowings: Wayahead, Iceberg and Crisp as Ice.

LETTUCE, ASPARAGUS. See Celtuce.

LETTUCE, LAMB'S. Corn Salad, which see.

LETTUCE, STEM. See Celtuce.

LETTUCE, WATER. Pistia Stratiotes, which see.

LEUCADENDRON—*Silver Tree* (Leucaden'-dron). Evergreen trees, some of them of great beauty in leaf and flower. They are natives of South Africa, and are planted in California and in similar mild, sunny climates. L. argenteum, the famous Silver Tree of Table Mountain, is the best-known kind. The downy, feltlike, silvery covering of the shoots and leaves renders them very attractive; the yellow flowers are in compact heads at the ends of the shoots.

Propagation is by seeds which germinate freely in a sandy, peaty soil. Leucadendron belongs to the Protea family, Proteaceae, and the name is from *leukos,* white, and *dendron,* a tree.

LEUCOCORYNE — *Glory-of-the-Sun* (Leucocory'ne). A small group, comprising four or five species and several varieties of very beautiful bulbous plants. They are natives of Chile and belong to the Lily family, Liliaceae. The name is derived from *leukos,* white, and *koryne,* a club, and refers to the three sterile or false anthers, which lie conspicuously on the perianth. The flowers, which superficially resemble those of a Scilla or Chionodoxa, though considerably larger, 1½ to 2 in. across, are in a loose umbel of from four or five to six or eight, on a graceful wiry stem, from 18 in. to 2 ft. or rather more tall. The onion-like foliage is insignificant.

Although Leucocoryne was sent to Britain as long ago as 1826, and had been grown, figured and described, it was not until a hundred years later, in 1927 and 1929, when Clarence Elliott collected bulbs and seeds in large quantity, that Leucocoryne became well known in Canada, the United States and Europe.

How to Grow Glory-of-the-Sun. The bulbs of Leucocoryne ixioides odorata are about the size of Snowdrop bulbs. The cultivation of the plant is still attended with a certain amount of difficulty and uncertainty, chiefly owing to the fact that a proportion of the bulbs persist in remaining dormant each year, and refusing to start into growth, though they are perfectly sound. The general treatment recommended is that which suits Freesia, but the temperature should be somewhat higher.

Suitable for a Warm Greenhouse. Leucocoryne is recommended for cultivation outdoors only in California and similar favored climates; it is

The fragrant, soft blue-flowered Glory-of-the-Sun, Leucocoryne ixioides odorata.

also best in a greenhouse with a minimum temperature of 55 degrees. The bulbs should be planted in October, in loamy soil, containing a large proportion of sand. Cultivation in pots has proved successful in some places, but planting out in a raised bed of soil in the greenhouse is probably better. The flowers appear in April and May.

Propagation is by seeds sown in sandy soil in early fall.

Fragrant Blue Spring Flowers. The flowers of Leucocoryne ixioides odorata are of a lovely blue or lavender-blue color, fading to white in the center; the three false stamens are yellow and add much to the beauty of the flower. They are powerfully fragrant with an almond or heliotrope scent, and a few heads of flower will scent a whole greenhouse. There is a good deal of variation in the flowers, some being paler or darker than others, while some are considerably larger.

LEUCOCRINUM MONTANUM—*Sand Lily, Desert Lily* (Leuco'crinum; Leucocri'num). The Sand Lily or Desert Lily, Leucocrinum montanum, is the only member of the genus, and belongs to the Lily family, Liliaceae. It is a native of North America from Nebraska westward to Oregon, and southward. The Sand Lily, although rare in some districts, is very abundant locally in others, as around the Garden of the Gods near Colorado Springs, where it grows in the sandy soil in amazing profusion. The name is derived from *leukos,* white, and *krinon,* a Lily.

Fragrant, Crocus-like Flowers. The Sand Lily is a low-growing herb with thick, fleshy, tongue-like roots joining in a crown near the surface of the soil, from which springs a spreading rosette of soft, narrow, grasslike leaves, 4-5 in. long, and great numbers of extremely beautiful crocus-like flowers, fragrant, pure white, and of a delicate, waxy appearance. These flowers are almost stemless, being only 2 or 3 in. high, and they appear in spring.

Propagation. The Sand Lily may be propagated by very careful division of the fleshy roots in spring, just as growth begins. Old established plants form several crowns, and these may be carefully separated from one another, and potted in separate pots. Propagation may also be effected by means of seed, which should be sown in pots of sandy soil in slight warmth in spring, the seedlings being pricked off when large enough to handle.

LEUCOJUM—*Snowflake* (Leuco'jum). Beautiful hardy bulbs which bloom in spring, early summer and fall; there are few kinds, but they are charming and indispensable garden flowers.

The Snowflakes are found wild in southern Europe; they belong to the same family as the Snowdrop, Amaryllidaceae. The name Leucojum is derived from *leukos,* white, and *ion,* a Violet.

The Spring Snowflake. The favorite kind is the Spring Snowflake, Leucojum vernum, which reaches a height of about 6 in.; its rather large, wide, drooping flowers are white with green tips, and open in early spring. At that time comparatively few plants are in bloom out of doors, and the Spring Snowflake is certainly one of the most fascinating of them. It should be grown by everyone who values choice spring flowering plants and likes to possess some of the less common kinds.

Chiefly suitable for planting in the rock garden, this plant thrives best in sandy, loamy soil, in a sunny or lightly shaded position. Heavy clayey ground can be made suitable by mixing in sand and compost; light land needs the addition of loam, together with leaf mold, compost, or peat moss.

When to Plant the Bulbs. Some disappointment is likely to result during the first year after planting because, as a rule, the Spring Snowflake does not bloom until it has become established. So that they may be given every chance to flower the first spring, the bulbs should be planted as

The Autumn Snowflake, Leucojum autumnale, is a slender kind suitable for choice locations in rock gardens or for growing in pans in an alpine house.

Leucojum aesti-
vum, the Summer
Snowflake.

early as possible—as soon as they can be purchased in late August or September—about 6 in.
apart, and 2-3 in. deep.

If it becomes necessary to lift and transplant
the bulbs, this should be done as soon as the
leaves have died down in early summer.

A variety of the Spring Snowflake called
Leucojum vernum carpathicum is more vigorous and has larger blooms tipped with yellow. It
is suitable for planting in the rock garden and,
because it is taller and more vigorous, it may be
set in grassy places or in open spaces among
shrubs.

The Summer Snowflake, Leucojum aestivum,
has long slender leaves, and bears rather small,
white flowers in May on stems 18-20 in. tall.
This plant is easily grown in a sunny or partly
shady place in ordinary garden soil that is
reasonably well drained. The bulbs should be
planted in September or early in October, about
5 in. apart, and covered with 2-3 in. of soil.

The Summer Snowflake is a charming and
graceful plant, suitable for planting in the rock
garden, in open woodland, or in spaces between
shrubs where it is not likely to be overshadowed
by the latter. The variety Gravetye has larger
blooms than those of the ordinary type.

The Autumn Snowflake, Leucojum antum-
nale, bears white flowers, tinged with pink, in

September. It should be planted in very sandy,
well-drained soil in a partially shady place in
the rock garden.

Other kinds, rare in cultivation, are Leucojum hiemalis, which bears white flowers in
spring, and L. roseum, with reddish flowers in
autumn.

For a Cool Greenhouse. The Snowflakes are
ideal bulbs for cultivation in pots in the cool
greenhouse, provided this is in a fairly sunny
position. The bulbs should be potted in September, several bulbs in a 5-in. pot, in a compost
of sandy loam, the tops of the bulbs being covered with soil.

When potting is finished, the pots of bulbs
must be watered thoroughly, through a spray nozzle, so that the soil is moistened right through.
They are then placed in a cold frame and shaded
from bright sunshine; the frame must be kept
perfectly cool, and ventilated freely in mild
weather. After 5-6 weeks the bulbs will be well
rooted and may be moved to the greenhouse.

LEUCOPHYTA. Calocephalus, which see.

LEUCOPOGON—*Australian Currant* (Leu-
copo'gon). Evergreen, flowering shrubs from Australia, which belong to the Epacris family, Epacri-
daceae. In Australia many of these grow 8 ft. in
height, but small plants in pots are useful for
greenhouses. They may be planted permanently
outdoors in California. They have small lance-
shaped heather-like leaves, and bear racemes of
small white flowers in May. The name Leucopogon is derived from *leukos,* white, and *pogon,*
a beard, and refers to the white hairs on the
corolla.

For a Greenhouse. These plants can be grown
in a greenhouse with a minimum winter temperature of 40 degrees. They should be potted in a
compost of three parts loam and peat and one
part sand; repotting is done after flowering. The
shoots are then slightly shortened and the plants
are syringed frequently to make them break into
fresh growth. As soon as the shoots are about
half an inch long, the plants are repotted in
slightly larger pots. In July they are placed out
of doors and are returned to the greenhouse before fall frosts. During the summer months abundance of water is required; in winter the soil is
kept moderately dry.

Propagation is by inserting shoots, 2 in. in length, in sandy peat, in the greenhouse, in late summer. They must be kept in a close atmosphere until rooted, and then potted singly in 2-in. pots and subsequently in larger pots. Seeds may be sown in pots of sandy peat under glass in spring.

The chief kinds are L. lanceolatus and L. Richei, both white, May. L. Fraseri is a low, spreading kind, 6-8 in. high, with pinkish flowers.

LEUCOTHOË (Leuco'thoë; Leucotho'ë). Evergreen and leaf-losing shrubs, widely distributed in North and South America, the Himalayas, Japan and other countries. A few kinds are in cultivation. They belong to the Heath family, Ericaceae. Leucothoë commemorates the daughter of the mythical king Orchamus; on being buried alive by her father she was transformed into a shrub by Apollo.

For Lime-free Soil. These shrubs thrive in acid loam and peaty soils, but, like most other members of the Heath family, they detest lime. Propagation is by sowing seeds in fine soil in a slightly heated greenhouse in March or in a cold frame in spring, or by taking cuttings in late summer or early fall. The cuttings are placed in a mixture of sand and peat moss in a close frame or greenhouse propagating bench which is kept close until the cuttings are rooted.

The Chief Kinds. L. axillaris is an evergreen shrub, 2-5 ft. high, with spreading, arching branches, leathery leaves, 2½-4½ in. long, and white flowers in April and May in short, dense, drooping clusters. It is a native of the southeastern United States and is hardy to southern New England.

L. Catesbaei, an evergreen also from the southeastern United States, grows 2-6 ft. high, forming a dense spreading mass of slender arching branches, with dark-green, leathery leaves and white flowers in May. It is somewhat hardier than L. axillaris.

L. racemosa, Sweetbells, is a leaf-losing shrub, 4-6 ft. high, with upright branches, rather small leaves, and white flowers in June. This is one of the most distinct kinds; it is from the eastern United States and is the hardiest kind. L. Davisiae, from Oregon to California, is an evergreen with erect heads of white flowers; it is hardy in mild climates only. L. Grayana, a semievergreen from Japan, has white or blush-colored flowers.

LEVISTICUM OFFICINALE—*Lovage* (Levis'ticum). A southern European perennial herb of the Carrot family, Umbelliferae. Its name is of uncertain origin. It is naturalized in parts of eastern North America.

Lovage is grown for its seeds and young stems, which are employed as condiments; for its leafstalks and leaves which are blanched and used as a vegetable; and for its roots, which possess medicinal qualities. It grows well in any ordinary soil and is easily propagated by division and by seeds.

LEWISIA (Lewis'ia). Perennial herbaceous plants which are natives of northwestern America and belong to the family Portulacaceae. The name commemorates Captain M. Lewis of the Lewis and Clark expedition. The Lewisias have fleshy leaves and roots, and many of them bear extremely beautiful flowers. They are, with the exception of L. columbiana, difficult to grow in the East.

For the Rock Garden. They are best grown in the rock garden in light, sandy, loamy soil, and must have perfect drainage. Some kinds are intolerant of lime, and it is safest to plant all in soil which contains little or none of this. They need light shade from strong summer sun.

Propagation. Seeds are the most satisfactory means of propagation. As soon as procured, they should be sown in pots or pans of light, sandy soil, and kept in a cool greenhouse or cold frame,

Lewisia Tweedyi bears the largest flowers of any kind. This specimen lived and bloomed for many years in a New York garden.

The apricot-yellow and pink Lewisia Howellii, a choice plant for the rock garden.

and carefully watered. Germination is often slow.

Several of the Lewisias vary greatly in the wild state, and intermediate forms occur, forming an almost perfect gradation from one species to another. In cultivation, too, some of them vary considerably; they have been crossed, and intermediate forms or hybrids have been produced. They are plants of great beauty and brilliance.

The Chief Kinds. Lewisia columbiana has rosettes of gray-green, fleshy, strap-shaped leaves, 4 or 5 in. across; the starry, ½-in.-wide flowers, which are very numerous, are in irregular clusters on 6-9-in. stems; they are pale pink with darker pink veins. Lewisia columbiana rosea is a distinct variety; its leaves are dark, glossy green,

and the plant forms numerous rosettes; it can be propagated by detaching these and potting them, or, alternatively, it can be propagated by seeds. The flowers are a fine purplish- or heather-pink, and are numerous, making it a very desirable plant.

Lewisia Heckneri has handsome rosettes of broad leaves, definitely tooth-edged, and the fine flowers are dark pink.

Lewisia Howellii is a beautiful plant; the edges of the leaves are markedly crimped and waved; the flowers are a fine combination of apricot-yellow and pink, with a band of paler color down the margin of each petal. These beautiful flowers, each about ½ in. in diameter, are carried in irregular heads upon 6-9 in. stems.

Lewisia Finchii somewhat resembles L. Howellii, but the leaves are broad and spoon-shaped, and the handsome flowers are striped with dark pink and white or pale pink. This plant dislikes lime.

Lewisia Purdyi, which is closely related to L. Howellii, has extra-broad leaves of bronze or reddish color.

Lewisia Cotyledon is distinguished from L. Howellii chiefly by its long, flat smooth-edged leaves. The flowers are pink, with paler edges to the petals.

A beautiful range of Lewisia hybrids has been raised by intercrossing L. Howellii, L. Cotyledon, L. Purdyi and L. Finchii. They produce large clusters of flowers in shades of cream, apricot and pink.

The Most Beautiful of All. Lewisia Tweedyi is perhaps the loveliest of all. The leaves are broad, spoon-shaped and fleshy, and the large flowers, 2 in. or more in diameter, and of waxlike texture, are of a charming soft apricot color. They look like some very waxy and exotic single Tea Rose. From one to four or five flowers are carried on each 5-6 in. stem in May or June.

L. oppositifolia is a very distinct plant and one of considerable interest and beauty. The leaves are long and blunt-ended, and the large, white flowers have ten petals. This plant loses its leaves in winter.

The State Flower of Montana. Lewisia rediviva, known in its native haunts as Bitter-root, was the first kind brought into cultivation, and for long the only one known. It is the state flower of Montana. From the rootstock spring a number of long, wormlike, fleshy leaves; these are followed by wonderful pink, satin-textured flowers.

LEYCESTERIA—*Pheasant Berry* (Leyceste′-ria). Leaf-losing shrubs, natives of the Himalayas and China, which belong to the Honeysuckle family, Caprifoliaceae. The name commemorates William Leycester, a judge in the Bengal Presidency.

The Leycesterias will grow in ordinary ground and, if planted in deeply cultivated loamy soil and an open sunny position, they are beautiful. Very few shrubs give more satisfactory results in shady borders beneath trees and in wind-swept

Leycesteria formosa, the Partridge Berry, is a shrub from the Himalayas and southwestern China, which thrives in any average soil and is excellent for planting in shady locations. Its white flowers are surrounded by claret-colored bracts and followed by red-purple berries.

positions near the ocean. Even when the soft ends of the branches are killed during the winter, new shoots grow from the base in spring. L. formosa is hardy in protected places as far north as southern New England.

Planting and Propagating. Planting is best done early in fall or spring. Seeds are freely produced on the bushes and provide an easy and rapid means of propagation. The seeds should be shown early in the year in a shallow box or pan filled with sandy soil, and placed in a greenhouse, garden frame or in a sheltered position out of doors.

Pruning is best done in early spring; it consists of the removal of worn-out stems of old bushes and the thinning of the branches of young bushes if they are crowded. There may also be some dead shoots to remove when growth is about to recommence in March or early April.

A Flowering Shrub for Shady Borders. Only one kind is commonly grown, Leycesteria formosa, a native of the Himalayas and southwest China. It is a leaf-losing shrub, averaging 5-6 ft. high, with smooth, hollow stems, glaucous or sea-green in color, and cordate-ovate to ovate-lanceolate leaves varying in size from 3-7 in. and of grayish or glaucous hue. From June to September the bushes produce attractive, claret-colored bracts surrounding the white flowers, the latter being followed by reddish-purple berries in autumn. Birds are fond of the berries. In addition to its utility for shady borders, Leycesteria formosa is a good town garden shrub. It is hardy in sheltered places as far north as New York City.

Leycesteria crocothyrsos, from Assam, is a most attractive and vigorous shrub, attaining a height of 8 to 10 ft. or more, with spikes of rich yellow blossoms terminating the arching branches. Unfortunately it is less hardy than Leycesteria formosa and of value only for gardens in the South and West.

LIATRIS—*Blazing Star, Button Snakeroot* (Lia'tris). Hardy perennial flowering plants, suitable for the herbaceous border, for wild gardens and for cut flowers. They grow about 2-6 ft. in height, have linear (long and narrow) leaves near the tips of the shoots, but they gradually become wider towards the base. The flowers, which are purplish or white, are in a wand-like spike and the bracts surrounding them are also colored. The flowers open from the tops of the stems downwards. These plants belong to the Daisy family, Compositae, and are natives of North America. The meaning of the name Liatris is obscure.

For a Sunny Border. These plants produce the

The Blazing Stars or Liatris are showy hardy herbaceous perennials that bloom in late summer and autumn. Unlike most flowers produced in spikes, those of Liatris open from the top downwards. L. pycnostachya, shown here, produces purplish flowers in 5-ft. spikes.

best effect when planted in groups of a dozen or more. They require an open, sunny position and light, well-drained soil. The roots should be planted in March or April, about 1 ft. apart. Although they require light soil, this must be fertile; therefore, poor ground should be enriched with compost or well-decayed manure. A light top-dressing of similar material in summer is also beneficial.

Propagation is by division of the roots at planting time in March or April. Seeds may be sown either in sandy soil in a cold frame in spring, or in well-prepared soil in the open in summer. When they are raised in pots or flats, the seedlings are pricked off into other flats filled with light soil, and kept in a cold frame until established. They are then planted out in nursery rows, where they remain until large enough to be set in their permanent quarters. The seedlings raised out of doors are thinned out, or pricked out into a nursery bed and treated in the same way as those raised in the frame.

The chief kinds are L. spicata, 6 ft., purple; L. pycnostachya, 5 ft., purple; L. scariosa, 3 ft., purple. L. September Glory, 6 ft., purple, and L. White Spire are improved varieties of L. scariosa. All bloom in late summer and fall.

LIBERTIA (Libert'ia). Evergreen perennial flowering plants which require well-drained soil and a sunny position and are hardy in the South. They grow wild in New Zealand and belong to the Iris family, Iridaceae. The leaves, which are dark green, 18 in. in length and ½ in. in width, are in a tuft rising straight from the rhizomes or rootstocks; the small white flowers are produced on long slender spikes in midsummer. The name Libertia commemorates Maria A. Libert, a Belgian botanist.

For Well-drained Soil. The roots should be planted in October or March in well-drained but fairly moist soil in a sunny position. Compost or other organic matter should be mixed with the soil. In cold districts the roots must be protected with leaves or salt hay in the winter. The plants should not be disturbed until they show signs of deteriorating when they are lifted, divided and replanted in fresh soil. Propagation is by dividing the roots at planting time. Seeds may also be

A clump of Libertia ixioides, a perennial plant from New Zealand, with narrow, dark green leaves and small white flowers clustered on stems 3 ft. tall in June. It likes a sunny, well-drained location.

sown in a cold frame in summer. The seedlings are pricked out into a frame and planted in their final position in April.

The chief kinds are L. ixioides, 3 ft., white, June; L. formosa, 1 ft., white, May; and L. grandiflora, 3 ft., white, June.

LIBOCEDRUS—*Incense Cedar* (Liboced'rus). Evergreen trees with a fragrant odor and cedar-scented wood, widely distributed throughout the world. The comparatively few kinds known are found in western North America, South America, China, Formosa, New Guinea, New Zealand and New Caledonia. Most kinds are too tender for cultivation out of doors except in mild climates.

Libocedrus is allied to Thuja and belongs to the Pine family, Pinaceae. The name is taken from the Greek *libanos,* the tree yielding frank-

incense, and *kedrus,* the ancient word for a cedar.

The Hardiest Kind. L. decurrens, the Incense Cedar, a tree of western North America, where it grows 100-150 ft. high with a trunk 12-18 ft. in girth, is the hardiest kind, and it succeeds as far north as southern New England. It is distinguished by its erect, stiff, columnar outline—in cultivation its branches are fairly short—but in a state of nature it has a much looser habit of growth. The branchlets are flattened and the leaves dark green. It is a most outstanding tree and one of the most distinct of all the Conifers.

Propagation. Cuttings will form roots if, in summer, they are inserted in a cold frame which is kept closed, but seeds provide a better means of propagation. These should be sown in pots or flats in a frame or cool greenhouse as soon as they can be obtained, early spring being the best time. Libocedrus decurrens and other kinds which are hardy enough to be grown out of doors should be planted in places where the atmosphere is reasonably free from impurities, in well-drained but moist loamy or peaty soil; they are unsuitable for lime soils. No regular pruning is required. The variety compacta is suitable for planting in rock gardens.

The Chilean Incense Cedar. The second hardiest kind is L. chilensis, a handsome tree 40 ft. high, in Chile and Valdivia. It has lighter-colored leaves and a looser habit of growth than L. decurrens, and can be grown in Florida and southern California. L. tetragona is a distinct kind, found wild in the Chilean Andes, in Patagonia, and in Tierra del Fuego. Under the most favorable circumstances it grows 120-150 ft. high, but is usually much smaller. It is grown out of doors in Ireland, and in a few favored gardens in the warmest parts of England.

Other Kinds. L. macrolepis is a tree 70 ft. high in south Yunnan, China, and in Formosa, where it is one of the most valuable trees. L. plumosa is from New Zealand, as also is L. Bidwillii.

Economic Uses. The wood of various kinds of Libocedrus is used for general carpentry where great strength is not required. It is gray, brown or reddish-brown, is durable, easily worked and has a spicy odor which is repellent to insects. The wood should not be used for boxes in which fatty or other absorbent articles are to be packed, as the odor may affect the goods.

LIBONIA. Jacobinia, which see.

LIFE PLANT. Bryophyllum pinnatum, which see.

LIFTING. A term in common use by gardeners to describe the practice of lifting or taking up trees, shrubs and plants for purposes of transplanting. Young fruit trees which make excessively vigorous growth but do not bear good crops of fruit are sometimes lifted out of the ground and replanted on the same site with the object of restricting root and branch growth.

To lift a tree, begin by digging a trench around the root mass at such a distance from the trunk that the main roots will not be damaged. Excavate the trench to a depth of 18-24 in. for trees of moderate size, deeper for large trees. Gradually, then, fork some of the soil from among the roots to allow the tree to be lifted without damage to them.

Trees and shrubs may be lifted bare-rooted, as described, or in such a manner that a ball of soil is maintained intact about the roots. Evergreens, except very small ones such as are used for forestry and nursery plantings, should always be moved with a ball. The soil ball is commonly wrapped tightly in burlap, and trees and shrubs so handled are said to be balled and burlaped.

A large tree lifted with a ball of earth that is tightly wrapped in burlap.

Preparing Trees and Shrubs for Lifting. When trees (especially evergreens) or large shrubs which have been undisturbed for many years have to be lifted, the work can be done most safely by a correct method of preparation. A year before the tree is to be moved, a trench may be dug at a suitable distance around the stem or trunk, and all the roots which are found there cut off close to the inner side of the trench. This practice checks the growth of the roots, but not violently, and restricts them within a certain area. Thus, when the tree is moved a year later, the shock to it is lessened, and it can be lifted and transplanted with far greater prospect of success than in other circumstances. This is especially important when transplanting trees from woods and wild, natural stands.

In nursery gardens, trees and shrubs are transplanted periodically for the purpose of restricting the area covered by the roots, and, in consequence, they can be lifted safely when the time comes for their removal. If this practice were not followed, there would be serious losses when the trees and shrubs, especially evergreens, were moved.

Very large trees can be lifted only by means of special equipment possessed by those who undertake this kind of work. After a circular trench has been dug at a suitable distance from the tree stem, it is usual to enclose the ball of soil and roots in tightly laced burlap or in a wooden

Lifting a herbaceous plant with a fork.

The roots of a young fruit tree lifted bare-rooted.

case. Next, by means of rollers, the tree, with roots enclosed, is pulled into and along a wide trench with a base sloping upwards until the ground level is reached; once on the surface, the tree can be transported to where it is required.

If it is merely a question of moving a large, valuable tree a few yards because it obstructs a view or for any other special reason, a wide trench is dug, leading to the new site, and the tree, after having been prepared in the way described, is moved along the trench on rollers.

Lifting Herbaceous Plants. No such elaborate preparation is needed when it is a matter merely of lifting herbaceous plants or small shrubs. These can be taken out of the ground if the spade or fork is thrust in the soil all around them to loosen their hold in the ground.

Lifting Bulbs. The proper time to lift bulbs is as soon as the leaves have turned yellow and are about to die down. It is, however, often necessary to lift spring-flowering bulbs while the leaves are still green, to make room for summer-blooming plants. The work can be done successfully only if care is taken to lift the bulbs so that the roots suffer the minimum of damage; moreover, the bulbs must be at once replanted in a reserve border, there to remain until the leaves have died down naturally.

LIGHT. All plants except fungi and other lowly kinds that contain no chlorophyll need light. It supplies energy for photosynthesis. When plants that normally contain chlorophyll grow in

darkness it is at the expense of food stored in their tissues during periods of light. This happens when Rhubarb, Lily-of-the-Valley and bulbs are forced in darkness. Growth is affected especially by the intensity of the light and by the length of time it is available during each 24-hour period. Optimum conditions vary with different plants and at different seasons. Lack of sufficient light causes weak growth; light that is too intense may damage plant tissues.

The sun is the chief source of light. Sunlight can, in some cases, be advantageously supplemented by using electric light. African Violets and other plants needing low illumination can be grown under artificial light alone. Light from fluorescent bulbs or such light supplemented with a small amount from incandescent bulbs is most satisfactory.

LIGNUM VITAE. Guaiacum officinale, which see.

LIGULARIA (Ligular'ia). A group of hardy and tender herbaceous perennials that have bold foliage and handsome flower heads. They belong to the Daisy family, Compositae, and are natives of Europe and Asia. The name is from *ligula,* a strap, and refers to the strap-shaped ray florets. Some of the plants are tender and are grown in greenhouses. But most are well adapted for waterside planting, for wild gardens and for large perennial borders. They prefer rich, fairly moist soil and full sun or part-day shade. They are easily propagated by division in spring or fall and by seeds.

Among noteworthy kinds are L. Clivorum, 4 ft. tall, with large leaves that are sometimes 20 in. across. The branched stems terminate in heads of flowers that have ray florets of orange-yellow and dark brown disc florets forming the center of the flowers. L. Kaempferi grows 2 ft. tall. It is not reliably hardy in climates such as that of New York City. It has 10-in.-wide leaves and 2-in.-broad flower heads of light yellow; the flower heads are borne in loose panicles. L. Kaempferi aureo-maculata, the Leopard Plant, has leaves that are blotched with yellow, cream-white and sometimes light rose, and is often grown in greenhouses and window gardens. It needs cool conditions and a fertile well-drained soil that is kept always moist. L. Veitchiana, a Japanese plant, grows 3-6 ft. tall. It is an unbranched plant with 16-in.-wide leaves and numerous heads of yellow flowers that are about 2½ in. across. L. Wilsoniana, the Giant Groundsel, has orange flowers in columnar spikes. All of the above bloom in late summer and fall.

LIGUSTRUM or PRIVET

Hardy and Tender Shrubs That Are Easy to Grow

(Ligus'trum). Evergreen and leaf-losing trees or shrubs, many of which are hardy and very easily grown under a variety of conditions. Many of them flower freely but the flowers are in some instances accompanied by a disagreeable odor. The seeds are enclosed in small pulpy fruits, containing a good deal of dyeing matter which may be purple, black, or yellow when the fruits are ripe. The wood is white, hard and strong, but it has no value, owing to the very limited supply. Ligustrum belongs to the Olive family, Oleaceae, and the name is the old Latin name for the common Privet (Ligustrum vulgare). The hardy kinds, with the exception of the one just mentioned, are natives of the Himalayas, China and Japan, but tender kinds are found wild in Australia and other countries.

As Specimens. Many Privets form handsome isolated bushes, but they must be given plenty of space for development, for they are spoiled by crowding and hard pruning. Any necessary prun-

ing for shaping purposes should be done as soon as the flowers fade; if severe cutting back is necessary, the work should be done in March in order to assure the longest possible growing period. When grown as specimens Privets look better unsheared than when trimmed into globes, cubes and other fancy shapes.

As Hedges. For planting as hedges in many locations the Privets can not be excelled. Both the deciduous and evergreen kinds stand shearing well, are tolerant of partial shade and require no special attention in the way of soil and fertilizers. They are especially useful in gardens near the sea and in city gardens.

To maintain formal Privet hedges in good condition they should be sheared regularly, usually three or more times each season. For the best results the sides of the hedge should slope inwards slightly towards the top so that the top of the hedge is somewhat narrower than its base.

Informal (unsheared) hedges of Privet may be

The California Privet, Ligustrum ovalifolium, is a favorite for planting to form hedges.

[6—10]
Hybrid Lily Golden Clarion

[6—11]
Lilium speciosum

[6—11a]
American Turk's-Cap Lily
(Lilium superbum)

[6—11c]
Goldband Lily
(Lilium auratum)

[6—11b]
Lilium leucanthum chloraster

Privets clipped into rounded shapes such as this lose their natural beauty and have little ornamental value.

used effectively as windbreaks, backgrounds and as screens. When left untrimmed, Privets are attractive in flower as well as in foliage.

To restore old, neglected hedges the best procedure is to cut them down to within 1 ft. of the ground in late winter or very early spring, then to fertilize, and to keep the roots well watered during dry weather throughout the following summer.

Planting. Privets may be planted in spring or fall. They thrive in any ordinary garden soil without special preparation, however, when they are planted as hedges faster and more favorable growth results if the soil, if of rather poor quality, is improved by spading into it deeply a liberal amount of compost, rotted manure, peat moss or other decayed organic matter and if some fertilizer is mixed in.

The best hedges are obtained by setting out young plants (specimens 2-3 years old) fairly closely together. Distances of 9-12 in. between plants set in a single row or 12-15 in. between plants set in a double row are appropriate. To insure the best results and promote a dense bushy growth at the bottom of the hedge the plants should be pruned back to a height of 6-12 in. of the ground surface at planting time.

Propagation. Although Privets are very easy to raise from seeds sown in well-drained, sandy soil in fall or in spring, this method of reproduction is rarely used because cuttings afford such

an easy and certain way of securing increase. For the same reason layering and air-layering are seldom employed as means of propagation although both methods are successful.

Evergreen Privets are most conveniently raised from leafy cuttings, each 3-4 in. long, made in summer and planted in a cold frame that is shaded and kept close (with minimal ventilation so that a humid atmosphere is assured). The cuttings may be planted directly in a bed made on the floor of the cold frame or they may be planted in flats and the flats stood in the frame. A sandy, peaty soil mixture forms an excellent rooting medium. If a cold frame is not available, small numbers of cuttings may be accommodated under a bell jar or even a mason jar. As an alternative to planting in a cold frame, summer cuttings of Privets may be rooted in a greenhouse propagating bench.

The leaf-losing (deciduous) Privets can be propagated by leafy summer cuttings in the way described above for evergreen kinds. They can also be raised very readily from hardwood cuttings taken in autumn after leaf fall. Hardwood cuttings consist of the current season's shoots cut into pieces 9-12 in. long. Where winters are not excessively severe they may be planted outdoors as soon as they are made, setting them 2-3 in. apart in rows spaced about 12 in. apart. The cuttings should be set so that only their upper inch protrudes from the soil. After planting, the soil must be trodden firmly against the cuttings. In

A hedge and foundation planting of Ligustrum lucidum in the South.

regions of severe winter freezing it is preferable to make the hardwood cuttings in fall, tie them in bundles of about 25 and bury them under about 8 in. of sand or sand and peat moss in a well-drained location outdoors. As soon as the ground is workable in spring the bundles of cuttings are dug up, untied and the cuttings planted separately as described above for fall planting.

Whether they are planted in fall or spring it is important not to permit the ground in which hardwood cuttings are planted to dry out during the summer. If kept moist, the cuttings will make good roots and top growth and become plants of such size that they will be ready for transplanting to nursery rows or to their permanent locations in the fall or following spring.

The Common Privet or Prim. This is L. vulgare, a native of the Mediterranean Region that has become naturalized in the eastern United States. L. vulgare forms a dense bush with long straggly branches and attains a maximum height of about 15 ft. It bears its white, heavily scented flowers in June and July and is hardier but less attractive than the California Privet, L. ovalifolium.

L. vulgare is a good hedge plant and thrives especially well near the sea; it may even be used for stabilizing shifting sand dunes. Several varieties of L. vulgare are grown of which argenteovariegatum, has leaves variegated with white, aureum has yellow leaves, aureo-variegatum has leaves variegated with yellow, leucocarpum produces white fruits, xanthocarpum has yellow fruits, pyramidale is of upright growth, and lodense is of dwarf, compact growth.

The California Privet, L. ovalifolium, forms a bush 12-15 ft. high, but it is more often seen as a hedge than a bush. It bears white flowers, but the odor is not pleasant. The variety aureomarginatum, Golden Privet, is one of the best-known colored-leaved shrubs. Although called California Privet, L. ovalifolium is a native of Japan. This kind is not hardy where winters are very severe. Even at New York City the tops are killed to the ground in exceptionally harsh winters.

The Chinese Privet. L. sinense, the Chinese Privet, retains its leaves in mild winters, but loses them when there is much frost. It has a decided treelike habit with a short trunk, 6-9 in. through, and a wide-spreading but compact head

of branches. Its great attraction lies in its upright clusters of white flowers which are freely produced in July. They are followed by small dark purple fruits. The flowers have not a disagreeable odor. It has been grown in gardens since 1852.

Ligustrum Quihoui is a shrub of rather stiff growth that was introduced from China about 1862. Its leaves fall in autumn, but it is worth growing for its panicles of fragrant white flowers in September–October.

Ligustrum amurense, the Amur Privet, is similar to the California Privet, L. ovalifolium, but is much hardier. It is not, however, such a good-looking hedge plant.

Ligustrum obtusifolium, from Japan, is also extremely hardy and is very popular. It is often, mistakenly, named L. Ibota, a name which correctly belongs to another and little-known kind. L. obtusifolium Regelianum is a low-growing, horizontally branched kind known as Regel's Privet.

Ligustrum Ibolium is a hybrid between I. ovalifolium and I. obtusifolium. It is hardier than L. ovalifolium.

More tender kinds include the following, which are generally not hardy in the North except in especially sheltered places.

L. lucidum is a Chinese shrub or small tree,

Of very compact habit, the evergreen Ligustrum japonicum rotundifolium is a favorite where winters are not severe.

When in bloom, Privets exhibit their close botanical relationship to Lilacs. This is the California Privet, Ligustrum ovalifolium.

18-20 ft. high, with large leathery, glossy, evergreen leaves and erect panicles of white flowers in autumn. The variety tricolor has white and pinkish leaves. L. japonicum, the Japanese Privet, is a shrub 6-8 ft. high, with dark, glossy evergreen leaves and terminal inflorescences of white flowers borne during summer. It should be chosen instead of L. lucidum where space is limited. L. japonicum rotundifolium (coriaceum) is a compact, slow-growing variety.

L. Delavayanum (Prattii) is another Chinese shrub of neat growth, with small evergreen leaves and white flowers, while L. compactum (yunnanense), which was introduced from Yunnan to France in 1888, is a large-leaved evergreen shrub, 10-15 ft. high, rather like L. lucidum. The flowers are creamy white.

LILAC. Syringa, which see.

LILAC, CALIFORNIAN. See Ceanothus.

LILAC, INDIAN. See Melia.

LILIUM or LILY
Aristocrats of the Flower Garden

(Lil'ium). The true Lilies, members of the genus Lilium, are distributed over the north temperate regions of both hemispheres, the greatest number being found wild in eastern Asia, while at least five kinds are known to grow wild in subtropical countries. The name Lilium is the old Latin name akin to the Greek *leirion,* a lily; the name was first given to the Madonna Lily, Lilium candidum. These plants belong to the family Liliaceae.

Lilies are among the most beautiful and ornamental of bulb plants for cultivation in the greenhouse and out of doors. Through countless ages the Lily has been used as a symbol of purity and beauty in literature and in art; whether the particular Lily referred to from time to time was a member of the genus Lilium, i.e., a true Lily, is open to doubt.

A number of details must be considered in the cultivation of a large group of plants with such a wide and varied geographical distribution as that of the Lilies. The bulbs vary greatly in size; those of L. pumilum (tenuifolium) are often little larger than a marble, while those of L.

Lilies, among the finest of summer-blooming bulbs, share their family name, Liliaceae, with such plants as Asparagus, Onions, Daylilies and Tulips. For most Lilies a well-drained, crumbly garden loam is satisfactory. Here is a border of the Madonna Lily, Lilium candidum.

Planting a bulb of Lilium regale. This is one of the kinds that should be set with at least 6 in. of soil covering the top of the bulb.

giganteum may be as large as, or larger than, a baseball. The variation in height is just as remarkable. L. rubellum grows only 15-24 in. high, while the stately L. giganteum reaches a height of 10-12 ft.

A Succession of Flowers. Out of doors a representative collection of Lilies will provide a succession of flowers from the end of May until October; under glass, if you force and retard the flowering of such Lilies as L. longiflorum and L. speciosum, blooms are easily available during every week of the year.

While the great majority of Lilies are hardy, a few require warm and sheltered positions and light, well-drained soil for their successful cultivation. A large number grow and flower best in partial shade, or at least in such a position that the lower half of the stem is shaded from the sun. A few Lilies cannot be grown successfully in soil containing lime in any appreciable quantity.

While it is necessary to choose certain positions and soils for some Lilies, a considerable number grow and flower freely in the ordinary deeply cultivated garden soil of the mixed flower border in sunshine in association with Delphiniums, Phloxes, and other familiar flowering plants.

The Lilies most in favor in small gardens are those which can be successfully grown in the mixed flower border in a sunny or lightly shaded position, in ordinary well-cultivated soil.

Planting Lilies

When to Plant. Autumn planting is desirable. There is little doubt that the failure to establish more than a meager percentage of the thousands of imported bulbs of L. auratum and L. speciosum which have been planted in gardens is due in part to their being out of the ground for several months. Under normal conditions the bulbs should be in the ground, making new roots, instead of being packed in boxes en route to their destination, or drying on the shelves of a bulb-dealer's store. The impaired vitality of many Lily plants is due to the loss of the fleshy basal roots, a circumstance which does not arise when we are able to plant home-grown Lily bulbs raised from seeds.

It is impossible to complete the planting of all Lily bulbs in the autumn months, since so many are imported from abroad and may not arrive until January. It is of great importance to obtain them as early as possible and to cover them with soil or peat moss as soon as they are received, if they cannot be planted at once; this will help to preserve the basal roots.

How Deep to Plant. The depth at which Lily bulbs are planted varies with the different kinds, because some root only from below the bulbs, while others develop roots freely from the bases of the bulbs and on the bases of the stems as well. Examples of those which need but a soil covering of an inch or two are L. candidum and L. giganteum. On the other hand, L. auratum, L. Henryi and L. myriophyllum variety superbum (sulphureum) cannot be considered happily placed unless the tops of the bulbs are covered with 6-8 in. of soil.

Set the Bulbs on Sand. While Lily bulbs delight in cool and moist conditions at the roots in summer, an excessive amount of moisture in winter may easily cause harm; for this reason, it is often helpful, when planting, to surround the bulbs with coarse sand.

Watering and Mulching. Lilies, as a group,

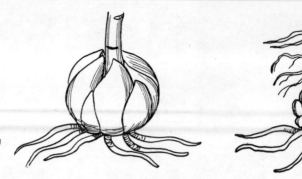

Base-rooting and stem-rooting Lilies.

need a reasonable amount of moisture in the soil at all times. They are especially likely to suffer if drought prevails in summer. To offset such conditions, watering must be done before the soil, at depths where the roots of the Lilies are, becomes excessively dry. When watering becomes necessary it should be done very thoroughly, enough being given each time to soak the ground to a depth of 6-8 in., then no more should be given for about a week. Frequent, shallow waterings are likely to be more harmful than helpful.

The practice of mulching the ground surface during the summer materially reduces the need for watering and helps to provide the cool soil conditions which are favorable to Lilies. Leaf mold, peat moss and compost are excellent mulch materials.

Fertilizing. Like other plants, Lilies respond to intelligent fertilizing, but they are easily harmed if fertilizers are used carelessly. It is especially dangerous to apply readily available nitrogen in considerable amounts; this is the reason why fresh or nearly fresh manure is likely to destroy Lily bulbs if it is placed near them. Very rotted, old manure is an excellent fertilizer to use; it may be applied as a mulch in early fall or early spring. Other organic fertilizers, such as tankage, cottonseed meal, tobacco stems and castor pomace are safe to use in moderate amounts and are beneficial. Commercial complete fertilizers, such as a 5-10-5, may be used effectively in small amounts; an application of 1 lb. of 5-10-5 to 100 sq. ft., made in early spring, is recommended.

Cutting Down Lily Stems. Growers of Lilies should be careful not to pull up the stems when the leaves turn yellow and begin to wither. They may be gradually shortened because of their untidy appearance, but 1-2 ft. of each stem should be left above ground to die away gradually; it should be removed in early spring when new shoots begin to grow. If the entire stem is pulled out from the center of the bulb, water is liable to collect there and may cause the bulb to decay.

Winter Protection. In sections where cold winters occur without a long-lasting, deep cover of snow, it is advisable to provide Lilies with a winter covering of some coarse, loose material such as salt hay, corn stalks, dry leaves or branches of evergreens; fine materials that tend to pack down should not be used for winter protection. The covering may be several inches thick and should be put in place after the ground has frozen to a depth of an inch or two. It is removed in early spring.

Where winters are severe and protection cannot be provided, consideration should be given to planting only those Lilies that are most hardy to cold. These include L. amabile, L. callosum, L. Davidii, L. philadelphicum, L. pumilum, L. superbum, and L. tigrinum.

When to Replant Lilies. The question of how often Lily bulbs should be lifted and replanted, when the question of increasing the stock does not arise, depends somewhat on the conditions under which they are grown. A safe rule to follow is to leave the bulbs undisturbed as long as the Lilies grow vigorously and flower freely. When a decline in health or crowding of the stems is noticed, it is time to lift the bulbs and give them fresh soil, or plant in new positions.

In the following notes on the chief kinds of Lilies, details on how to cultivate each are given.

Propagation

Raising Lilies From Seeds. While it may be

desirable to sow the seeds of rare and uncommon Lilies in pots or pans under glass, most kinds can be successfully raised in a cold frame or even in a cool and moist border out of doors where shelter from the midday sun is afforded. The lime-loving Lilies and, in fact, all except the lime-haters, can be raised in ordinary well-cultivated garden soil. Fork in a little leaf mold or peat moss and then make the surface moderately firm and level, after having raked off stones and lumps. Draw shallow drills 1-1¼ in. deep, and 12-15 in. apart, scatter the seeds thinly in the drills, and cover with about 1 in. of finely sifted soil. Sowing the seeds in drills is recommended in preference to broadcast sowing, for it is then much easier to keep the ground free from weeds. For the lime-hating Lilies a compost of sandy peat and leaf mold should be provided. The end of September and early October are the best times to sow seeds of Lilies. They do not begin to appear above the soil until early spring.

If seeds are kept dry during the winter and not sown until March or early April, some kinds, e.g., L. auratum, L. monadelphum and L. giganteum, often remain dormant in the ground for a year before sprouting. Those kinds which germinate quickly, like L. regale, L. philippinense formosanum, and L. pumilum (tenuifolium) may be sown in early spring.

Sowing under Glass. The grower who has seeds of choice and rare kinds usually prefers to sow the seeds in sandy soil in a cool greenhouse or garden frame. The seeds should be sown thinly so that the seedlings may remain in the pans or boxes for a year after germination, when they should be carefully transplanted to a sheltered border. Seedlings raised out of doors, or in a prepared bed in a garden frame, also must be carefully set out in lines on a sheltered border when they are large enough to be easily moved.

Managing the Seedlings. It is important to move the seedlings without damage to the roots. Set the plants 3-6 in. apart and allow 12-15 in. between the rows according to the vigor of the kind. Early spring is a good season to transplant seedling Lilies. This will be about eighteen months after sowing the seeds.

Give the seedlings a mulch of leaf mold or peat moss early in June; during dry weather spray freely morning and evening during the summer, and give water liberally, remembering always that Lilies dislike dry conditions at the roots.

Seedlings bloom in 1 to 6 years. The strongest seedlings of L. regale, L. pumilum, and L. philippinense formosanum will produce a flower bud the first year when the seeds are sown in a heated greenhouse early. Under outdoor treatment several kinds bear flower stems the second year; among them are the three already mentioned and L. Leichtlinii Maximowiczii, L. rubellum and L. pomponium. The majority of lilies flower in the third and fourth years from seeds. The notable exceptions are L. cordatum

Planted in rows in a cut-flower garden, these Regal Lilies send up many stout shoots each spring.

In summer every shoot is terminated by a cluster of gorgeous, fragrant flowers.

and L. giganteum and its variety yunnanense, which take five or six years.

Growing Lilies from Bulbils. At least four Lilies produce bulbils (small bulbs on the stems) freely in the axils of the leaves. These are L. bulbiferum, L. Sargentiae, L. myriophyllum variety superbum (sulphureum) and L. tigrinum. The bulbils should be removed shortly after the blooms fade. Dibble them an inch apart in sandy peat and leaf mold in a cold frame or cool greenhouse for the winter.

Quite a number of Lilies produce bulbils on

A bulb of Lilium longiflorum showing the formation of bulbils above the mother bulb and just beneath the ground surface.

the stem between the surface of the ground and the top of the bulb. The most common example is the Easter Lily, Lilium longiflorum.

Growing Lilies from Scales. Next to propagation from seeds, the raising of Lily bulbs from scales provides the most rapid means of increasing stock. For ordinary requirements it is usually sufficient to remove a few of the loose outer scales from the bulbs, but when large numbers

Bulbils clustered along a stem of Lilium bulbiferum.

Removing scales from a Lily bulb to be used in propagation.

The bulbils taken from the Lily stems are planted 1 in. or so apart in flats of sandy, peaty soil.

Planting the scales in a mixture of peat moss and sand.

are required the bulbs can be carefully and entirely dismembered.

A simple way to cause the formation of the bulblets on the scales is to bury the bases of the scales in coarse sand. March is the best time to set the scales, but it may also be done in October or November previous to planting and when replanting the bulbs. The shallow pans containing the scales are placed on a bench in a cool greenhouse, in a well-protected garden frame, or even in a cool cellar, and covered with a sheet of glass.

In due course the bulblets must be transferred to the ordinary soil suitable to the particular Lily. Most Lilies produce bulblets freely on the scales, and particularly L. Henryi, L. auratum, L. testaceum and L. chalcedonicum.

Lifting and Separating Lily Bulbs. The propagation of Lilies by lifting and separating the groups of bulbs is the simplest and easiest method. Generally October, when the stems and leaves have turned yellow, is the best time to lift, divide and replant the bulbs.

Important exceptions, however, are the Madonna Lily (L. candidum) and the Nankeen Lily (L. testaceum). These two Lilies produce a tuft of leaves in autumn and should be lifted and replanted during August or early in September.

Lily bulbs should not be disturbed more than once every third or fourth year for the purpose of increasing the stock.

Kinds, Some Easy, Some Difficult

Provided vigorous bulbs free of virus diseases are planted and soil and other growing conditions are reasonably suitable, the Lilies described below are mostly relatively easy to cultivate. The exceptions, those generally considered difficult to grow in gardens (except perhaps in favored parts of the Pacific Northwest), are: Lilium columbianum, L. Duchartrei, L. japonicum, L. Kelloggii, L. Leichtlinii and its variety Maximowiczii, L. leucanthum chloraster, L. Parryi, L. parvum, L. rubescens, L. Wardii, L. Washingtonianum.

The Goldband Lily, L. auratum, attains a height of 4-7 ft., sometimes more, with large, open, white flowers flushed with yellow and spotted with dark brown. It blooms in August–September. The variety platyphyllum has broad yellow bands but fewer spots; pictum has rose-colored markings down the centers and on the tips of the petals; rubro-vittatum, white flowers with deep red or crimson markings and freely spotted; virginale, white flowers with faint yellow spots and bands. Crimson Queen is double-flowered, and the vigorous Esperanza strain, raised in British Columbia, embraces a wide range of good forms of this Lily. Roots develop freely on the stems of L. auratum, so the bulbs should be planted 6-8 in. deep in positions where the bottom half of the stem is shaded and in peat or lime-free loam and leaf mold. A mulch of leaf mold or compost is very beneficial. Unfortunately, this Lily is subject to many diseases.

L. bulbiferum. This European Lily grows 2-4 ft. high and in June bears orange-red, upright blossoms resembling those of L. hollandicum (umbellatum). It thrives in ordinary cultivated garden ground in sun or partial shade. The bulbs are stem-rooting and should be planted 5-6 in. deep in autumn. L. bulbiferum is so-named because bulbils are produced in the axils of the leaves, affording an easy means of propagation.

The Orange Lily of the Alps of Savoy, Corsica

Lilium canadense is an American native that blooms in early summer. It thrives best in partial shade.

and Lombardy is L. bulbiferum croceum, a variety that is often listed as a distinct species (L. croceum). It thrives in a sunny position in ordinary garden soil and is particularly vigorous in rather heavy loam. The upright orange-colored blooms are freely produced on stems 4-6 ft. tall, in June and July. Like the type, it is a stem-rooting Lily, and the bulbs should be planted 4-5 in. deep in autumn or early spring.

The Meadow Lily is L. canadense. There are two forms of this Canadian Lily, one called flavum, having golden-yellow flowers, and coccineum (rubrum) with orange-red flowers. The flowering season is July and the average height of the stems 4-6 ft. Plant the bulbs 6-8 in. deep in a compost of sandy peat and leaf mold or lime-free loam. It is a woodland Lily, thriving in partial shade.

The Madonna Lily. L. candidum, the beautiful Madonna Lily or White Lily, is a native of southern Europe. It thrives in good garden ground containing lime. In rather heavy soil, mix sand or grit and decayed organic material freely with the soil before planting. The bulb roots only from the base and thrives best when covered with only 1-2 in. of soil. The Madonna Lily is practically an evergreen plant; almost as soon as the flowering stems die down, new leaves begin to grow.

August and early September are the best times for planting and transplanting. This is one of the Lilies that should be left undisturbed so long as the stems are vigorous and flower freely. It grows 3-4 ft. high and blooms in June and early July.

Several varieties of the Madonna Lily are in cultivation. The best known are one with black stems, named cernuum (peregrinum), and variety salonikae, with wider-opening flowers, a free seeder, and considered more disease-resistant than the type.

The Scarlet Turk's-Cap Lily. L. chalcedonicum is a native of Greece, thriving in loamy soils and doing especially well in limestone districts. It likes a sunny position, grows 3-4 feet high, and in June–July bears five to eight waxlike scarlet flowers on each stem. The bulbs form roots only at the base, so they are planted 3-4 in. deep in autumn. The bulbs do not usually flower freely

the first season after planting. Variety maculatum has purple-spotted flowers.

L. Davidii. This Lily is widely distributed in China and Tibet. An elegant and graceful plant, 4-7 or 8 ft. high, it is readily raised from seeds. The reflexed flowers are cinnabar-red and open in July–August. This is a stem-rooting Lily and should be planted 8 in. deep in a compost of gritty loam and leaf mold in sun or partial shade. Notable varieties and hybrids of it include macranthum, larger, scarlet flowers; Willmottiae, flowers heavily speckled with brown; and Lady Byng, orange-vermilion, spotted purple.

Lilium Duchartrei (Farreri) is a Chinese Lily of slender and graceful growth about 3 ft. high, producing in June and July recurved white flowers, slightly spotted with purple. It is a stem-rooting Lily; the small bulbs should be planted in autumn, 5 in. deep in ordinary garden ground with which plenty of coarse grit and decomposed organic material has been mixed. The bulb produces stolons freely and of some length; growth sometimes appears a foot or more from the parent bulb. It will grow in sun or partial shade.

The Giant Himalayan Lily. There are three distinct Asiatic Lilies which are similar in growth and require the same treatment. They are L. giganteum (Himalayas) and its variety yunnanense (China), and L. cordatum (Japan). All three grow best in partial shade and are ideal Lilies for the open woodland and shrub borders in regions where they thrive. Unfortunately they are difficult to cultivate in most parts of Canada and the United States; they thrive best in the Pacific Northwest.

These Lilies require a compost of loam, leaf mold and thoroughly decayed manure. The bulbs should be planted an inch below the surface and given a heavy mulch. The flowering season is July. When the bulb has flowered, it decays, and in early autumn the offsets or small bulbs should be lifted and replanted; otherwise the decay set up by the old bulb may spread to the offsets. The offsets will flower in three or four years. Seeds of these Lilies may not germinate for a year or two and the seedlings usually take 5 or 6 years to reach the flowering stage.

L. giganteum bears an immense spike, 10 or

Lilium Hansonii, an early summer-blooming kind that is easy to grow.

12 ft., with from twelve to thirty long, tubular, white flowers; variety yunnanense has similar flowers, but they are fewer in number on stems 4-5 ft. high. L. cordatum has similar flowers, on stems up to 6 ft. tall, but is not so showy or hardy as L. giganteum.

Hanson's Lily. L. Hansonii, from Korea, thrives in the soil of the mixed flower border in sun or partial shade and grows 3-5 ft. high; the reflexed, orange-colored flowers with yellow spots are freely borne on the stems in whorls during June and early July. Roots develop on the base of the stem, so the bulbs should be planted 8 or 9 in.

deep. In strong sun the flowers bleach, so a partially shaded location is preferable.

Henry's Lily. L. Henryi, a Chinese Lily, grows 6-8 or 9 ft. high and bears twelve to twenty nodding apricot-colored flowers in August. This is a stem-rooting bulb and should be planted 8 in. deep in rich loamy soil in sun or partial shade; the latter is preferable because the flowers bleach when exposed to strong sunshine.

L. hollandicum. This name is applied to a group of hybrid Lilies that are often known in gardens under the name L. umbellatum. They differ from the true L. maculatum varieties in

Two beautiful Lilies that rank among the easiest to cultivate successfully. (Left), the Tiger Lily, L. tigrinum splendens, with salmon-red, purple-spotted blooms. (Right), the apricot-colored blooms of L. Henryi.

being rather taller, but otherwise are similar. Notable kinds are erectum, red, suffused orange; Golden Fleece, golden-yellow, tipped scarlet; grandiflorum, orange, shading to red at the tips; Incomparabile, crimson; Invincible, deep-orange shading to red; and Orange King, rich orange, with red tips.

L. Humboldtii. A showy California Lily with reflexed orange-red flowers on stems 5 ft. high. It flowers in July and does well in sunny positions if the lower part of the stem is shaded by other plants. Plant in sandy loam and leaf mold; the bulbs root only from below and should be planted 4-5 inches deep. Two varieties are worthy of attention—ocellatum, a strong-growing Lily with rich orange-red, crimson-spotted flowers, and Bloomerianum, a smaller-growing variety, 2¼-3 ft. high, with flowers of similar coloring.

L. leucanthum chloraster (centifolium) is one of the most distinct of the Chinese Lilies. Growing from 5-8 ft. high, it produces ten to twenty large, trumpet-shaped white flowers on a stem. The flowering season is August. It is a stem-rooting Lily; the bulbs should be planted 9 in. deep in gritty loam and leaf mold in sun or partial shade.

The Easter Lily, L. longiflorum, is more largely grown under glass to supply cut flowers and pot plants than any other Lily; it is planted com-monly as a garden plant in the South. It is available in several named strains or varieties such as Croft, Creole, Estate and Giganteum. With good winter protection the hardier forms or varieties of it live outdoors as far north as New York City. Even bulbs that have been forced in pots for Easter, if they are kept watered and are planted in the garden after danger from frost has passed, will usually recover and bloom again in late summer. In climates where they are hardy, such bulbs will live through the winter outdoors and will bloom even better in succeeding years. Bulbs that have been forced are of no

The richly colored Lilium hollandicum (umbellatum) Orange King.

The Easter Lily, Lilium longiflorum, and its varieties are produced in huge quantities by florists for the pot-plant trade.

use for growing indoors the following season.

The stems of the Easter Lily grow 2-4 ft. high, each stem being crowned with several large trumpet-shaped white flowers. The normal season of flowering is July and August, but, by forcing and retarding the bulbs, market growers can maintain a supply throughout the year. The bulbs are stem rooting and should be planted about 8 in. deep in a compost of gritty loam and leaf mold.

L. maculatum. This is the original and therefore valid name of the group of Japanese Lilies commonly listed as L. Thunbergianum or L. elegans. They are interesting and attractive, dwarf-growing Lilies with cup-shaped flowers, growing 1-2 ft. high. They thrive in sandy loam and leaf mold or peat moss, are stem rooting, and should be planted 6 in. deep in sun or partial shade. They are attractive in the rock garden and the front of the sunny flower border. Numerous named varieties are in cultivation. The following six are distinct: Alice Wilson, lemon-yellow; alutaceum, apricot-yellow; atrosanguineum, dark red, crimson center; Orange Queen, orange-yellow; Prince of Orange, orange, shaded apricot; and sanguineum, dark red spotted with black. However, there are many other equally showy sorts.

The Martagon Lily. L. Martagon is the old Turk's-Cap Lily, with tall slender spikes of pink to purple blooms. The average height of the flower spikes is 4-5 ft. and the flowering season June and July. The bulbs root only from the base and should be planted 3-4 in. deep; it thrives best in sandy loam and leaf mold. The variety album with its lovely white flowers is among the best dozen Lilies for the small garden. The variety sanguineopurpureum (dalmaticum), from Dalmatia, is often taller in growth than the ordinary L. Martagon and has wine-red or wine-crimson flowers, while those of Cattaniae are rich purple-claret.

L. monadelphum. Considerable confusion exists in gardens with regard to this Caucasian Lily and L. Szovitsianum; they are now generally regarded as distinct species. L. monadelphum has deep yellow reflexed flowers. The stout stems of plants are 3-5 ft. high, each carrying ten to twenty or more pendent flowers in June. This Lily thrives in rich loamy ground in sun or partial shade. The bulbs root only from the base and should be planted 4-5 in. deep in autumn. Often this Lily does not make much growth above the soil the first season after planting.

The Leopard Lily. L. pardalinum is one of the best native North American Lilies. It grows and flowers best in lime-free loam and peat in the semishade of woodland; the rich orange-red flowers are freely produced on stems 5-8 ft. high in July. The bulbs have no stem roots and should be planted 5 in. deep. There are numerous forms and variations.

L. pomponium, from Italy, grows 3-4 ft. high and bears blooms of sealing-wax red in June. The bulbs root from the base only. They should be planted 4 or 5 in. deep in loamy soil which does not lack lime.

L. pumilum (tenuifolium), a dainty Lily from China and Siberia, bears up to twenty small, reflexed, scarlet flowers on 18-in. stems in June. Notable varieties are Golden Gleam, golden-orange, and Red Star, deep scarlet. The small, stem-rooting bulbs should be planted 4-5 in. deep in sandy loam and leaf mold or peat moss. They thrive in sun or partial shade in the rock garden or near the front of the mixed flower border.

The dainty scarlet Lilium pumilum (tenuifolium), which bears numerous flowers on 18-in. stems.

The Pyrenean Lily. L. pyrenaicum, known as the Yellow Turk's-Cap, is one of the first Lilies to bloom; its waxlike, greenish-yellow flowers open in May and early June. Growing 2-3 ft. high, this Lily roots from the base of the bulb only and should be planted about 4 in. deep in autumn. It thrives in ordinary garden soil in sun or partial shade. L. pyrenaicum rubrum has

The American Turk's Cap Lily, Lilium superbum.

orange-scarlet flowers spotted with maroon.

Chinese Regal Lily. Introduced from China in 1903 by Dr. E. H. Wilson, the Regal Lily, Lilium regale, now occupies first place in popular favor as a good garden Lily. It is readily raised from seeds and is particularly accommodating with regard to soil, doing equally well in light soils and heavy loam, with or without lime. The stems reach a height of 3-6 or 7 ft., are crowned with five to twenty white, funnel-shaped flowers, the outside streaked with brown and shaded with pink, the inside flushed with yellow.

One of the easiest of all Lilies to grow outdoors is the Regal Lily, Lilium regale.

When grown under glass, the flowers are white or nearly white. The flowering season is the end of June and in July. As this is a stem-rooting Lily, the bulbs should be planted 7 or 8 in. deep in autumn or early spring.

L. Sargentiae. A strong-growing Lily from China, 4-5 ft. high, with large, funnel-shaped flowers, creamy-white inside, reddish-brown on the exterior, in August. It thrives in rich, gritty loam that contains generous amounts of decayed organic matter, is stem rooting, and should be planted 8 or 9 in. deep in autumn.

Lilium speciosum is a popular Lily. It flowers in August and in September and it has stems

Lilium speciosum Kraetzeri is a white-flowered variety of great merit.

3-5 ft. tall. The bulbs are stem-rooting and should be planted 6-8 inches deep in early spring. The most suitable soil is sandy loam and leaf mold, with a liberal mulch applied at the beginning of summer. Numerous named varieties are listed in the catalogues of bulb dealers. The following are four of the best: Kraetzeri, white, with green stripes; magnificum, ruby-red, margined with white; Melpomene, crimson, margined with white, and rubrum, rose-pink to carmine pink.

The American Turk's-Cap, L. superbum, is an

The canary-yellow Lilium Szovitsianum.

ideal Lily for the moist and shady conditions of the open woodland and partially shaded shrub border. The bulbs should be planted 4-5 in. deep in leaf mold and sandy peat or lime-free sandy loam. The average height is 5-6 ft.; the rich orange-red flowers flushed with crimson are freely borne in late July and August.

Lilium Szovitsianum, closely related to L. monadelphum and thriving under similar conditions, bears large canary-yellow, black-spotted, bell-shaped flowers on 4-6 ft. stems in June.

The Tiger Lily. L. tigrinum, the well-known Tiger Lily, is a native of Japan and China. It is one of the oldest Lilies in cultivation, is easily grown and thrives in ordinary soils in full sun. The reflexed, orange-red flowers spotted with purple, on stems 4-5 ft. high, are beautiful in August. The bulbs should be planted 6-8 in. deep in late autumn or spring, for roots form on the stem. Distinct forms of the Tiger Lily are splendens, salmon-red flowers with purple spots, 4-5 ft. high, flowering in August; Fortunei, a giant Tiger Lily, 5-7 ft. high, each stem with twenty to thirty large flowers, salmon-orange, spotted with purple, in August and September; and plenescens, the double-flowered Tiger Lily, with orange-red flowers in August and September, on stems 3-4 ft. high. The Tiger Lily produces bulbils in the axils of the leaves and these may be detached and planted to raise an increased stock, as explained earlier.

Some West Coast Lilies. L. Parryi is a distinct and charming Californian Lily, 4-6 ft. high, with citron-yellow, funnel-shaped flowers, spotted with purple-brown, in July. It is a woodland Lily, thriving in leaf mold and peat or lime-free sandy loam. Plant the bulbs 5 or 6 in. deep.

The following West Coast Lilies thrive under similar conditions to L. Parryi: L. rubescens, 3-5 ft., tubular white flowers passing to purple, with dark spots, in June–July: L. Washingtonianum, 4-5 ft., white flowers, suffused and dotted with purple, June–July; and L. parvum, 4-5 ft., small bell-shaped, orange-red flowers, spotted with purple, in July.

A Lily from Tibet. L. Wardii is a beautiful Tibetan Lily, discovered by Captain Kingdon-Ward in 1924, and often called the pink-flowered Martagon. It averages 4 ft. high and bears

The Tiger Lily, Lilium tigrinum, is a hardy Lily that increases by bulbils formed in the axils of the leaves. It is a very easy kind to grow.

purplish-pink flowers in August and September. Plant the bulbs 4-5 in. deep in ordinary garden soil to which plenty of leaf mold has been added.

Some Other Lilies. The following kinds, of which brief details are given, should find a place in the gardens of all Lily enthusiasts who wish to cultivate a representative collection.

L. amabile, from Korea, grows 3-4 ft. high, and bears red flowers spotted with black, in July. It is stem rooting; plant at 6-8 in. deep in partial shade in sandy loam, leaf mold and grit. Variety luteum has golden or orange-yellow flowers.

L. Brownii, a Chinese Lily, 3-4 ft., bears large trumpet-shaped, fragrant flowers which are chocolate-colored outside and cream or pale yellow inside; it blooms in July. It is stem rooting; plant it 8 in. deep in ordinary well-cultivated garden soil. The variety Colchesteri is similar in habit, but the flowers are more funnel-shaped, reddish-purple outside and cream-white inside.

L. callosum, a Japanese Lily, is 2-3 ft. high, with red, reflexed flowers in August and September; it is stem rooting; plant it 6-8 in. deep in ordinary well-drained soil in a sunny position.

L. cernuum, a Chinese Lily, 2 ft. high, bears lilac-pink, fragrant flowers in June–July; it is stem rooting; plant it 4-5 in. deep in sandy loam on a sunny border or in the rock garden.

L. columbianum, from northwestern America, reaches a height of 3 ft. and bears reflexed, orange-yellow flowers with purple spots in July. This Lily roots from the bulb only; plant 4-5 in. deep in a sunny position in ordinary well-drained soil.

L. concolor, a Chinese Lily, 1½-2 ft., has orange-red flowers in June–July. It roots from the bulb only; plant 4 in. deep in sandy loam and leaf mold in a sunny position in rock garden or border.

L. Grayi, from North Carolina, 3-4 ft., bears two to four orange-red, funnel-shaped flowers on each stem in July. Roots form only from the bulb; plant 4 in. deep in partial shade in sandy peat.

L. japonicum (Krameri), from Japan, 2-4 ft. high, bears pink, trumpet-shaped flowers, two to five on a stem, in June and July; it is stem rooting; plant the bulbs 6-8 in. deep in very sandy loam and leaf mold in a sheltered position.

L. Kelloggii, from California, 2-3 ft., has reflexed pale pink flowers which deepen in color as they age. It is base rooting; plant it 4 in. deep in partial shade in sandy peat and leaf mold.

L. Leichtlinii is a Japanese Lily, 3-4 ft., with reflexed, pale yellow flowers with purple spots in July–August. It is stem rooting; plant it 6-8 in.

The dainty pink-flowered Lilium rubellum, from Japan.

deep in sandy peat and leaf mold in partial shade. Its variety Maximowiczii, 2-3½ ft., has orange-red flowers with dark spots.

L. philadelphicum, a North American Lily, 2-3 ft., bears clusters of cup-shaped, orange-scarlet flowers in June–July. It has few roots on the stem, and should be planted 5 in. deep, in a sunny position in sandy loam and leaf mold among dwarf shrubs. It is not an easy Lily to grow.

L. rubellum, from Japan, 1¼-1½ ft., has fragrant, pink, trumpet-shaped flowers in June. It is stem rooting; plant it 6 in. deep in well-drained loam, leaf mold and sand in the rock garden and among dwarf shrubs. This Lily is readily raised from seeds.

Hybrid Lilies. An early example of a really good hybrid or cross-bred Lily is L. testaceum, a cross between L. candidum and L. chalcedonicum, said to have been raised by an Erfurt, Germany, nurseryman about 1846. This beautiful Lily grows 4-6 ft. high and bears flowers of pale apricot color. The bulbs should be planted in September, 6 in. deep, in loam, leaf mold and sand.

L. Marhan, a hybrid, between L. Martagon and L. Hansonii, grows 4-6 ft. high and bears orange-colored flowers with reddish spots in June and July. Plant the bulbs 8 in. deep in ordinary garden soil.

The Golden Chalice Hybrids are suitable for a sunny, dry corner of the June border.

L. Dalhansonii is the result of crossing L. Martagon Cattaniae (dalmaticum) with L. Hansonii. Growing about 4 ft. high, the slender stems bear glossy purple-brown flowers in June and July. Plant the bulbs 4-6 in. deep in ordinary well-drained garden soil.

The Lilies known as Backhouse Hybrids were raised by Mrs. R. O. Backhouse, of England, by crossing and intercrossing L. Martagon album, L. dalmaticum and L. Hansonii. They are stem-rooting Lilies and the bulbs should be planted 8 in. deep in sandy loam and leaf mold. Several have been given names. They flower during June and July. Some of the best are Brocade, orange-yellow suffused pink, chocolate spots, 5-6 ft.; Mrs. R. O. Backhouse, orange-yellow, spotted purple, often 15-30 flowers on a stem, 5 ft.; Golden Orb, straw-yellow with crimson spots, 3-4 ft.; Sceptre, pink-buff shade with dark spots, 5-6 ft.

L. Burbankii is a showy Lily reputed to be a cross between L. pardalinum and L. Parryi, raised by Luther Burbank. It grows 5-6 ft. high,

and has rich orange-colored flowers spotted with red, in July. It roots only from the bulb and should be planted 3-4 in. deep.

L. sulphur-gale is a hybrid between L. sulphureum and L. regale raised in Germany,

Serenade, with clear orange flowers, is a fine garden Lily, one of the Mid-Century Hybrids.

Parade, a Mid-Century hybrid, has broad petals of yellow-orange spotted with dark maroon or black.

The Olympic Hybrids are a modern strain of Trumpet Lilies for July flowering.

where it first flowered in 1916. The plants grow 4-6 ft. high and bear large cream-white flowers in July and August. Plant the bulbs 9 in. deep in fibrous loam, leaf mold and sand.

In recent years many fine hybrid Lilies have been raised by North American breeders; as the work continues, there is every promise that the list of handsome, easy-to-grow hybrid kinds will be substantially extended.

Among the best of the hybrids raised by American breeders are the Aurelian Hybrids, the Bellingham Hybrids, the Fiesta Hybrids, the Golden Chalice Hybrids, the Green Mountain Hybrids, the Mid-Century Hybrids and the Rainbow Hybrids. Many selections of these have been given individual varietal names, are being propagated vegetatively, and will be found described in the catalogues of dealers specializing in Lilies.

Hollywood Hybrid Lilies, with star-shaped flowers, resulted from crossing Preston Hybrids with Mid-Century Hybrids.

Lilies for the Rock Garden

Some of the dwarf Lilies are admirable plants for the rock garden. The well-drained, yet cool, moist soil in the lower parts of a rock garden which is in slight shade, provides ideal conditions for the bulbs. The slender flower spikes, 1-2 ft. high, serve to break the flatness of trailing and other low-growing plants and add beauty and interest to the display.

Some of the best kinds for the rock garden are L. pumilum, L. rubellum, L. concolor, and its varieties coridion and pulchellum, L. cernuum, L. bulbiferum and the dwarfer varieties of L. maculatum.

Cultivation in Pots

The cultivation of Lilies in flowerpots is an easy procedure, and splendid results can be obtained. Although the bulbs must be started into growth under glass, during the summer months most of them may be placed out of doors. The bulbs of some kinds can be purchased in autumn, others early in the New Year. It is important that they be obtained at the earliest possible opportunity, for the longer they are kept out of the soil the more they deteriorate.

The best compost for Lilies suitable for growing in pots consists of fibrous loam, two thirds, and leaf mold and peat, one third, with a free scattering of sand. Pots 5- to 7-in. in diameter should be chosen, according to the size of the bulbs. The pots must be clean, and drained by placing a layer of crocks at the base. Sufficient compost is placed in the pots to fill almost one third of the depth and on this the Lily bulbs are placed, one in each pot. The bulbs are just covered with soil; the soil is then watered.

When all are potted, the bulbs should be placed in a slightly heated greenhouse or frame; if no artificial warmth is available the Lily bulbs must be kept safe from frost in severe weather.

In from five to eight weeks, according to the time when they were potted and the temperature of the greenhouse or frame, the bulbs will start into growth. Care must be taken not to overwater the soil while roots are few in number: it should be moistened only when it is moderately dry. Later on, when the plants are growing freely, the soil must be kept always moist.

Top-dressing the Bulbs. As soon as top growth begins, sufficient soil is added to fill half the remaining space in the pot, and the plants must then be fully exposed to the light in the greenhouse or frame.

Later on, as growth advances, the flowerpot should be filled to within half an inch or so of the rim with the prepared compost. The Lilies must be kept in a cool greenhouse or frame until all danger from late frosts has passed, when they may be placed out of doors, preferably in slight shade. When the flower buds show, an occasional watering with weak liquid fertilizer is advised.

When the Lilies begin to die down, watering is discontinued gradually: during winter the soil should be watered merely to prevent its becoming dust-dry. The following spring, the bulbs should be repotted.

Favorite Lilies for cultivation in pots are L. auratum, L. speciosum, L. regale, L. longiflorum, L. tigrinum, L. bulbiferum croceum, L. hollandicum (umbellatum), and many of the modern hybrids that have been raised by American breeders.

Lilium longiflorum, and often Lilium auratum, cannot be relied on to continue satisfactory, but L. speciosum, L. regale, L. tigrinum and others may be "grown on" from year to year. Many amateurs experience disappointing results with Lily bulbs after the first year because they neglect the plants when the flowers have faded. The roots must be kept moist until the leaves have changed color, though, when active growth has ceased, less water is required than during the summer months.

The bulbs, left in the pots, should be kept in a frost-proof greenhouse during the winter months, care being taken not to place them near the hot-water pipes, where they might become very dry. It is merely necessary to keep them safe from frost. In January they should be turned out of the pots, all offsets or small bulbs being removed; they must then be repotted and managed in the way already advised.

Forcing Easter Lilies. When Easter Lilies (Lilium longiflorum and its varieties) are to be forced into bloom for a late winter or early spring display it is necessary to grow them in higher temperatures than those recommended above. The bulbs should be potted in fall, and be kept in a temperature of 40-50 degrees for 4-6 weeks or longer. They should then be transferred to a greenhouse where the night temperature is held at 60 degrees and the daytime temperature is somewhat higher.

From the time when the first leaves expand to the time the flowers open will be approximately 12 weeks, but this varies somewhat according to the kind of Lily and prevailing weather conditions. For example, the Creole variety comes into bloom more quickly than the Croft variety; in sunny weather, progress will be more rapid than in cloudy weather.

Once the plants have filled their pots with roots, weekly applications of very dilute liquid fertilizers are beneficial. At no time must the soil be allowed to become dry or the plants to suffer from lack of moisture. The atmosphere should be humid; on bright days, syringing the plants with clear water is beneficial.

LILY. Lilium, which see.

LILY, ADOBE. Fritillaria pluriflora, which see.

LILY, AFRICAN. Agapanthus africanus, which see.

LILY, AMAZON. See Eucharis.

LILY, ARUM. See Zantedeschia.

LILY, ATAMASCO. See Zephyranthes.

LILY, BELLADONNA. See Amaryllis Belladonna.

LILY, BLACKBERRY. Belamcanda chinensis, which see.

LILY, BLOOD. Haemanthus, which see.

LILY, BRISBANE. See Eurycles.

LILY, CHILEAN. See Alstroemeria.

LILY, CHINESE SACRED. Narcissus Tazetta orientalis, which see.

LILY, CORFU. Hosta subcordata, which see.

LILY, CORN. Ixia, which see.

LILY, DAY. Hemerocallis, which see.

LILY, DESERT. See Leucocrinum.

LILY, FAWN. Erythronium californicum, which see.

LILY, FOXTAIL. See Eremurus.

LILY, GINGER. Hedychium, which see.

LILY, GLORY. See Gloriosa.

LILY, GUERNSEY. Nerine sarniensis, which see.

LILY, JACOBEAN. Spreckelia formosissima, which see.

LILY, KAFIR. Clivia and Schizostylis, which see.

LILY, MARIPOSA. Calochortus, which see.

LILY, MILK AND WINE. See Crinum.

LILY OF THE NILE. Agapanthus africanus, which see.

LILY OF THE VALLEY
A Delightful Fragrant Flower for Shady Places

A native of the north temperate regions, the dainty, fragrant white Lily of the Valley, Convallaria majalis, has long been a favorite in gardens. It is also grown extensively in pots for decoration, and is forced in large quantities to provide cut blooms.

When to Plant. Planting is best done in late September or in October, in deeply dug soil enriched with compost or decayed manure, in a shaded or partly shaded place. Single crowns or roots—often called "pips"—are planted 3-4 in. apart, with the tips an inch below the ground surface. Every year, in October, top-dressing of

leaf mold or compost should be given and each spring an application of a complete fertilizer (see Fertilizers).

Lily of the Valley should be left undisturbed as long as possible, but when the plants begin to deteriorate through overcrowding, which may not happen for many years, they should be lifted and separated into single crowns for replanting. This work is best done in late September or October.

Growing Lily of the Valley in Pots. In October or November single crowns or roots are placed 1 in. apart in 6-in. pots, the tips of the crowns

Trimming the ends off the roots of retarded crowns of Lily of the Valley before potting them for forcing.

Potting retarded crowns of Lily of the Valley for forcing in a mixture of peat moss and sand.

Lily of the Valley may be forced into bloom very quickly. In a month or less from the time of planting, retarded pips (plants from cold storage) may be had in full flower.

level with the tops of the pots. The best compost consists of equal parts fibrous loam and leaf mold, well shaken among the roots, and made moderately firm. The pots are placed in a cold frame, and covered with ashes or peat moss until

January; then they are set in a greenhouse, temperature 50-60 degrees, and are shaded and watered freely as growth advances. After flowering, they are again placed in the cold frame and kept there until danger of frost has passed, when they are taken out of the pots and planted out of doors.

For Blooms at Any Time. Retarded crowns, or roots that have been kept dormant in a temperature of 28 degrees F., can be forced quickly into bloom throughout spring, summer, autumn and winter. They are placed close together in 6-in. pots or flats, and light sandy soil or peat moss is shaken between the roots and left fairly loose, the tips of the crowns being 1 in. above soil level. They are placed in a greenhouse with a temperature of 65-75 degrees. The pots or boxes are covered with inverted pots or boxes, to exclude light for 10-14 days; light is gradually admitted as growth starts, and the covering removed entirely as growth advances. Bottom heat causes the flower spikes to develop in advance of the leaves. Water is given freely when growth is active. Retarded crowns can be forced into bloom in three or four weeks.

There are several varieties: one with double flowers; rosea, in which the flowers are tinged with pink; and variegata, which has variegated leaves. Fortin's Giant is particularly fine; it is more vigorous than the ordinary kind and bears larger flowers.

LILY OF THE VALLEY TREE. See Clethra.

LILY, PERUVIAN. See Alstroemeria.

LILY, PLANTAIN. See Hosta.

LILY, PRAIRIE. See Cooperia.

LILY, RAIN. See Cooperia.

LILY, ST. BERNARD'S. Anthericum Liliago, which see.

LILY, ST. BRUNO'S. Paradisea Liliastrum, which see.

LILY, SAND. See Leucocrinum montanum.

LILY, SEGO. Calochortus Nuttallii, which see.

LILY, SPEAR. See Doryanthes.

LILY, SPIDER. Hymenocallis, which see.

LILY, TOAD. Tricyrtis, which see.

LILY, TORCH. See Kniphofia.

LILY TURF. See Liriope and Ophiopogon.

LILY, WATER. Nymphaea and Victoria, which see.

LILY, ZEPHYR. Zephyranthes, which see.

LIMB. A term sometimes used by gardeners to denote a large branch of a tree.

LIME. See Citrus and Tilia.

LIME. When chalk or limestone, as dug from quarries and pits, is roasted in kilns, it changes into lime; this lime is known as quicklime, burnt lime, caustic lime, shell lime, lump lime or, if reduced to powder in a mill, as ground lime. Lime in this form absorbs about half its weight of water yet still remains dry; it swells up, becomes very hot, and eventually falls into a powder known as slaked or hydrated lime. In gardening the term is now used loosely to cover all forms of calcium carbonate.

Liming the Soil. The practice of liming soil is one of the oldest methods of improving soils and crops.

When lime is dug into a stiff or clayey soil, it tends to make it friable and more easily worked. It breaks up the clay, lowers the tenacity of the plastic mass, reduces the cohesiveness of the particles and so promotes better drainage, while at the same time it makes it easier to secure that fine condition of the soil which is so necessary for good cropping.

There is nothing better than a dressing of lime in first efforts to improve clayey soil, and no better proof of its efficiency than to see how much easier it is to get fine surface soil for seed sowing in spring on land so treated. In render-

Applying lime with a spreader. Many dealers in garden supplies lend or sell spreaders.

ing the clay more friable, it reduces the amount of labor that need be expended upon it, and makes it warmer, thus ensuring earlier cropping in spring and earlier maturity of crops in autumn.

On the other hand, a loose sandy soil that dries up too quickly during drought is rendered more compact by the use of lime, more retentive of moisture and better able to carry crops through a spell of dry weather.

Lime Sets Free Plant Foods. Lime acts on humus, setting free plant foods. Soils should contain a fair amount of humus, and, when lime comes into contact with this, it sets free chemical substances that provide the food of plants. It is said, sometimes, to reduce fertility by lowering the humus content of soils in this way, but such a statement is a false explanation of the action of lime; lime really feeds plants indirectly by ensuring plenty of food for them. Lime also acts chemically on heavy soils and sets free potash that would otherwise be locked up, i.e., not available to the plants.

Counteracts Acidity and Sourness. In most cases land used for general garden and farm crops must not be of a very acid or sour character. Land of this nature seldom carries good crops, and, since it is inimical to the development and good work of helpful soil bacteria, it must usually be modified. The addition of lime

Lime may be applied by hand if the area to be fertilized is not too large.

corrects acidity and improves the cropping power of excessively acid soil.

Lime Is a Soil Tonic. Many diseases, such as club root, Clover sickness, etc., stem from the soil and attack certain crops. Lime checks some of these diseases and thus promotes health and vitality in plants. Moreover, lime is distinctly distasteful, if not actually injurious, to some soil pests, such as slugs, leatherjackets and wireworms; an application is of undoubted benefit in efforts to ensure immunity from these soil pests.

Lime Is a Plant Food. It is sometimes overlooked that most plants need a supply of lime in order to grow, and this they secure in solution from the soil through the roots. Some crops need more than others; Peas, Beans, Cabbages and Turnips revel in soils containing lime. It must not be forgotten, however, that a few, notably the plants belonging to the Heath family, Erica, Azalea and Rhododendrons, and so on, actually dislike lime in the soil, while others, like Potatoes and a few cereals, are not at their best if lime is applied to the ground immediately before they are planted or sown.

Plants That Are Harmed by Lime. Lime should not be applied to soil in which the plants mentioned above or in which other definitely acid-soil plants are grown, but for the majority of vegetables and flower-garden plants a soil that is neutral or slightly acid is best, and it is often necessary to lime periodically to maintain this condition.

How to Know When Soil Lacks Lime. Land which requires lime betrays its deficiency in various ways. If grass is growing on it, as on the lawn, stronger-growing, coarse grasses and weeds are apt to assert themselves to the detriment of the finer grasses. Arable or cultivated land in need of lime does not respond to cultivation and manuring as it ought to; weeds, sheep sorrel, and so on, flourish, and often a green scum grows over the surface. A soil test that reveals excessive acidity indicates the need for liming.

Different Kinds of Lime. For small gardens, hydrated (air-slaked) lime is probably most economical because it can be distributed so uniformly and so easily. Moreover, it acts at once and good results are ensured from its application shortly afterwards. Ground limestone (lime-

stone powdered but not roasted) is often used instead of lime. One third more by weight is needed to secure similar results.

Quicklime, obtained in lumps, is placed in a heap on a vacant part of the garden and water dashed over it. The lumps swell visibly and become very hot; finally they begin to crumble, and, after a time, a heap of dry powder called slaked lime is obtained.

How Much Lime to Use. Use ½ lb. per sq. yd. or up to 1 lb. where a heavy dressing seems necessary; 1 lb. per sq. yd. is roughly equal to 2 tons per acre. While acid soils may need a heavy dressing, it must be remembered that light dressings, in alternate years, give the best results.

How to Apply Lime. The efficiency of lime depends on an even distribution and good admixture with the soil; poor results follow careless application. As it tends to work lower in the ground as time goes on, it must not be dug in deeply. It is best broadcast on to surface of newly dug soil in late winter or early spring for the rains to wash in, the dry residue left being forked in when preparing the ground for sowing or planting.

It is unwise to apply lime and fresh manure together. Apply the lime a month or more after the manure.

Lime-loving Plants. In gardens situated on soils in which limestone is present, priority should be given to those plants which favor such conditions. Many of the trees and shrubs included in the Rose family, Rosaceae, give excellent results on lime soils. Many Conifers are not very partial to lime; though they may grow and live for many years on lime soils, they do not reach their best dimensions.

Still, a good deal depends upon the depth of soil overlying limestone rocks, for well-grown trees are often found where the soil is deep. Some Conifers, such as Junipers, thrive on lime soils, and the Yew may often be seen in excellent condition on limestone land.

How to Prepare Lime Soil. Naturally, the best results are obtained on lime land when the surface soil is moderately deep and the subsoil more or less broken up by stones and boulders among which roots can penetrate and spread about. Under such conditions it is possible to cultivate many plants, for by digging deeply, then adding available humus or decayed vegetable matter, the depth of soil can be increased.

Large Holes Must Be Dug for Trees. Because fine old trees may be found growing in places where very shallow soil overlies limestone, it does not follow that success can be assured by planting trees reared in nursery gardens without due preparation of the ground. In all cases where trees of any importance are to be planted, large holes should be dug and filled with good soil, in order that the trees may become established and be in a good state of health by the time the roots have to push their way into the surrounding ground and stones.

Limestone screes on hillsides are often excellent positions for establishing alpine plants, and very beautiful rock gardens can be formed with comparatively little trouble among natural limestone. This, when weathered, is often very picturesque.

Conifers for Lime Soil. Suitable Conifers for limestone soils are Pseudotsuga taxifolia, Cupressus Lawsoniana, the Yews (Taxus), and most Junipers. The European Larch will thrive where the soil is moderately deep, though it may not grow very fast. For shallow soils, Pinus nigra and Taxus are most satisfactory. Numerous smaller trees are available.

Suitable Flowering Trees. All the ornamental Crabs, the flowering Plums and Cherries, Whitebeam trees, Pears, Mountain Ash and Hawthorn give excellent results on limestone soils; and fruit-bearing trees, especially Plums and Damsons, frequently bear very good crops of richly colored fruits in these soils. The Whitebeam, Pyrus Aria, thrives under very adverse conditions.

The Spindle tree, Euonymus europaeus, grows well on lime soils and fruits freely, as also does the False Acacia, Robinia Pseudoacacia and allied kinds. Hollies in variety are suitable trees and bushes, while the more vigorous kinds of Magnolia, such as M. acuminata, succeed, though usually Magnolias are better suited to soils that are moderately free from lime.

Shrubs for Lime Soil. There are many kinds of shrubs that succeed in lime soils. Roses give good results, both cultivated varieties and wild kinds,

but the ground must be well worked before they are planted. Shrubby Spiraeas do very well, also Exochorda, Kerria japonica, the various Chinese and Japanese Quinces, the numerous kinds of Rubus, Flowering Currant, Mock Orange (Philadelphus), Deutzia, Honeysuckle (bush and climbing forms), Diervilla, and shrubby kinds of Cornus.

Cotoneaster Is Particularly Suitable. The numerous kinds of Cotoneaster are among the very best shrubs for establishing in places where there is not much soil overlying limestone.

Evergreen and leaf-losing kinds of Sun Rose and Rock Rose, species and varieties of Helianthemum and Cistus, respectively, are peculiarly adapted for planting on sunny banks where the soil is shallow; once they are established they withstand considerable drought and look after themselves.

The different kinds of Buckthorn (Rhamnus), although not very showy shrubs, thrive on lime soils, as do some of the more attractive allied shrubs, the Ceanothus.

Boxwood and Clematis. The common Boxwood, Buxus sempervirens, grows wild on lime soils, and it and allied kinds can be used freely. Forsythia also thrives. Clematis, both wild and cultivated kinds, succeeds much better on lime soils than on those which show a deficiency of lime.

Various kinds of Daphne are suitable, as are also Viburnum, Elderberry, Privet, Lilac, Juniper, Tamarix, Hazel, Buddleia, Berberis, Laurus, Elaeagnus, Lavender, Phillyrea, Escallonia, Yucca and Ivy.

Herbaceous and Alpine Plants. An indefinite number of herbaceous and alpine plants succeed on lime soil, particularly after it has been well worked. Such vigorous kinds as the herbaceous Phlox, Delphinium, Aster, Geum, Helianthus, Inula, Salvia, Poppy, Oenothera, Monarda, Hypericum and Helenium all do well, while smaller plants, as the Pink and Carnation, many kinds of Primula and Campanula, Wallflower, Stock, Sweet William, Silvery Saxifrage, Sedum, hardy Geranium and many others also thrive.

Bulbs such as Crocus and Narcissus can be naturalized in grassland on lime soil. In fact anyone who has to make a garden on lime soils, though he may be denied the pleasure of cultivating certain very attractive plants that enjoy an acid type of soil, has many compensations. He can experiment with numerous woody and herbaceous plants, many of which give far better results on lime than on acid soil.

LIME, OGEECHEE. Nyssa Ogeche, which see.

LIMEQUAT. This name is given to hybrids between the Kumquat and the West Indian Lime. They are propagated by grafting on Trifoliate Orange and require the same culture as Kumquat, which see. See also Hybrid Citrus, under Citrus.

LIMESTONE CHIPS. Crushed limestone, usually of a size that will pass through a sieve with a half-inch or three-quarter-inch mesh and with all fine, dustlike particles removed. Limestone chips are used for mixing with the soil for certain rock garden plants and other kinds that need lime.

LIME, SUPERPHOSPHATE OF. See Fertilizers and Manures.

LIME, TEST FOR. See Soil Testing.

LIMNANTHEMUM. See Nymphoides.

LIMNANTHES DOUGLASII (Limnanth'es). A beautiful hardy annual which grows wild in the western United States. It belongs to the Limnanthes family, Limnanthaceae. The name is derived from *limne,* a marsh, and *anthos,* a flower.

A Beautiful Edging Flower. This annual is chiefly suitable for sowing as an edging to flower beds and borders; it blooms most profusely and is very attractive when in full flower. The plants grow only about 6 in. high and the comparative-

The dainty annual Limnanthes Douglasii, with yellow, white-edged flowers, makes a very attractive dwarf edging.

ly large flowers are yellow with white margins. They do not thrive where summers are excessively hot and humid.

A Good Bee Flower. Limnanthes is a splendid bee flower. It is seen at its best only in sunny weather, and must be grown in a place fully exposed to the sunshine. Ordinary garden soil is suitable for Limnanthes, provided it has been well broken by digging and raking. Some compost or thoroughly decayed manure will improve clayey ground.

When to Sow Seeds. Seeds may be sown either in early autumn in mild localities, or in spring, to yield flowers in May–June and in July–August respectively. The best time to sow in spring is as soon as the soil is reasonably dry. Autumn sowing should be done early in September, but only on light or well-drained soil. If Limnanthes is sown in September on heavy, clayey ground that becomes sodden in winter, there are sure to be serious losses among the seedlings during the winter months, and for that reason autumn sowing is to be recommended only on light land. When seeds are sown in September, the chief thinning of the seedlings should be left until spring.

When thinning is finished, the seedlings should be about 5 in. apart. Those raised in autumn are generally more vigorous than others from a spring sowing.

LIMNOCHARIS (Limnoch'aris). Tender aquatic flowering plants, from South America, which belong to the Alisma family, Alismaceae. These plants grow about 16 in. in height, have lanceolate (lance-shaped) leaves which stand erect out of the water, and the flowers, which are pale yellow, are produced in small umbels, or bunches, in summer. The name Limnocharis is derived from *limne,* a marsh, and *charis,* beauty.

Outdoors in Warm Weather. They should be planted in March or April, in shallow tubs or aquaria, which are kept in a greenhouse having a minimum winter temperature of 50 degrees. The tubs are filled to within 9 in. of the top with a mixture of equal parts of rich soil and leaf mold, compost or rotted manure and a layer of sand is placed on the surface. After the roots are inserted, the tubs are filled with water, which is added gently to avoid disturbing the soil. Very little attention is required, but when the plants become overcrowded, they should be lifted and divided and the strongest pieces replanted in new compost.

As soon as the weather is warm and settled, the plants may be transferred to outdoor pools, but this should not be done while the water is yet cold.

Plants are easily increased by dividing and replanting in spring.

The chief kind is L. flava, which has pale yellow flowers bordered with white.

LIMONIUM—*Sea Lavender* (Limo'nium). Annual and perennial plants that are found naturally mostly on seacoasts and in salt marshes and are widely distributed over the Northern Hemisphere. They belong to the Plumbago or Leadwort family, Plumbaginaceae. Limonium comes from the Greek *leimon,* a meadow, and alludes to salt meadows.

The flowers in many species are in loose panicles, in others they are in branching spikes. The flower colors are white, yellow, rose, lavender and blue. Although natives of salt marshes, they will grow and thrive in any good garden soil. The Limoniums, together with the Armerias (Thrifts), were once included in the genus Statice and are still often known by that name in gardens.

Treatment of Hardy Kinds. The border and rock garden kinds require well-drained soil and a sunny site. Heavy clay soil must be excavated and replaced with suitable compost, or lightened by adding quantities of sand or cinders. Planting is done in spring; firm planting is essential. The plants are not disturbed for many years, as they flower best when well established. Those showing signs of poor growth need a top-dressing of well-decayed manure in spring.

When to Sow Seeds. New plants may be obtained in various ways. Seeds are sown in April in a well-drained pot or pan filled with light soil. They are set in a cold frame or slightly heated greenhouse to germinate, and the seedlings pricked off into a large pan or seed flat. Towards the end of May, or early in June, they are hardened off and planted out, 6 in. apart, in a nursery bed. The smaller kinds are best grown separately in small pots, from which they can be planted in the rock garden.

Taking Cuttings. Small side shoots bearing rosettes of leaves can be detached and inserted in pots of sandy soil in summer. If set in a shady frame, they quickly form roots and will be large enough for planting in the spring. Young plants are also obtained by lifting and dividing the old ones in spring, the divided portions being set out where they are to grow.

Annual Everlastings. L. sinuatum, which grows 18 in. in height, and has compact terminal clusters of blue, mauve, pink or white flowers, is extensively grown as an annual, and the flowers are cut and dried for winter decoration. L. Bonduellii, which is similar but has yellow flowers, is also extensively grown in the same way.

The seeds are sown out of doors in early spring where the plants are to grow, the seedlings being thinned to 9 in. apart. Another method, which is widely adopted, is to sow the seeds in a pan of fine soil in the greenhouse (minimum temperature 45 degrees) about 8 weeks before it is safe to transplant the young plants to the outdoor garden.

The seedlings are pricked out into flats of soil, hardened off, and planted in the border, or in the cutting garden to provide cut flowers in May. A sunny position and a well-drained soil are necessary.

For winter decoration, the flowers are cut when fully expanded, and hung in bundles in a cool shed or room to dry.

For the Greenhouse. L. Suworowii is the most beautiful of all for the greenhouse. It may also be grown as an annual and planted out of doors in May, but it is most useful as a pot plant for decorating the greenhouse in late spring or summer. The seeds are sown from August to March, and the seedlings pricked off into flats. When large enough, they are potted separately in 3-in. pots, and, when well rooted, are set in 5-in. pots, in which they will bloom. The best compost consists of fibrous loam, two parts, and leaf mold, one part, with a little sand and decayed manure.

Water must be carefully applied to the soil at all times, as these plants are very liable to decay at the soil level. The best method is to wait until the soil becomes moderately dry before being moistened. Good drainage is necessary. The plants must not be coddled, and need shading only from the fiercest rays of the sun. They should be given a cool, well-ventilated position, and, when coming into flower, an occasional dose of weak liquid fertilizer.

Limonium sinuatum and its varieties, and L. Bonduellii also make attractive pot plants. Another greenhouse kind is L. macrophyllum. This is a perennial, subshrubby plant, 2 ft. in height, with large, smooth, spatulate (spoon-shaped) leaves and a tall branching spike of blue and white flowers. It is raised by inserting cuttings in a bed of coarse sand in spring. They are covered with a bell jar until rooted, then potted separately in small pots, and subsequently in larger pots. The old plants may be repotted in larger pots each year, but a few young plants should be raised annually, as they are more vigorous and floriferous.

Hardy Perennials for the Border and Rock Garden. The most popular of the hardy border kinds is L. latifolium, which grows 2 ft. in height and has wide-spreading sprays of small, purplish-blue flowers in Summer. L. tataricum nanum is a beautiful free-flowering kind, also about 12 in. in height, bearing numerous small pink flowers in spreading clusters. There is also a white variety, alba; the variety nanum grows only 6 in. in height, and is suitable for the rock garden. L. Gmelinii is a good border plant, with branching panicles of blue flowers, and L. tataricum is suitable for the front of the perennial border or a sunny rock garden. Its average height is 12 in., and it has red and white blossoms in attractive sprays.

In addition to L. tataricum nanum, which is also known as L. incanum nanum and is mentioned above, several other kinds are available for the rock garden. L. binervosum, 6 in., blue; L. caesium, 8 in., rose; L. minutum, 9 in., red; L. spathulatum, 1 ft., purple and white; and L. eximium, 9 in., lilac, are easily grown and flower freely.

Shrubby Kinds. In California and similar mild climates certain tender shrubby kinds can be grown outdoors in light, well-drained soils in sunny locations. These are mostly kinds that are natives of the Canary Islands, and include L.

macrophyllum, mentioned above, L. brassicaefolium, L. imbricatum, L. puberulum and some others.

LINARIA—*Toadflax* (Lina'ria). A group of plants embracing more than a hundred species; most of them are hardy herbaceous plants, a few are subshrubs. They are mostly distributed in the Old World regions of the Northern Hemisphere outside the tropics. The name Linaria is derived from *linon*, Flax, from the resemblance of the leaves to those of Flax plants. Linaria belongs to the Snapdragon family, Scrophulariaceae.

The flowers are in spikes or racemes, or solitary in the axils of the leaves; they are spurred, the petals being shaped like a mouth, as in Snapdragon.

As Greenhouse Plants. Garden varieties of the annual L. maroccana are attractive for growing in cool greenhouses, both as flowering pot plants and as sources of cut flowers. They are easily raised from seeds sown from September to January. Plants raised in this way bloom in late winter and spring and may be flowered in 4-5-in. pots. They need porous, fertile soil and a sunny location where the night temperature is about 50 degrees and the day temperature 5-10 degrees higher.

Hardy Flowering Plants. There are many highly ornamental flowering plants among the

Garden varieties of Linaria maroccana.

Toadflaxes which are valuable in the flower border, for cutting, in the rock and wall garden, and for growing in the crevices of flagged or paved paths. There are both annual and perennial kinds, and almost all are of the very easiest cultivation in light well-drained soil. The perennial sorts are easily propagated by division of the roots in spring or autumn, while the annuals may be sown in pans of light soil in a cold frame in March, and pricked out when large enough, or sown in spring where they are to flower in summer.

A Handsome Border Toadflax. Linaria dalmatica is a herbaceous perennial for the flower border rather than the rock garden, and admirable for cutting. It is an erect branched plant about 2 ft. tall, with blue-green leaves, and blunt spikes of handsome golden snapdragon-like flowers. This fine plant has a long summer flowering season and is easily propagated either by seeds sown in a cold frame in spring, or by division of the roots at the same season. L. macedonica, 3-4 ft., is similar to L. dalmatica, but has larger flowers.

Linaria genistifolia, the Genista-leaved Toadflax, is a perennial plant for the flower border, coming from southern Europe and Asia Minor. It grows from 2-3 ft. high, and has panicles of light yellow flowers in summer.

The Alpine Toadflax, Linaria alpina, is without doubt the best of all the Toadflaxes for the rock garden. It is a dwarf perennial, forming low spreading mats from 3 or 4 up to 8 or 9 in. across, and with very numerous flower spikes, 2-3 in. high. In the typical plant, the flowers, which resemble minute, spurred Snapdragons, are a brilliant violet, with the lips of the dragon mouth bright golden-yellow. The narrow leaves with which the stems are clothed are gray-green, often tinged or shot with a purplish hue.

This brilliant and extremely beautiful little Alpine is common throughout the Alps of Europe, and is often abundant, starring the high alpine screes, moraines and shingles, which it chiefly haunts, with countless splashes of splendid color.

Easy to Grow. Linaria alpina is of the easiest possible cultivation. It thrives in any reasonably good soil, is better on a light soil than a heavy one, and it grows and looks best in the scree or moraine garden; there it lives longer and flowers more freely than in loam, and it shows its intense coloring to the fullest advantage among the subdued tones of gray stone chips.

Raising Seedlings. Propagation by means of seed is by far the easiest and most satisfactory method with the typical plant, though cuttings may be resorted to if necessary. Seeds may be sown thinly in pans or pots of light soil in spring, and kept in a cold frame. Germination is usually very quick. Prick off the seedlings while still quite small into boxes of light soil, putting them 2 in. apart. In a few weeks they should be ready to plant in the permanent flowering quarters in the rock garden.

There are several very attractive varieties or color forms of Linaria alpina, notably alba, white, and rosea, pink.

Other Attractive Kinds. Linaria bipartita is a pretty annual from Portugal, growing from 9-12 in. high, with loose racemes of violet-purple flowers with orange-colored lips and narrow leaves. It flowers from June to September. Linaria canadensis, the Canadian Toadflax, is a hardy annual species, a native of North America, 6 in. to 2 ft. in height, with racemes of violet flowers.

Linaria crassifolia is a beautiful plant from southwestern Europe, 3-6 in. high, with bright blue-purple flowers with yellow lips, and red-purple throat; the leaves are of leathery texture, smooth and roundish.

Linaria heterophylla is an annual Toadflax from Morocco, growing 2-3 ft. tall, and flowering in July. The flowers are rather large, about 1 in. long, straw-yellow, and carried in branched racemes. It is best sown where it is to flower, and the seedlings thinned severely.

Linaria maroccana, the Morocco Toadflax, is a purple-flowered annual, with whorled, narrow, glaucous leaves. It grows from 9-12 in. high.

Linaria purpurea, the Purple Toadflax, a perennial species from southern Europe, makes a good wall plant. The bluish-purple flowers with white, velvety lips and striped spurs, are carried in long racemes. The plant grows from 1-3 ft. high, according to soil and situation, and flowers from July to September.

Linaria reticulata is a brilliant, popular and

easily grown annual, growing 12-18 in. high, with heads of fine purple flowers with golden or coppery-orange colored lips. It is a native of Portugal. There is a variety, aureo-purpurea, with flowers of even richer coloring than the type. Seeds are best sown thinly in spring, where the plant is to flower. They are good for cutting.

Linaria triornithophora is a pretty perennial, a native of Spain and Portugal, 5-6 in. high. The fine purple flowers with golden lips are so arranged as to look like three birds, as the plant's species name denotes—three-bird-bearing. This plant flowers July to September.

The Common Toadflax. Linaria vulgaris, the Common Toadflax, or Butter and Eggs, is a native of Europe and Asia Minor and is naturalized freely in North America. It is a handsome plant, growing 2-3 ft. high, with showy spikes of rich, yellow flowers with deeper golden lips, which it produces with the utmost freedom from spring until autumn. Although such a handsome, free-flowering plant, it is also a free seeder, and the gardener may well hesitate to introduce it into his flower borders, or the garden proper, though if a place can be found where its rapid increase does not matter, it is certainly well worth cultivating in the wild garden.

LINDELOFIA (Lindelof'ia). A small group of hardy herbaceous plants which are closely related to the Hound's-Tongue (Cynoglossum). They are natives of the Himalayas and belong to the Borage family, Boraginaceae. They grow about 2 ft. in height, have lanceolate (lance-shaped) leaves, and dense racemes of purplish tubular flowers $1/4$ in. in length. The name Lindelofia commemorates Friedrich von Lindelof, a German botanist.

The chief kind is L. longiflora. It makes an effective display when grouped in the herbaceous border, in a sunny position and well-drained soil, where it will grow 2 ft. tall, producing spikes of purple flowers in May.

Planting is done in fall or spring, and the plants are set 10 in. apart; no staking is required unless the position is very exposed. The plants may be kept growing vigorously for many years by forking decayed manure or compost into the surface soil in spring.

Propagation is by division or by sowing seed.

When it is desired to divide them, the plants are lifted in April, the roots being severed with a sharp knife. Each division should consist of a portion of root with one growing point (bud); the separated pieces may be planted immediately into their permanent positions.

LINDEN. Tilia, which see.

LINDERA—*Spice Bush* (Lin'dera; Linde'ra). Evergreen or leaf-losing trees and shrubs with a spicy odor, two kinds being found wild in North America and numerous others in eastern and southern Asia. They bear small, yellowish flowers in April. They are easily increased by seeds sown in a greenhouse or outdoors in spring, or by cuttings inserted in a frame in summer. They flourish in ordinary garden soil in a sunny or partly shaded position and may be planted in autumn or spring. Lindera belongs to the Laurel family, Lauraceae, and the name commemorates Johann Linder, a Swedish botanist of the early eighteenth century.

There are a number of kinds in cultivation. L. Benzoin, the Spice Bush, grows 6-12 ft. high, with light green leaves which become clear yellow and fall in autumn; it is native of moist soils in the eastern United States. L. megaphylla, a shrub or small tree with large evergreen leaves, is a native of China. L. melissaefolia, 10 ft., leaf-losing, is a native of the southeastern United States. L. obtusiloba, from Japan, Korea and China, is a leaf-losing shrub or tree, 18-25 ft. high. L. praecox, a leaf-losing shrub or tree, 20-25 ft. tall, comes also from Japan and Korea.

LINDSAYA (Lindsa'ya). Tender Ferns which have creeping rhizomes, and fronds resembling those of the Maidenhair Fern (Adiantum). The fronds average 6 in. in length and are evergreen. The name Lindsaya commemorates Dr. John Lindsay, an English botanist. The plants belong to the family Polypodiaceae.

These beautiful Ferns are not easy to grow and are chiefly cultivated in botanical collections. In their native habitats they grow on stony, impoverished soil and their roots are often drenched with heavy rain.

The most successful method of cultivation in greenhouses is to grow them in deep pans, nearly filled with crocks. The best compost consists of equal parts of peat, loam and sand. An inch layer of this is spread over the crocks and the rhizomes are pegged into it or held down by pieces of stone. The minimum temperature for the hothouse kinds is 55 degrees and, for the greenhouse kinds, 45 degrees.

These Ferns require a moist atmosphere at all times, and often do best under a large bell jar. During the summer the soil is kept moist, but throughout the winter less water is required, although the compost must not be allowed to become dust-dry.

Propagation is by division of the rhizomes in spring, when they are detached and treated as advised for potting. Spores may also be sown, as soon as they are ripe, on the surface of finely sifted compost. The spores are not covered, but a pane of glass is laid over the pot (which is set in a saucer of water) and kept there until the young Ferns are large enough to transplant. They are then pricked off, 1 in. apart, in deep pans of sifted compost and treated as advised for the mature plants.

The chief kinds are L. guianensis, 6 in., for the hothouse, and L. linearis, 18 in., for the cool greenhouse.

LINE. A garden line is invaluable when marking out paths, flower beds and borders, and when setting out vegetables or other plants which are arranged in rows. It is indispensable also for use when trimming the edges of the lawn. It is made of stout cord, one end of which is tied to a short iron stake, the other end being wound

around another iron stake so that the line can be unwound easily. A special iron reel, so made that the portion on which the cord is wound revolves, thus allowing of easy winding and unwinding, can be purchased.

LINEAR. A botanical term meaning long and narrow with parallel margins. See Leaf.

LINNAEA BOREALIS—*Twin Flower* (Linnae'a). This hardy trailing shrubby plant belongs to the Honeysuckle family, Caprifoliaceae, and was named in honor of Linnaeus. It has slender, creeping stems, the little evergreen leaves are ovate, and in opposite pairs, and from the axils of the leaves appear the nodding flowers, in pairs, on slender stems ½ in. high.

Almond-scented Flowers. The flowers are bell-shaped, pale pink, marked inside with deeper pink, and have a delicious and powerful almond fragrance. This beautiful little plant is a native of the cold regions of the Northern Hemisphere. The North American form, distinguished as variety americana, has rather larger flowers than the European form.

For Peat Soil in the Rock Garden. Linnaea borealis is grown in leaf mold, peat or the acid sandy soils in which Heathers and Rhododendrons flourish; it may also be grown in pans in soil of a peaty nature in the unheated alpine house. It flowers in May and June, and is a very beautiful plant for the rock garden and in open woodland, either in sun or in partial shade. It is best suited for cool climates.

Propagation. This plant may be propagated by means of seed or by cuttings in July, but most readily by division of the plant in September or April, the stems rooting at intervals where they touch the soil.

LINOSYRIS VULGARIS—*Goldilocks* (Linosy'-ris). The name of this Old World hardy perennial is taken from Linum, the Flax, and *osyris*,

A garden line with a metal stake and reel.

For planting in a sunny location in the front of a perennial border, the Goldilocks, Linosyris vulgaris, is well adapted.

a plant with yellow flowers. It is an attractive aster-like plant that has a profusion of yellow flowers late in the season. It belongs to the Daisy family, Compositae.

Linosyris grows easily in any good garden soil; it needs a sunny location. Propagation is readily carried out by dividing the plants in spring or early fall and by sowing seeds in spring. This plant is well adapted for a position at the front of the perennial border. It attains a height of about 2 ft.

LINSEED. The seed of the Flax plant, Linum usitatissimum.

LINUM—*Flax* (Li'num). The Linums or Flaxes form a fairly large group of annual, biennial and perennial herbs and subshrubs, and are natives of the temperate regions of the world. They belong to the family Linaceae. The name Linum is from *linon,* the old Greek name given by Theophrastus. The flowers may be yellow, or-

ange, red, blue, pink, or white; although the individual flowers last but a short time, they are extremely numerous and succeed one another over a long period.

For Light Soils and a Sunny Place. Many Flaxes are highly ornamental and most desirable plants for the flower border and the rock garden. All prefer a light, well-drained soil to a heavy one, and must be given a fully sunny position.

Propagation is most easily effected by means of seeds. The perennial kinds should be sown in March or April, in a cold frame; the seedlings are pricked out into boxes or small pots and finally planted out in their permanent flowering quarters later in the summer. The annual Flaxes are sown in early spring where they are to flower in summer.

Taking Cuttings. Cuttings of perennial kinds may be taken in August; half-ripened, not too

The Yellow Flax, Linum flavum, bears a profusion of flowers in early sum er.

[6—12]
Regal Lily
(Lilium regale)

[6—12a]
Tulip Tree
(Liriodendron Tulipifera)

[6—12b]
Lupine
(Lupinus polyphyllus variety)

[6—12c]
Yellow Skunk Cabbage
(Lysichitum americanum)

[6—13]
Lithospermum diffusum

[6—13a]
*Sweet Alyssum
(Lobularia maritima
variety)*

The blue-flowered Linum perenne is one of the most beautiful of flowering plants for rock gardens and for planting at the front of perennial borders.

hard shoots, should be selected. These may be rooted in sand in a cold frame, which should be kept close and shaded, or they may be rooted in sandy soil out of doors under a bell jar. A few kinds, especially Linum narbonnense, may be increased by simple division, rooted underground suckers being removed from the parent plant in June.

The Alpine Flax. Linum alpinum, which is a native of Europe, and plentiful in many parts of the Alps, is a very beautiful dwarf Flax 6-9 in. high. It is of tufted habit, throwing up numerous slender wiry stems, clothed with narrow, almost heathlike leaves, and carrying a number of large, pale, clear blue flowers in June and July. It is a first-rate subject for the rock garden, and should be given a sunny position in light well-drained soil, or may be given a place in the scree or moraine. The white-flowered variety, alba, is rare, but is less attractive than the type.

The Yellow Tree Flax and Others. Linum arboreum, the Tree Flax, a native of Crete, forms a low woody-based subshrub, 12-18 in. high. The yellow flowers, which are very handsome, are carried in heads, and appear in May or June. It is not hardy in the North.

Linum austriacum is like a rather larger and more erect-growing Linum alpinum, with flowers of a more telling blue. It grows about 9-12 in. high, and is a very beautiful and easily cultivated rock garden plant. It is a native of Austria.

Linum flavum is a fairly strong-growing herbaceous perennial, 1½-2 ft. tall, with a forest of erect stems, each carrying a head of fine golden flowers. It is a handsome plant either for the front of the flower border, the larger rock garden, or the wall garden. It is a native of Europe.

The Crimson Annual Flax. Linum grandiflorum, which is a native of northern Africa, is an extremely beautiful and handsome annual. It grows 18 in. or rather more in height, and is much-branched at the base. It blooms from June until autumn or at least until very hot weather comes. The large flowers of the best variety, rubrum, are of a fine blood-red color with a beautiful satin sheen on the petals. This lovely plant is invaluable in the flower border, where it may be sown in early spring. The seedlings should be well thinned out so that they may develop to their full size and beauty.

Linum grandiflorum rubrum is one of the easiest, showiest and most beautiful of all hardy annuals.

Linum monogynum is a subshrubby Flax from New Zealand, 9-12 in. high, with white flowers in June and July. It may be raised from seeds sown under glass in spring, and makes a pretty rock garden plant, but it is not reliably hardy in the North.

A Lovely Blue Flax. Linum narbonnense, the

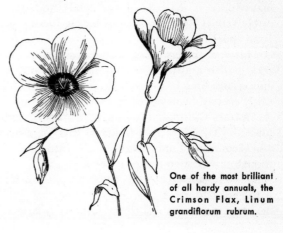

One of the most brilliant of all hardy annuals, the Crimson Flax, Linum grandiflorum rubrum.

Narbonne Flax, is one of the finest of the whole group, either for the rock garden or wall garden or for the front of the flower border. A hardy perennial, it is a native of southern Europe, growing 18-24 in. tall, and making a handsome evergreen bush 2-3 ft. across, of branched wiry stems, semiwoody at the base, and clothed with narrow, green, pointed leaves. The large flowers of satin texture are deep azure-blue, and are produced in great profusion from June until August.

Linum perenne, a native of Europe, is almost as valuable and beautiful a plant as Linum narbonnense. It is more erect-growing and less branched than L. narbonnense, with narrower, softer leaves, of a somewhat lighter green, and the flowers are clear sky blue. The plant grows about 18 in. tall, its erect stems forming a mass of heathlike wiry growth, and the lovely blue blossoms are produced with amazing profusion during June and July. They have been aptly likened to "a cloud of blue butterflies."

The flowers only last a day or part of a day and, when the petals fall, they form a carpet of blue beneath the plant, but they are succeeded by fresh crops of blossoms day after day for many weeks on end.

A Beautiful Rock Garden Flax. Linum salsoloides, a native of southern Europe, is one of the most beautiful of the Flaxes suitable for the rock garden. Growing to a height of some 5-8 in., it is of wiry habit, almost woody at the base, with erect, branching stems clothed with fine narrow leaves, and carrying large flowers of a lovely silky pearly texture, white, with a stain of palest mauve-pink at the base of the petals, and delicately veined with the same color. It flowers in June and July.

This Flax prefers a hot, sunny position in the rock garden and light, well-drained soil, and it appreciates lime in the soil. Propagation is most easily effected by means of seeds, which, however, are scarce. Cuttings, taken with a "heel" and placed in sand in a cold frame in early summer and kept close and shaded, will form roots, though this is often a slow process.

So lovely, however, is this Flax that no trouble is too great to get it established in the rock garden and, once established in suitable quarters,

it is not difficult. Full sun and perfect drainage are the two main essentials to success. This Flax is excellent for the scree or moraine (which see).

The common Flax, Linum usitatissimum, a native of Europe, is the Flax used in the manufacture of linen. It is an annual, growing 4 ft. high, with beautiful blue flowers, and is a plant of sufficient beauty to be worth a place in any flower border, though it is seldom used in this manner.

Linum viscosum is a very distinct and handsome Flax, a native of south Europe. It grows 18 in. to 2 ft. tall, with a few erect stems, broad, roundish leaves, and few-flowered, branched heads of large blooms of pinkish-mauve. It is common neither in nature nor in the garden, but it is so distinct and handsome that it deserves a special effort to bring it more commonly into cultivation. It must be increased by seeds, which, when obtainable, should be sown in pots of light soil in March in a cold frame or cool greenhouse. This is an attractive perennial either for the rock garden or the choice flower border.

LION'S-EAR. See Leonotis Leonurus.

LION'S-LEAF. See Leontice.

LION'S-TAIL. Leonotis Leonurus, which see.

LIPARIS—*Twayblade* (Lip'aris). Terrestrial Orchids, belonging to the Orchid family, Orchidaceae. The name comes from *liparos,* smooth, oily, and refers to the shining leaves. These interesting plants have a few broad leaves and small flowers of dull white, green or yellow color. They are sometimes planted in the wild garden, for which purpose plants collected from the wild are used. Some are hardy; others are tropical. The two listed here are hardy natives. L. liliifolia, 10 in. high, has racemes of greenish-white flowers 6 in. long, May to July; L. Loeselii, 10 in. high, has racemes of yellowish-green or whitish flowers. They should be planted in fairly moist, rich woodsy soil in partial shade. They benefit from a light mulch of leaf mold applied to the ground each fall. No other special care is needed, but nearby plants must be prevented from spreading and choking them out.

LIPPIA—*Lemon Verbena* (Lip'pia). A genus of shrubby and herbaceous plants, chiefly natives of North and South America. The only kind commonly grown is the Lemon Verbena, Lippia ci-triodora, sometimes called Aloysia citriodora. The genus belongs to the family Verbenaceae, and is named in honor of the Italian botanist Auguste Lippi.

Lemon Verbena is a leaf-losing shrub from Chile, valued for its deliciously scented leaves, which give off a lemon-like fragrance; it bears small pale lilac flowers in August. It is not hardy in the North and is commonly grown as a pot plant in cool greenhouses and sunrooms. It may be planted permanently outdoors in mild climates.

Lemon Verbena needs well-drained soil of a sandy loam type. Pruning, which should be done in spring, is practiced by shortening the branches of the previous summer's growth as may be necessary to keep the plant shapely and within bounds.

When to Take Cuttings. An increased stock of plants is raised by means of cuttings made from the young shoots in March–April; these are placed in sand in a glass-covered box or beneath a hand light in a frame or greenhouse having a temperature of 50-55 degrees. When well rooted, the cuttings are potted separately in 3-in. pots of sandy, loamy soil and finally in pots 6-8 in. wide.

During the summer the soil must be kept always moist. When the leaves begin to fall, the supply of water should be discontinued gradually; in winter the soil need be moistened only sufficiently often to prevent its becoming dust-dry. In February–March the plants are pruned; the shoots may be cut back much or little according to requirements, and the soil is again kept moist. If repotting is needed, it should be done as soon as the plants start into fresh growth.

LIQUIDAMBAR STYRACIFLUA — *Sweet Gum* (Liquidam'bar). A handsome native leaf-losing tree which reaches a height of 100-130 ft. in eastern North America. It belongs to the Witch Hazel family, Hamamelidaceae. The first name comes from the Latin *liquidus*, fluid, and the Arabic *ambar*, amber, and refers to the fragrant balsam obtained from a related species L. orientalis.

The leaves are maple-like in outline and fragrant when bruised; they can, however, be dis-

The Sweet Gum, Liquidambar Styraciflua, is one of the finest native North American trees. Its foliage colors brilliantly in fall.

tinguished from those of the Maple because they are arranged alternately on the shoots, whereas those of the Maple are opposite.

Autumn-tinted Leaves. With little pruning, this species grows into a shapely pyramidal tree and is conspicuous in summer because of its glossy leaves. It is, however, in autumn that this tree is seen at its best, for the leaves color brilliantly, taking on shades of red, orange and bronze before they fall. The flowers have no special attraction.

Propagation of this and other kinds is by seeds, though it is possible to increase them by cuttings of short shoots inserted in sand in a frame during summer. Moist, loamy soil that is not waterlogged is suitable for this tree, and it should be planted in an open location.

The timber is of considerable importance. It is known as Yellow or Red Gum, according to color. American storax, a balsam or viscid resin with medicinal uses, is obtained from the tree.

Two related species, neither of which is very hardy, are in cultivation. L. orientalis, Oriental Sweet Gum, is a native of Asia Minor. From this tree we obtain liquid storax, a balsam used in medicine for the alleviation of certain chest complaints, and in the treatment of certain skin diseases; it is also used in perfumery. L. formosana is a native tree of China, and is hardy in the southern United States only.

LIQUID FERTILIZER. Plants absorb, through their roots, the nutrient chemicals and salts that are known as fertilizers. When solid fertilizers are applied to the soil, they have to be dissolved by soil moisture before the plants can utilize them; however, when the solids are first dissolved in water to make what are called liquid fertilizers, the nutrients are more quickly available to the plants.

Excellent results can be obtained from the regular use of liquid fertilizers. The frequency of their application must be varied according to the needs of different plants. Those that have almost exhausted their available soil of nutrients benefit from being given liquid fertilizers more often than others. Rapidly growing plants can use with advantage more frequent applications than can slowly growing plants. Many potted plants respond well if they are given liquid fertilizers every week or ten days when they are growing actively.

In all cases the soil should be given one or more soakings with clear water between successive applications of the fertilizer. Since liquid fertilizers encourage continued growth, supplies should cease when the plants approach the stage of maturity; the fertilizers should not be applied to plants during their dormant seasons. Sickly plants, other than those that are unhealthy as a result of starvation, should not be fertilized.

Liquid fertilizer can be made from all forms of animal manures and from other fertilizers that contain soluble nutrient matter, such as nitrate of soda, nitrate of potash, sulphate of potash and urea. They should not be applied when the ground is dry; the soil must first be thoroughly moistened with water.

Manure Water. When prepared from animal manure, liquid fertilizer is often called manure water. To make this, stir into a 2-gallon pail of water a heaped trowelful of fairly fresh cow manure, or use a gallon of manure to 10 gallons of water. Stir well and macerate the manure; allow to settle, then remove the clear liquid and leave the sludge. The liquid fertilizer so prepared has the color of tea; the sludge may be thrown back on the manure heap or the compost pile. The clear liquid contains all the soluble matter in the manure, and it is this that the plants absorb.

Chicken manure, used at the rate of 1 pound to 5 gallons of water and steeped as advised for cow manure, provides an excellent liquid fertilizer. Sheep manure used at the rate of 1 quart to 4 gallons of water is also good.

An easy way to make liquid manure is to place the manure in a coarse sack or infuser; this is suspended in the water and allowed to steep for 48 hours before being used.

The liquid that drains from a manure heap makes excellent liquid fertilizer; it should be used at the rate of 1 pint to the gallon of water.

Soft-coal soot may also be used at the same rate; it makes a liquid that gives foliage a beautiful green color.

All these forms of liquid fertilizer should be

Here liquid fertilizer is prepared by dropping a small amount of a moistened soluble fertilizer into a can of water.

The water containing the fertilizer is thoroughly stirred before it is applied to the plants.

Applying a commercial completely soluble liquid fertilizer.

used as clear solutions. If sludge is present, it tends to cake on the soil surface, thus preventing aeration and souring the soil. The soil should be hoed the day after liquid manure is used.

Concentrated complete liquid fertilizers containing nitrogen, phosphorus and potash can be purchased from horticultural dealers, and only need to be diluted according to the manufacturers' directions for use. These are excellent for promoting well-balanced growth and are especially useful for older plants, when luxuriant growth is not so desirable.

To stimulate rapid growth, a soluble nitrogenous fertilizer may be used in liquid form. To prepare this, stir into a gallon of water a heaped teaspoonful of either nitrate of soda, sulphate of ammonia, nitrate of ammonia, or urea.

To "finish" plants for exhibition, growers sometimes use expensive but highly efficient liquids made by dissolving other chemicals in water. Try using 1 teaspoonful per gallon of one of the following: phosphate of potash; an equal mixture of phosphate of potash and nitrate of ammonia; or a mixture of saltpeter and a good grade of superphosphate. Plants derive even greater benefit if the type of liquid fertilizer applied to them is changed every week or two. See also Foliar Feeding.

LIRIODENDRON—*Tulip Tree* (Lirioden'-dron). Two deciduous or leaf-losing kinds of trees are included under this heading: L. Tulipifera, of the eastern United States, and L. chinense, from China. They belong to the family Magnoliaceae. The name is from the Greek *lirion*, a Lily, and *dendron*, a tree.

Propagation should be by seeds whenever possible, but the Chinese kind (when seeds are unobtainable) and varieties of L. Tulipifera have to be grafted on seedlings of the latter.

The Tulip Tree, Liriodendron Tulipifera, is a native of eastern North America.

The upright-growing form of the Tulip Tree, Liriodendron Tulipifera variety fastigiatum, has a compact, columnar growth habit.

Planting and Pruning. Tulip Trees should be planted in deep, loamy soil, and it is an advantage to place peat or leaf mold about the roots at planting time. After the trees have been set out in permanent places, root disturbance must be avoided.

Young trees should be pruned to check the undue development of wide branches at the expense of the trunk. Care should be taken to train the leading shoot in such a way that a single trunk is carried well into the head of the tree, for if Tulip Trees are allowed to develop a number of rival trunks or heavy branches lower down, they are very liable to injury by storms.

The American Tulip Tree. L. Tulipifera, the Tulip Tree or Tulip Poplar, grows to 200 feet high. Its leaves are of a curious shape and are truncate; that is, they look as though they had suddenly been cut off instead of being continued to a point. They are 3-8 in. long and 4-9 in. wide, according to the age and vigor of the tree.

The flower is like a Tulip in shape; greenish-yellow marked with orange, it is about 2-3 in. across, and opens during early summer. This is a very handsome and remarkable tree.

Several varieties have been given definite names, notably aureo-maculatum, with yellow-blotched leaves; aureo-marginatum, leaves edged with yellow; integrifolium, with leaves which are not deeply lobed; and fastigatum, with the habit and growth of a Lombardy Poplar.

L. Tulipifera is a very important timber tree. The wood is greenish-gray or brown, or sometimes yellowish; it is easily worked, polishes well, and is much used in general carpentry and in furniture work. It is obtainable in large sizes and is free from knots, and is variously called Tulip Poplar, Yellow Poplar, and Whitewood.

The Chinese Tulip Tree. L. chinense, the Chinese Tulip Tree, was introduced during the

The Tulip Tree, Liriodendron Tulipifera, has curiously truncate leaves, and greenish-yellow, orange-marked, tulip-like flowers produced in early summer.

early years of the present century. It seems to grow as well as the American kind and is very similar in appearance, but the flowers are a little smaller.

LIRIOPE—*Lily Turf* (Li'riope). A small group of evergreen perennial plants, natives of Cochin China, China, Japan and the Philippines, that are hardy in fairly sheltered places as far north as New York City. They are named after the nymph Liriope, and belong to the family Liliaceae.

The plants will thrive in ordinary well-drained garden soil and they are also commonly grown in greenhouses having winter temperatures of 45-50 degrees.

For Greenhouse and Window. The best known of these plants are Liriope Muscari and its variety variegata. The latter is slightly less hardy than the former, or green-leaved kind. It is a valuable plant for the greenhouse, growing 12-18 in. high; the yellow and green leaves are attractive at all seasons. In July and August plants established in 5-in. and 6-in. pots bear numerous spikes closely set with dark purple or violet flowers. Both the green-leaved and variegated kinds are useful and attractive window plants.

Liriope spicata differs from L. Muscari in hav-

In this rock garden, located close to New York City, Liriope Muscari variety variegata thrives and flowers freely.

ing a more shallow root system that spreads or creeps horizontally; in being lower (it is 4-12 in. high); and in having pale lilac to almost white flowers.

Liriope is readily propagated by division of the clumps immediately after flowering or early in April.

LISSOCHILUS (Lissochi'lus). Orchids found wild in Africa, from Natal upwards into the tropics. All are terrestrial and have long leaves, deciduous or nearly so, which spring from a cormlike rootstock. The flower spikes are tall and erect and on the upper portion bear numerous attractive blooms, often curiously twisted and with petals larger than the sepals. The labellum, or lowest petal, is three-lobed and the base is contracted into a short spur. Lissochilus belongs to the family Orchidaceae; the name is derived from *lissos,* smooth, and *cheilos,* a lip.

Owing to the unusual conditions under which some of the kinds grow in a wild state, cultivation is often difficult. L. giganteus grows on the edges of the River Congo; as the river recedes it is subjected to severe drought.

Hothouse Orchids. The treatment required seems to be tropical heat and abundance of water when the plants are growing and, after the leaves have fallen, a very decided rest in a temperature of not less than 60 degrees. Success has been attained with L. Horsfallii and L. Krebsii by growing them in a warm greenhouse and, as the flower spikes develop, placing the plants in a sunny, airy one; they must be replaced in the warm greenhouse after flowering. A compost of fibrous loam, leaf mold and sand with a little chopped sphagnum moss and osmunda fiber makes a suitable potting mixture. Repotting, if necessary, must be done early in the year, as soon as fresh growth is seen.

The Chief Kinds. L. giganteus produces a flower spike often 16 ft. tall, bearing 30-40 flowers with rose-colored sepals and petals and bright purple lip marked with yellow. The spikes of L. Horsfallii, from Old Calabar, may reach a height of 6 ft., and bear purple and magenta flowers. L. Krebsii, from South Africa, is less tall; the petals are bright yellow and the sepals are greenish, the lip being red and yellow.

LISTERA (Lis'tera). Terrestrial Orchids

belonging in the family Orchidaceae and natives of the North Temperate regions. The name commemorates Martin Lister, a British botanist. L. cordata, the Heart-Leaved Twayblade, is the one most likely to be cultivated.

Listeras are occasionally planted in wild gardens and rock gardens. They need a deep, dampish, loamy soil that is well supplied with humus and moderate shade.

LITCHI CHINENSIS (Li'tchi). A Chinese tree that belongs to the Soapberry family, Sapindaceae. The name is of Chinese origin. It is an ornamental tree, suitable for cultivating in warm regions only, and valued, particularly by the Chinese, for its fruits, which, when dried, are the Litchi nuts of commerce.

Litchi chinensis succeeds only in frost-free or nearly frost-free climates. It is planted to some extent in southern California and in parts of Florida. The trees grow best in rich, loamy soils that are somewhat acid. They are propagated by grafting and inarching (which see) and by cuttings and seeds. The fruits ripen in early summer.

LITHOPHRAGMA (Lithophrag'ma). A small group of hardy herbaceous plants that are natives of western North America. They are closely related to Tellima and are sometimes planted in rock gardens and woodland gardens. Lithophragma belongs in the Saxifrage family, the Saxifragaceae. The name is derived from *lithos,* stone, and *phragma,* a fence, and refers to the rocky locations in which some kinds grow naturally. The name is sometimes spelled Lithofragma.

Lithophragmas thrive in a woodland soil that contains a generous proportion of organic matter and tends to be moist rather than dry. They prefer a partial shade. Propagation is by seeds, which are produced plentifully, and by the tiny bulblets that some kinds produce.

The kind most likely to be cultivated is L. affinis, Woodland Star, which grows to 15-16 in. tall, has white flowers, and foliage that is often of a bronze hue. This kind is a native of California. Others are L. parviflora, 12 in., flowers white or pinkish, a native from Alberta to California; and L. tennella, 6 in., flowers pink, a native from Alberta to Wyoming.

Lithops bella.

LITHOPS—*Pebble Plant, Stone Plant* (Li'thops). A curious genus of small succulent plants, of the family Aizoaceae, natives of South Africa. The name is from *lithos,* stone, and *ops,* appearance, and the plants do resemble small stones. The growth consists of two fleshy leaves, united except for a small split across the top, with markings similar to the pebbles among which they grow. When these leaves die, two more appear. As with some other plants of this type, some of the species have "windowed" growths, that is, they are translucent on the upper surface. In cultivation these plants should be rested in April–May. For details of cultivation, see Mesembryanthemum, in which genus they were previously included.

A few notable kinds are L. bella, 1 in. high, flowers white; L. Fulleri, grayish with brown markings, flowers white; L. olivacea, dark olive-green, paler at the edges, flowers yellow; L. optica, gray or fawn, with translucent (windowed) tips, flowers white; L. opalina, gray-blue,

Lithops optica.

flowers white; and L. turbiniformis, brownish, with darker markings, flowers yellow.

LITHOSPERMUM — *Gromwell* (Lithosper'-mum). A small group of hardy herbs or sub-shrubs, natives of North America, Europe (especially the Mediterranean region), and northern Asia. They belong to the Borage family, Boraginaceae. The name comes from *lithos,* a stone, and *sperma,* a seed, and refers to the hard seeds. The species previously named Lithosper-mum intermedium and L. petraeum have now been separated into the genus Moltkia, which see.

Nearly all of these plants are best grown in the rock garden or alpine house. All require light sandy soil and a sunny, well-drained position. Propagation may be effected by means of seed sown in spring in a cold frame, or, in July, by cuttings of the young shoots placed in sand in a cold frame kept close and shaded.

A magnificent specimen of Litho-spermum diffusum Heavenly Blue, one of the loveliest of all trailing rock-garden plants.

Rock-Garden Plants. Lithospermum canescens is the beautiful North American Puccoon, with erect stems 9-18 in. high, clothed with narrow, silky gray leaves, and carrying heads of orange-yellow flowers in June. It requires light, sandy, well-drained soil and full exposure to sun. The best means of propagation is by seed.

Lithospermum Gastonii is a rare and rather difficult plant from the Pyrenees, with large pale blue flowers. It thrives best in a well-drained pocket of soil facing west; lime should be added to the soil.

The Finest of All. Lithospermum diffusum, often grown in gardens as L. prostratum, is the finest, the most brilliant, and the most widely grown of the family. Of wiry, subshrubby habit, it is a strong, rapid trailer, forming wide mats of dark, evergreen foliage and covering itself in early summer with heads of flowers of an intense, pure, deep blue of the utmost brilliance and magnificence. Apart from this main flowering in early summer, Lithospermum diffusum keeps up a succession of stray flower heads practically all through the year with surprising and delightful persistence.

Needs Peat or Leaf Mold. Unfortunately, this plant is difficult to grow in some soils and where hot summers prevail. It is best in acid, sandy soils, or the soils in which Heathers and Rhododendrons are at home. It has a reputation for disliking lime, which is, in general, quite justified, although cases have been reported in which it has flourished on limestone soils. This species is very suitable for planting in the wall garden, down the face of which it will fall in a cascade of azure splendor.

There is a variety called Heavenly Blue, with flowers of a lighter color which is even lovelier than the type, and its constitution is rather more vigorous. Equally desirable is the deeper blue, slightly larger-flowered variety Grace Ward.

How to Raise Plants from Cuttings. Lithospermum diffusum is best propagated by means of young shoots of the current year's growth which should be taken off in early summer and planted in sand, or very sandy peat in a cold frame kept close. Seeds are rarely obtainable, but seedlings may be expected to be strong and vigorous. The Heavenly Blue and Grace Ward varieties can only be increased by this technique of cuttings.

There is a white variety, album prostratum, which, though quite pretty, is not to be compared with the blue type. There is also an erect-growing variety with blue flowers, which, however, does not seem to possess any virtue other than its novelty.

Flowers Which Change Color. Lithospermum purpureo-caeruleum is a European native, a rapid grower and spreader, and so should only be planted where it can enjoy ample room and where its invasive habits can do no harm. But it is a beautiful plant, with arching stems, 12-18 in. high, each carrying a head of ½ in. wide flowers, opening red and changing to blue-purple, in early summer. It makes a fine ground cover in thin shrubbery, and half-shady places, and is increased by division of the roots in spring or autumn. The rooted pieces will soon become re-established if kept moist in dry weather.

For the Alpine House. Lithospermum rosmarinifolium is a dwarf shrubby kind with bright green, rosemary-like leaves, and heads of brilliant, pure, light-blue flowers in winter and early spring. For this reason, and because it is not very hardy, it is best grown as a pot plant in the alpine house, except in warm and favored localities, where it can enjoy its winter flowering unharmed. It is best propagated from soft-shoot cuttings placed in sand in a cold frame in spring.

LITTLE PICKLES. Othonna crassifolia, which see.

LITTONIA MODESTA (Litto'nia). A tender climbing plant with attractive flowers in April. It grows wild in South Africa, and belongs to the Lily family, Liliaceae. This plant has soft-stemmed branches, 3-4 ft. in length, clothed with ovate leaves having tendrils at the tips. The flowers, produced singly towards the ends of the shoots, are bell-shaped, pendulous, orange-yellow and 1 in. in diameter. The name Littonia commemorates Dr. Samuel Litton, professor of botany in Dublin, Ireland.

A Greenhouse Climbing Plant. This plant requires a minimum winter temperature of 45 degrees and a sunny position. The best compost consists of two parts of loam and equal parts of leaf-mold and peat, with a generous sprinkling

Littonia modesta is closely related botanically to Gloriosa. Its orange-yellow flowers are produced in summer.

of sand. The plants are set in large pots or tubs, or planted in a prepared bed of soil in the greenhouse in March. Wires are fixed to the wall or sides of the greenhouse to which the shoots attach themselves by their leaf-tip tendrils. Water is applied moderately to the soil until the plants are established, after which the soil is kept moist throughout the summer.

During the autumn, winter and early spring the soil is moistened only when it becomes quite dry. The shoots are syringed with clear water, mornings and evenings, until flowers are produced; syringing is then discontinued until the flowers are over. The plants need to be shaded only from very strong sunlight.

Propagation is by division of the plants at potting time, or by seeds. The seeds, which are scarlet and about the size of Peas, are sown in pots of finely sifted soil in spring. They are set 1 in. apart and ½ in. deep; the pot is covered with a pane of glass and set in a temperature of 65 degrees. When the seedlings are 2 in. in height they are potted separately in 3-in. pots and subsequently in larger ones, in which they are kept until the flowering stage is reached.

The principal species is L. modesta, 4 ft., orange, April. In mild climates such as that of

Florida and southern California it may be grown outdoors.

LIVE-FOR-EVER. Sedum, which see.

LIVE OAK. Quercus virginiana. The Coast Live Oak is Quercus agrifolia. See Quercus.

LIVERLEAF. Hepatica, which see.

LIVING FENCE. Rosa multiflora, which see.

LIVISTONA—*Fan Palm* (Livisto'na). Palms from Australia, China, Japan and Java; some are useful for room and greenhouse decoration when grown in pots, and for planting outdoors in the far South. They belong to the family Palmaceae.

The most popular kind is L. chinensis (often wrongly called Latania borbonica), which reaches 30 ft. in height and has a terminal cluster of large, fan-shaped leaves. The lower part of the leafstalk is armed with hard, brown spines.

The best potting compost consists of three parts of fibrous loam and one part of equal quantities of well-decayed manure and sand. Repotting is done in February or March, or as soon as new growth commences. The plants are removed from their pots, the crocks and all loose soil removed with a pointed stick and the plants are then set in pots two sizes larger. To keep plants in large pots or tubs growing vigorously, top-dress them with fresh compost annually, removing a little of the old soil from the top of the ball of soil to make room for the fresh material.

Summer and Winter Management. The cool greenhouse kinds require a minimum winter temperature of 45 degrees. In the summer they may be used for room decoration or plunged in the soil out of doors to create a subtropical effect. The hothouse kinds need a winter temperature of 55 degrees, and require shading from strong sunlight in summer. During the summer the soil in the pots must be kept moist; in winter far less water is needed but the soil must not be allowed to become dry.

Raising Fan Palms from Seeds. Seeds are sown 1 in. deep in pans of sandy compost, and these are plunged in a propagating case where a temperature of 60-75 degrees is maintained. When the seedlings are 2 in. in height, they are potted separately in 3-in. pots and subsequently in pots of larger sizes.

In their young stages the plants grow more

vigorously if the pots are set in a bed of peat moss with bottom heat. The atmosphere must be kept moist by frequently damping the floor and benches of the glasshouse, and the leaves should be sprayed with water twice a day in hot weather in summer.

The chief kinds, for the cool greenhouse, are L. chinensis (Latania borbonica), L. australis, L. rotundifolia, and L. humilis.

LIZARD'S-TAIL. Saururus, which see.

LLAVEA CORDIFOLIA (Lla'vea). An evergreen Fern for the warm greenhouse or outdoors in the far South. It grows about 2 ft. in height and has tripinnate (thrice divided) fronds. The upper portions of the fronds are contracted into the spore-bearing parts and the lower portions are broad and barren. This Fern is a native of Mexico, and belongs to the family Polypodiaceae. The name Llavea commemorates La Llave, who discovered the plant.

A Fern for a Warm Greenhouse. This Fern requires a shaded position in a greenhouse with a minimum winter temperature of 55 degrees. The best potting compost consists of equal parts of loam, peat and sand. Repotting is done in March, or as soon as the new fronds commence to uncurl. Well-drained pots are used. After a little of the old soil has been removed from the roots, the plants are set in slightly larger pots. The soil must not be rammed, but simply pressed firmly with the fingers.

After potting, very little water is applied to the soil until new roots are formed; afterwards the plant must be kept moist during the summer; in the winter, it is, however, moistened only when it becomes dry. The atmosphere must be maintained in a moist condition by damping in summer; the fronds must not be syringed.

Propagation is effected by division or by sowing spores (see Ferns).

The only species in cultivation is L. cordifolia, 2 ft., evergreen.

LLOYDIA (Lloyd'ia). Dwarf bulbous plants suitable for a cool position in the rock garden. They are found growing wild in Europe on high alpine pastures in northern Asia and in the Rocky Mountains. They belong to the Lily family, Liliaceae, and are closely related to Erythronium.

These plants grow from small bulbs and bear two kinds of leaves; those near the base are filiform (threadlike), while higher up they are much stouter and broader. The flowers, which are borne singly on stems 6 in. in height, are white, veined with red, and each of the six perianth segments (petals) has a nectar-bearing cavity at the base. The name Lloydia commemorates Edward Lloyd, who first discovered the plant on the Welsh Mountains.

Bulbs for the Rock Garden. The bulbs are planted in September or October, in a well-drained position in the rock garden. The site is prepared by making a hole 2 ft. deep and placing small stones to 1 ft. in depth in the hole. Upon this a few pieces of turf are laid to prevent the compost from washing into the drainage and so blocking it up. The hole is filled with a compost of three parts of loam and one part of sand. This is pressed in firmly and the bulbs are then planted 3 in. deep and 3 in. apart. When the plants become established they should not be disturbed until they show signs of deterioration.

Propagation by Offsets. If the plants appear to be deteriorating, it is best to lift them in the autumn, pick out the largest bulbs for replanting, and replenish the site with fresh soil. The smaller bulbs can be used as a means of increasing the stock of plants. These small bulbs or offsets, which are formed on the ends of underground shoots, are planted 1 in. deep in a flat filled with sandy loam. They are carefully watered when growth commences, and "grown on" in the flat until large enough to be planted in their permanent positions in the rock garden.

The chief kind is L. serotina, 6 in., white and red, June.

LOAM. This term is frequently used by gardeners, but beginners often find difficulty in understanding exactly what is meant by it. Technically, loam is a soil that has physical characteristics approximately midway between those of a sandy soil and a clay soil. This does not mean that loam consists of clay and sand in about equal proportions. It is a mixture of clay, silt, and sand, and, if fertile, it normally contains an appreciable proportion of organic material. The sizes of the particles that comprise loam vary considerably and, because of this, loam does not pack together and become impervious as does clay, nor does it remain loose and shifting as does sand.

A good loam possesses the good qualities (from the gardeners' point of view) of both sandy soil and clayey soil without exhibiting the undesirable qualities of either. Most good topsoils are loams.

Sandy soils, loams, and clayey soils grade into each other imperceptibly, so that, in loam classification, we get as extremes sandy or light loams and clayey or heavy loams, with medium loams representing an in-between group.

Loam for Potting. In a more restricted sense, gardeners use the word loam for specially prepared topsoil that is used for potting and planting in greenhouses. When gardeners speak of loam in this sense they mean a top layer of turf which has been cut from a meadow and stacked in a heap for several months. By then the grass has completely died and the roots have partially decayed, leaving a mass of rough fiber and mellow soil. This is also known as turfy loam, and forms the chief ingredient in soil composts in which most plants in pots are grown.

Such loam is important for success in the cultivation of pot plants for it is rich in plant foods, and contains much fibrous material which helps to keep the compost well drained and sweet. Plants in pots cannot be grown to perfection as easily if ordinary garden soil is used in the pots; turfy loam is much to be preferred as a basis for potting soils.

Loam varies considerably. There is clayey loam, which consists of decayed turf cut from pasture on heavy, clayey land, and there is light loam, which is obtained from light or sandy land. The quality of loam depends chiefly on the quantity of root fiber it contains, and on the kind of soil which is found among the fibers.

When used in potting composts, clayey loam needs a larger proportion of leaf mold or peat and sand mixed with it than sandy loam does, to make it suitable for most plants.

Turfs for conversion into loam should be stacked grass-side downwards, with, if possible, layers of fresh farmyard or stable manure between. At the end of six months or thereabouts the heap of turf will be well decayed and will be

"turfy loam." It will be excellent material to use in the cultivation of pot plants, for digging into flower beds and borders, or for placing around the roots of trees and plants at planting time.

It is not necessary to use alternate layers of manure and turf when making up the stack, but this practice ensures that the loam will be richer in plant food than if turf alone were stacked.

The quality of the loam will depend on the meadow from which the turf was cut; though it may not be the ideal "mellow loam," which the professional gardener likes best of all, it will serve its purpose and yield results far superior to those that can be obtained in soil taken from the garden.

LOASA—*Chilean Nettle* (Loa'sa). Tender annual, biennial, and perennial flowering plants, from Chile and Peru, which belong to the family Loasaceae. Some are climbing plants, others erect herbs. They grow 2-3 ft. in height, and have deeply lobed leaves, with serrate (notched) edges, and measure 3-6 in. in width. The flowers, which are showy and borne in the axils of the leaves, are produced in small clusters or sometimes singly. They measure 1 in. in diameter and are red, white or yellow.

Stinging Plants. Although these plants are very attractive they are not widely cultivated, because the leaves sting to such an extent that they cause acute pain for several days. The meaning of the name Loasa is unknown. It is the old original South American name for the plants.

When to Sow Seeds. The seeds are sown, early in March, in a greenhouse with a minimum temperature of 55 degrees in a compost of equal parts of loam, leaf mold and sand, which is passed through a sieve with $1/8$-in. mesh, and pressed down lightly.

As soon as the seedlings have formed two pairs of leaves, they are potted singly in small pots; later they are transferred to 5-in. pots. When well rooted in these, they are gradually hardened off and planted out of doors in June. They require a sunny position. Ordinary garden soil is suitable, but it must be deeply dug and enriched. The climbing kinds are supported by stakes or planted against a trellis, to which the shoots readily cling.

Sowing Outdoors. Seeds may be sown thinly outdoors in well-drained soil as soon in spring as the weather is warm and settled. The seedlings should be thinned to 6-8 in. apart.

The chief kinds are Loasa (Eucnide) urens (hispida), lemon-yellow, marked with green and white; and L. vulcanica, white, with red and white center. Both bloom in August and September.

LOBELIA (Lobe'lia). Hardy and tender annuals and perennials, natives of widely separated countries of both the Northern and Southern Hemispheres, and belonging to the Lobelia family, Lobeliaceae. Lobelia is named after M. de l'Obel, who was physician to James I of England and a well-known botanist of his day.

There are over 200 species, with numerous varieties, of Lobelia, though comparatively few are of garden value. The Lobelias chiefly grown range in size from the dwarf, compact bedding varieties, which are only a few inches in height and are grown as annuals, to the perennial Lobelias, which are 3 ft. or more tall. The giant of the race is Lobelia Tupa, from Chile, which, when given generous treatment, will grow 8 ft. tall; it is a noble herbaceous plant bearing reddish-scarlet flowers.

Bedding Lobelias. The popular Lobelias which are used for summer bedding purposes have been raised from Lobelia Erinus, a blue-flowered plant introduced from the Cape of Good Hope in 1752. The wild plant is of somewhat straggling habit and grows about 6 in. high, but the seedsman has evolved many compact, free-flowering varieties with flowers in shades of blue, purple, and white. There is also a crimson, white-eyed variety.

Raising Bedding Lobelias. Though strictly tender perennials, for garden purposes these plants are best grown as annuals from seeds sown in a greenhouse, temperature 55-60 degrees, in February. The seedlings are transplanted to flats filled with loam, leaf mold and sand, and grown in the greenhouse until May. They are planted out of doors early in June.

These Lobelias thrive in ordinary, well-drained garden soil. They prefer an area where summers are moderately cool, and they stand light shade.

Another method of propagation, though it has

A variety of bedding Lobelia.

been superseded in most gardens by raising seedlings in the way described, is to pot a few of the old plants in October, and keep them in a greenhouse with a minimum temperature of 50 degrees during the winter. In late January or early February they will start into fresh growth; the new shoots, when 2-3 in. long, are taken off as cuttings and inserted in a propagating bench, in sand or vermiculite.

Perennial Lobelias. These have considerable merit. They are quite different from the varieties of bedding Lobelia, for they are erect, stout-stemmed plants, bearing rich green or crimson

Lobelia siphilitica, a native of North America, has spikes of bright blue flowers.

leaves, and large flowers, chiefly of bright scarlet, though a number of recent varieties are of pink and mauve shades, and some have blue flowers. There is, too, a white-flowered variety of L. siphilitica.

The perennial species (kinds as they occur in the wild) may be propagated by seeds sown in early fall or spring and by division at those same seasons. The latter method must be used to increase hybrids and garden varieties.

Of the tall-growing Lobelias, the best-known are L. cardinalis (Cardinal Flower or Indian Pink) and L. siphilitica (Blue Lobelia), both hardy, wet soil plants that are natives of North America. They are splendid for watersides and wild gardens, and for ordinary flower borders, provided the soil is not too dry. L. fulgens (usually misnamed L. cardinalis in European gardens) is a Mexican plant that is not hardy in the North. Varieties of it and hybrids between it and L. siphilitica and L. cardinalis are much grown in Great Britain and are well suited for cultivation in the Pacific Northwest. They are not hardy in the North and do not thrive where summers are very hot.

Reddish Leaves and Scarlet Flowers. The oldest of the L. fulgens varieties, Queen Victoria, is still grown; it has reddish-crimson foliage and bears vivid scarlet flowers. Other handsome varieties are Blue Bird, blue; Silver Queen, light blue; Delight, purplish-mauve; Purple King, Purple; Excelsior, blue-mauve; Lady Gregory, cerise; Princess, red-cerise; Mrs. Humbert, the best of the pink varieties; and Ibis, deep carmine. The Bishop, Elstead Scarlet, Huntsman and Arthur Humbert all have scarlet flowers.

Hints on Cultivation. These handsome, tall-growing Lobelias respond to generous treatment and the soil can scarcely be made too rich for them. The average height of the plants is 2 ft. 6 in., but if deep, rich soil is provided, and the plants are given copious waterings when needed during the growing and flowering season, most of them will reach a height of 3 ft. or more. They are of branching habit and if the central spike is removed as soon as it has finished flowering, the side shoots will continue the floral display until well into late autumn; this is the time to give extra nourishment in the form of dilute manure water (see Liquid Fertilizers) or a good fertilizer.

Hardy Only in Mild Districts. As these varieties and hybrids of L. fulgens are true herbaceous plants, they form little colonies of growth at the base of the old stems during late summer, and these provide next year's plants. Unfortunately, Lobelias of this type are hardy in the United States only in the milder parts, so in many places it is necessary to lift the offsets and winter them in a frostproof greenhouse or frame.

For Flower Beds and Borders. In the mixed flower border, the tall Lobelias are very effective when planted in groups of nine or more, according to the width of the border, at about 3 ft. from the front. As they are moisture-loving plants they may also be used at the margins of pools and streams, but they must not be planted in boggy soil. The plants should be set 15 in. apart.

Lobelias for Baskets. Seedsmen have raised a type of Lobelia of spreading habit of growth, principally from Lobelia Erinus, which gave rise to the dwarf bedding Lobelias. These are admir-

The native American scarlet Lobelia cardinalis.

able plants for growing in wire baskets to hang in the conservatory or porch. There are varieties with dark blue, light blue, and white flowers.

The wire baskets, which may be purchased, are lined with moss to hold the soil and the Lobelias are planted firmly in a compost of loam and leaf mold. Turf makes an even better lining for the basket than moss and provides an additional rooting medium. The turf should be placed grass-side inwards. When planting the baskets, the need for thorough watering should be remembered and the surface should be finished off slightly saucer-shaped.

Lobelias for the Greenhouse. As a pot plant for the cool window garden and greenhouse (having a minimum temperature of 50 degrees), Lobelia tenuior (L. ramosa), a western Australian species, is of great value. This Lobelia grows 12 in. or more in height and, when well furnished with its deep blue, white-eyed flowers, is exceedingly attractive.

If the seeds are sown in January or early February in a greenhouse having a temperature of 60 degrees, the plants will flower throughout the summer and autumn months. As the seedlings grow, they should be reduced to three in each pot; the potfuls of seedlings, undisturbed, are finally placed in 6-in. pots, in which they will bloom.

LOBIVIA (Lobiv'ia). A group of South American Cacti, family Cactaceae, that are generally similar to Echinopsis and require the same general care. For their culture, see Cactus. Many different kinds are cultivated by fanciers and specialists and may be offered by dealers. The name is an anagram of Bolivia.

LOBLOLLY BAY. See Gordonia.

LOBSTER'S-CLAW. See Clianthus.

LOBULARIA MARITIMA—*Sweet Alyssum* (Lobular'ia). This is the invaluable summer bedding annual often grown under the name of Alyssum maritimum, which botanists have now decided is invalid. It belongs to the Cruciferae or Mustard family and is quite hardy, though often raised under glass for early flowering. It forms compact cushions up to 9 in. high and more across, smothered with white fragrant flowers from June to September. The dwarf varieties, like compactum, Little Gem, Snow Queen and

Sweet Alyssum, Lobularia maritima, is a favored garden annual.

Little Dorrit, are invaluable as edging plants for beds and borders. Two valuable dwarf colored varieties are Lilac Queen and Violet Queen.

Seeds may be sown in March in a greenhouse —temperature 50 degrees—or out of doors in April, and later, to provide a succession of flowers in summer. Plants should be set 6-8 in. apart or, if seeds are sown outdoors, thinned to that distance from each other early. Sowing seeds out of doors in April gives least trouble but the plants do not bloom so early as others raised under glass. Self-sown seedlings often appear abundantly.

LOCKHARTIA (Lockhart'ia). Orchids from Central America, which can be grown in a warm, moist greenhouse. They are epiphytal, with evergreen leaves, and are without pseudobulbs. The flowers are rather small but usually of bright yellow color. The name was given in honor of Mr. David Lockhart, onetime curator of the Trinidad Botanic Garden.

These Orchids require a warm, moist greenhouse with a tropical temperature and atmosphere in the summer, and a minimum winter temperature of 60 degrees. They may be affixed to small blocks of wood or placed in small flower pans, using a compost of two parts osmunda fiber and two parts sphagnum moss.

Careful watering is necessary throughout the year and shading is required from early March

[6—14]
Cardinal Flower
(Lobelia cardinalis)

[6—14a]
Honeysuckle
(Lonicera variety Goldflame)

[6—14b]
Bush Honeysuckle
(Lonicera tatarica)

[6—14c]
Loosestrife
(Lythrum virgatum variety)

[6—15]
Star Magnolia
(Magnolia stellata)

[6—15a]
Magnolia Soulangeana

to the end of September. Repotting may be done in February. Most kinds are summer-flowering.

The chief kinds are L. acuta, L. elegans and L. verrucosa. All have bright yellow flowers, the lips being marked with red.

LOCUST. See Robina.

LOCUST, BLACK. Robinia Pseudoacacia, which see.

LOCUST, HONEY. Gleditsia, which see.

LOCUST, SWAMP. Gleditsia aquatica, which see.

LOCUST, SWEET. Gleditsia triacanthos, which see.

LOCUST, WATER. Gleditsia aquatica, which see.

LODOICEA MALDIVICA (SEYCHELLA-RUM)—*Coco de Mer, Double Coconut* (Lodoi'-cea). A very interesting and decorative Palm found only in the Seychelles, where it grows 50-100 ft. high; it has very large, fan-shaped leaves and what are regarded as being the largest and heaviest seeds of any known tree. The fresh nuts in the husk often weigh 40-50 lb. The male inflorescences are also interesting for they are cylindrical bodies, 4-5 ft. long and 3-4 in. in diameter. The nuts are usually two-lobed, sometimes three- or four-lobed.

Before the discovery of the Seychelle Islands and the growing trees, these fruits and seeds were sometimes found floating in the Indian Ocean, and their peculiar shape led to several curious legends. Such seeds were often sold at high prices. They have actually no economic value but are sometimes carved and sold as fancy objects.

Unfortunately the tree is difficult to establish in other countries and does not live very long when grown in greenhouses. It belongs to the Palm family, Palmaceae.

LOGANBERRY. See Blackberry, Trailing.

LOISELEURIA PROCUMBENS — *Alpine Azalea* (Loiseleur'ia). A very dwarf, evergreen, alpine shrub found in cold regions of Europe, Asia and North America. If cultivated (it is rare in cultivation) it should be given a place in the rock garden. It thrives only in the colder parts of North America, in moist, peaty soil, such as would suit alpine Rhododendrons. Seeds and cuttings can be used for propagation of the shrub.

Loiseleuria belongs to the Heath family, Ericaceae, and the name commemorates a late eighteenth- and early nineteenth-century French botanist and physician, J. C. A. Loiseleur-Deslongchamps.

LOLIUM—*Rye Grass* (Lol'ium). Annual and perennial Grasses, family Gramineae, that are used horticulturally as "nurse" grasses in lawnseed mixtures and as cover crops. Lolium perennis is the Perennial or English Rye Grass; L. multiflorum is the Italian Rye Grass. Both are perennials.

LOMARIA. Blechnum, which see.

LOMATIA (Loma'tia). Tender evergreen flowering shrubs, natives of Australia and South America, belonging to the Protea family, Proteaceae. Most have large, feathery leaves resembling those of Grevillea robusta, and some, particularly L. obliqua, have ovate to lance-shaped leaves. In their young state, the shoots and leaves of Lomatia are covered with a mat of downy hairs. The name Lomatia is derived from *loma*, an edge, and refers to the winged seeds.

Can Be Grown Out of Doors in Mild Regions. Lomatia can only be grown out of doors in the warmer parts of the United States, where, if the shrubs are allowed full room for development, flowers are produced. These are formed in racemes (loose spikes) 2-3 in. in length; they are tubular, ½ in. in length, and creamy white, sometimes tinged with red.

Cultivation Out of Doors. The site should be sheltered and perfect drainage is necessary. The existing soil, if unsuitable, must be replaced with equal parts of loam, peat and sand. Planting is done in spring, and wires or trellis are fixed to the wall; the shoots are tied to these as they develop. Pruning consists of slightly shortening the shoots after the flowers have faded.

Treatment in Greenhouses. These shrubs require a sunny, airy position in a greenhouse with a minimum winter temperature of 40 degrees. Repotting is done in March, and a potting compost of equal parts peat, loam and sand is used. Two or three weeks before this, the shoots are slightly shortened to trim the plants into shape. The plants are frequently syringed until new growth appears; at this time they are taken out of the pots, and the crocks and loose soil around the ball of roots and earth are removed with a pointed stick. For repotting, use well-drained pots two sizes larger, and make the compost firm with a potting stick. Good drainage is assured by placing an inch or two of crocks in the bottom of the pot.

After potting, the shrubs are shaded from bright sunlight and syringed twice a day until they are established, after which they are exposed to full sunlight and given the maximum amount of fresh air. Well-rooted plants must be watered freely during the summer. The soil must not be allowed to become very dry during the growing season or wholesale leaf dropping will result. Throughout the winter much less water is required by these shrubs, and the soil is only watered when it is noticed to become quite dry.

The chief kinds are L. ferruginea, 8 ft., golden-yellow flowers, pinnate foliage; L. longifolia, 10 ft., lanceolate (lance-shaped) foliage, greenish-white flowers; and L. obliqua, 20 ft., brownish-yellow. L. obliqua and L. ferruginea are the hardiest kinds.

LOMBARDY POPLAR. See Populus nigra italica.

LONAS INODORA — *African Daisy* (Lo'nas). A dwarf yellow-flowered annual plant of little horticultural value, though sometimes grown as an "everlasting." It grows 12 in. in height, has alternate, coarsely toothed leaves and bears dense clusters of yellow flowers 1/2 in. in diameter in summer. The plant is a native of the Mediterranean region and belongs to the Daisy family, Compositae.

For a Sunny Position. This plant requires a position which is exposed to sun and is thoroughly well-drained: a light, sandy, rather poor soil suits it best. The seeds are sown in April where the plants are to grow, and the seedlings thinned to 6 in.

LONDON PLANE. See Platanus acerifolia.
LONGAN. Euphoria Longana, which see.

LONICERA: THE FRAGRANT HONEYSUCKLE
Favorite Climbers and Shrubs for Spring, Summer, and Winter Bloom

LONICERA (Loni'cera; Lonice'ra). Leaf-losing (or rarely evergreen) shrubs and climbers, many of them hardy; they are natives of Europe, North America, and Asia—particularly central and northern Asia.

Honeysuckles are divided into two definite groups, one with climbing branches and dense clusters of flowers, the other of bushy habit with the flowers appearing in pairs from the leaf axils. There are, however, some modifications of these general characteristics, particularly in the climbing kinds. The flowers are often fragrant and are succeeded in many instances by attractive fruits. (See Berried Trees and Shrubs.)

Lonicera belongs to the Honeysuckle family, Caprifoliaceae, and is named after Adam Lonicer, a German naturalist of the sixteenth century.

Honeysuckles thrive in well-drained, loamy soil.

Propagation may be by seeds or cuttings. Seeds are sown in March in a greenhouse in a mixture of two parts sandy loam and one part leaf mold. The young plants should be placed singly in small pots as soon as they are large enough to handle, and should eventually be planted out in a nursery bed. Cuttings of young shoots about 4 in. long (short side shoots are better than long, sappy growths) should be taken in August or September and dibbled in a bed of sand in a propagating case in a greenhouse or cold frame kept close. Roots form in the course of a few weeks. The young plants should be kept in a cold frame for the winter and planted in a nursery bed in spring.

Pruning. The ends of the shoots of young plants may be cut off to ensure that a good foundation of branches is laid. Regular pruning of old plants is unnecessary, but, when the climbing Honeysuckles have to be kept within certain bounds, any pruning required should be carried out as soon as the flowers are over. Some of the old wood is cut out and vigorous young shoots are retained. Bush Honeysuckles may be thinned occasionally if they are becoming too dense; this should be done as soon as the flowers fade, or in winter. Similarly, when plants are outgrowing their places, they may be cut back after flowering.

Tender Honeysuckles. A few kinds require growing in a cool greenhouse in the North but are excellent for outdoor planting in the South. Notable among these is the giant L. Hildebrandtiana, from Burma and Assam, which may reach a height of 40-50 ft.; it bears tubular, deep orange flowers, 5 in. long. L. etrusca and its variety superba, from the Mediterranean region, and L. affinis, from China and Japan, also require greenhouse cultivation in many parts of North America.

Hardy Climbing Honeysuckles. Of the hardy climbing kinds, those next described will be found attractive. L. sempervirens has fine coral-colored or red flowers. This native American is well worth planting, and its variety magnifica is especially good. L. Brownii, which is a hybrid of L. sempervirens, is hardier than the latter and bears rich red and orange flowers freely in summer. L. Caprifolium is a vigorous European kind 15-20 ft. high, with clusters of fragrant, yellowish, pink-tinged flowers in summer; L. Giraldii, a Chinese plant, has very slender branchlets, densely hairy leaves, and yellowish flowers.

L. flava, which occurs as a native from North

The Japanese Honeysuckle, Lonicera japonica, is a vigorous ground cover that may be used on banks and other places where it is not likely to invade choicer plantings.

Carolina to Oklahoma, is one of the finest of American Honeysuckles; its flowers are orange-yellow and very fragrant.

L. Henryi, an evergreen climber with very slender branches, bears reddish-purple flowers in June. L. italica, a hybrid between L. Caprifolium and L. etrusca, has flowers which are 2 in. long, yellow suffused with red, and borne freely in summer. L. Heckrottii, a hybrid with yellow and wine-red blooms, flowers continuously throughout summer and fall; variety Goldflame is an even better kind of similar habit, with creamy-yellow and flame-pink flowers.

Japanese Honeysuckle. L. japonica (Japanese Honeysuckle) is a hardy variable plant found in Japan, China and Korea; it forms a dense tangle of slender stems that grow to a considerable height, sometimes 20 ft. The flowers are almost white when they first open, but change to yellow in a short time. Of several varieties, aureo-reticulata, with the leaves variegated with yellow, is one of the best colored-leaved plants throughout summer; the variety flexuosa has flowers that are pale-red on the outside and white within, and Halliana is very free blooming.

The Japanese Honeysuckle has established itself and become a difficult-to-eradicate weed in

Lonicera Heckrottii is a climbing plant that flowers continuously from early summer until fall.

The fragrant white and buff flowers of Lonicera japonica Halliana.

Hardy Bush Honeysuckles. Of the bush Honeysuckles, one of the best is L. fragrantissima, a Chinese shrub 6-8 ft. high, bearing fragrant cream-colored flowers on leafless branches during late winter or earliest spring. L. Standishii, another Chinese shrub, bears sweet-smelling creamy white flowers at the same season. L. tatarica is a vigorous shrub, 8-10 ft. high, found wild from Russia to Turkestan; its flowers are usually pink and are produced freely in May–June; some varieties have white flowers and others red, and the flowers are followed by attractive red fruits. L. Korolkowii, a native of Turkestan, and its variety floribunda, are graceful shrubs with attractive bluish-green foliage and pale-pink flowers which are followed by red fruits. These shrubs grow 8-10 ft. tall.

the eastern United States, yet under some conditions it is an excellent plant to use as a ground cover on banks and in other difficult places. Neither it nor its varieties should ever be planted where they cannot be kept under control.

The Woodbine. L. Periclymenum, the Woodbine or Honeysuckle of English hedgerows, is a valued plant by reason of its attractive fragrant flowers and scarlet fruits. Selected varieties, of which belgica, the early Dutch Honeysuckle, and serotina, late Dutch Honeysuckle, are two of the best, are worth planting in gardens. L. tragophylla from China has attractive flowers, 2½-3½ in. long. L. Tellmanniana, a hybrid of recent introduction, has exceptionally large yellow flowers tipped with red.

The flowers of the Bush Honeysuckle, Lonicera tatarica, are attractive when cut and arranged in a vase. The shrub is easy to grow under ordinary garden conditions.

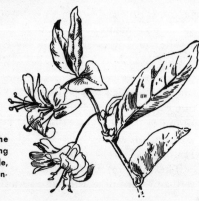

Flowers of the winter - blooming Bush Honeysuckle, Lonicera fragrantissima.

L. Maackii is a graceful bush with spreading branches 6-10 ft. high. It flowers freely in May, the flowers being first white, then yellowish; they are followed by red fruits. This Honeysuckle is a native of China.

L. syringantha is a wide-spreading bush with slender branches and very fragrant pinkish or lilac flowers. It is a native of China and Tibet.

Its variety Wolfii has narrower leaves and car-mine· flowers.

L. alpigena, the Cherry Woodbine, a native of central Europe, bears yellow flowers in May that are followed by large red fruits. L. Ledebouri, a Californian shrub 6-9 ft. high, is very distinct by reason of the two large reddish bracts that surround each pair of orange, red-tinged flowers; after the flowers fall the bracts remain and their color becomes intensified, until the black fruits are thoroughly ripe.

Evergreen Shrubs. L. nitida is a charming small-leaved evergreen bush from China. It makes a compact plant, 4-5 ft. high, and is a good hedge plant as far north as Philadelphia, especially for small gardens. It is easily increased by cuttings. L. pileata is another evergreen shrub of about equal hardiness. It grows about a foot tall and has horizontal branches. L. pileata is adaptable as a ground cover and is useful in rock gardens. Cuttings provide an easy means of increase.

LOOFAH OR DISHCLOTH GOURD. See Luffa.

LOOSESTRIFE. See Lysimachia and Lythrum.

LOOSESTRIFE, FRINGED. See Steironema ciliatum.

LOPEZIA (Lope'zia). Annual plants from Mexico. They belong to the family Onagraceae. These dainty annuals grow 18 in. tall, and form branching plants bearing racemes of small purple, red or pink flowers in summer. They have ovate, dentate (toothed at the margins) leaves, 1½ in. in length, and the flowers are composed of four heart-shaped petals. The name Lopezia commemorates T. Lopez, a Spanish botanist.

For a Sunny Border. The seeds are sown out of doors in spring in a sunny position. Any ordinary garden soil which is not clayey or heavy will grow them. When the seedlings are well developed, they are thinned out to 12 in. apart; as they increase in height, they must be supported by twiggy sticks inserted among them. Early flowers may be obtained by sowing in March, indoors, in a temperature of 55-60 degrees. The seedlings are pricked out into flats of light compost, gradually hardened off, and planted out of doors in May.

The chief kinds are L. cordata, 18 in., purple;

L. coronata, 12 in., red; L. grandiflora, 3 ft., red; and L. lineata, 3 ft., pink.

LOPHOCEREUS (Lophoce'reus). A genus of Cacti. The only species is L. Schottii, with stout, columnar, ribbed stems furnished with short, strong spines. The small reddish flowers open at night. Variety monstrosus is a curiously distorted, spineless form. The plants belong to the family Cactaceae, and were previously included in the genus Pilocereus. The name Lophocereus is derived from *lophos,* crest, and refers to the bristly top of the flower stem. For details of cultivation see Cacti.

The Peyote, Lophophora Williamsii, a Cactus that is native to southern Texas and Mexico.

LOPHOPHORA — *Peyote* (Lophoph'ora). Dwarf, flattened Cacti, with broad, rounded ribs, each areole (spine cluster) being furnished with a tuft of hairs, hence the name, derived from *lophos,* a crest, and *phoreo,* to bear. The chief kind is L. Williamsii (Echioncactus Williamsii), from Mexico and Texas, of grayish coloring, with small, pale pink or cream flowers produced from the center of the plant. For cultivation, see Cactus.

LOPHOSPERMUM. Maurandia, which see.

LOQUAT. See Eriobotrya.

LORD ANSON'S PEA. See Lathyrus magellanicus.

LORETTE PRUNING. A system of pruning fruit trees, introduced by M. Lorette, a Frenchman, which is only carried out in summer and upon new growths that have reached a certain thickness. No winter pruning is done at all. This method has never become popular in North America, yet when carried out in its entirety, and properly, it undoubtedly gives excellent results.

Chiefly Practiced on Apple and Pear Trees. This type of pruning is applied principally to Apple and Pear trees and is most generally adopted for espaliers, cordons and dwarf pyramid trees, and to the somewhat unorthodox forms of training known as the vase, goblet, winged-pyramid, etc.—forms commonly grown in France. The system may appear somewhat complicated to the inexperienced gardener, and practical demonstration is necessary to obtain a clear understanding of the smaller details involved in the operations.

Chief Pruning Done in Spring and Summer. It is important to note that the main pruning is carried out in the late spring and summer months; it is directed to shoots that have attained the thickness of a pencil and have become woody. The object of pruning is to direct the sap towards the stipulary eyes (the inconspicuous buds in the axils of the stipules near the base of the shoot) of the lateral shoots by cutting them off at a point just above the basal leaflets.

Experiments carried out by M. Lorette showed that the stipulary eyes are much more fruitful than the axillary eyes—the buds higher up on the shoot. By the repeated summer prunings these stipulary eyes or buds are strengthened; they get the benefit of the sap which would have been utilized by the useless lateral growth, and the result is seen in better nourished and more productive fruit buds.

By this means, too, the vigor of certain varieties of Apples and Pears is checked and the trees bear fruit much sooner than they would do naturally. At the same time, the branches are given the maximum amount of light and air by being spaced at least 16 in. apart all over the tree, and the largest amount of nourishment is provided for them by so regulating the lateral growth that energy is not dissipated in the lengthening of unwanted shoots.

The pruning is begun in April, towards the end of the month. This first pruning is confined to the extension growths, that is, the leader shoots which extend the main branches. These are shortened by about one-third, or by half if growth is weakly. This is necessary to drive the sap back to the buds lower down and cause them to break into short laterals all along the branch.

The next pruning takes place towards the end of June and is applied to the half-woody shoots that are then about the thickness of a pencil. The soft, green and shorter shoots are not touched, but left until they have strengthened. The pencil-thick, half-woody shoots are shortened to within ½-1 in. of their base, leaving just a short piece of growth with two or three basal leaves.

This treatment is repeated at the end of July, on new laterals which were not sufficiently matured and thick to be cut back in June. The result of this "stopping" is that, in the same season, fruit buds are produced at the base of the growths, or short "dards," which turn into fruit buds and then into short spurs which become ultimately an inexhaustible source of fruit buds for future years.

The Final Pruning in September. In late August or September, all late "secondary" growth, which has developed as a result of the earlier shortening of the laterals, is cut hard back to immediately above a fruit bud. Any shoots that have by then become half-woody and about the thickness of a pencil, but which were not sufficiently matured to cut back at the previous prunings, are shortened as advised above. So that by the end of September, pruning is completed, except for the thinning of crowded spurs and the removal of damaged or badly positioned small branches which were overlooked earlier.

When the Lorette pruning is applied to Cherry, Plum and Apricot trees, trained as cordons or espaliers, the only operations to carry out are the pruning of extension growths or leaders in April and the drastic shortening of all lateral shoots during June and July.

Bark-ringing and Bark-slitting. In addition to this shortening of the lateral growths as they become sufficiently thick and woody, M. Lorette advocates modified forms of bark-ringing and bark-slitting to encourage fruit buds and lateral growth in bare places along the branches. The vigor of any branches that spoil the balance of the tree is also curtailed by removing a quarter or half of the blade of the leaves as soon as they have attained their full size. Shoots slow in developing their basal buds are temporarily bent down and fastened with their ends towards the ground, to check the flow of sap to the more forward branch tops.

How to Ensure the Best Results. It is probable that the best results are obtained only when this system of pruning is practiced from the very beginning of the making of the tree. Upon the accurate spacing of the foundation branches and sub-branches, and the early development of stipulary eyes all along the branches, a very great deal depends. The transition from the old system of pruning to the Lorette method can be made without great difficulty, however, and after three seasons, it will be completed.

Lorette Pruning for Old Trees. When applying the Lorette pruning to old espalier, fan-shaped and pyramid trees, the branches should first be thinned, for in the ordinary tree they are invariably too crowded and numerous. An evenly balanced framework of branches is essential. The branches should be spaced out some 18 in. or 2 ft. apart all over the tree. In April the branches should be shortened by cutting off the top quarter or so, this being necessary to concentrate the flow of sap upon the lower half of the tree and encourage dormant buds to break into leaf.

All fruiting laterals should be pruned back to within 2-4 in. of their base at the same time. From these hard-pruned growths many new lateral shoots will be produced in early summer; as soon as they are about a foot long and become woody, they must be cut back to near their base, to induce growth from the stipulary or basal buds. In this first year it will be found that new growth develops more rapidly and profusely from the top half of the tree; to counteract this, the top half should be pruned earlier than the middle, and the growths from the middle part of the tree earlier than those at the base.

Details of Chief Importance. Throughout, the pruner must remember that the aim is to produce fruit growths as near as possible to the main branches; that, in spring, all new growth must be allowed to develop freely—except the leaders

which are shortened in April. In June, July and August, when young growths have reached the pencil-thickness stage, they must be pruned back, leaving a short piece not more than ½-1 in. long at the base of each. Further growth from these short stumps is pruned back in late summer.

At the end of the second or third year after adopting the Lorette pruning, short fruiting "knobs" will have formed all along the main branches; once these are obtained the future stopping of the new growths, each summer, is a simple matter.

Great importance is attached to correct manurial treatment, and a mulch of rotted manure in late spring, coupled with applications of fertilizers according to the soil and the behavior of the tree, is necessary to ensure the best results.

LOROPETALUM CHINENSE (Loropet'-alum). An evergreen shrub, 4-5 ft. high, closely related to the Witch Hazels (Hamamelis), but less hardy and only suitable for cultivation out of doors in the warmer parts of the United States. It is a native of China, whence it was introduced in 1880. The flowers have very narrow petals, as in the Witch Hazels, but they are white. The shrub succeeds out of doors as far north as Washington, D. C., but in colder climates it should be grown in pots, plunged out of doors in summer, and removed, on the approach of winter, to a cool greenhouse, where it will flower during the late winter and early spring.

The shrub can be increased by cuttings of young shoots in early summer; these are placed in a close and warm frame. It succeeds in a

The creamy white flowers of Loropetalum chinense are borne in great profusion during late winter and early spring.

mixture of two parts loam and one part peat, with a fair quantity of sand.

Loropetalum belongs to the Witch Hazel family, Hamamelidaceae. The name is taken from *loro*, a thong, and *petalon,* a petal, and alludes to the strap-shaped petals.

LOTUS (Lo'tus). Tender and hardy perennial flowering plants which belong to the Pea family, Leguminosae. Some are natives of North America; others are found growing wild in the Canary Isles, Cape Verde Islands, the Mediterranean region and other parts of Europe and Asia.

Lotus Berthelotii, which is sometimes called the Coral Gem, is an attractive plant for growing in pots and hanging baskets.

A Showy Plant. L. Berthelotii, the Coral Gem from the Canary Islands, may be grown outdoors in California and similar mild climates. It is also a popular window garden and greenhouse kind; it requires a minimum winter temperature of 40 degrees. The best potting compost consists of two parts of sandy loam and one part of leaf mold. When it is grown in baskets, these are lined with moss and filled with soil. Two or three small plants are planted in each basket; they must be shaded and syringed until established, after which full exposure to sunlight is necessary. During the summer the soil is kept moist, but, throughout the winter, water is only applied when the soil becomes quite dry. These plants may also be grown in pots, and the shoots allowed to hang over the edge of the greenhouse benches. When flower buds are forming, weak liquid fertilizer should be applied twice a week. The coral-red flowers of L. Berthelotti show to advantage against its finely divided, silvery gray foliage.

Propagation. L. Berthelotii is propagated by sowing seeds in a pot of sandy soil in March. The pot is covered with a pane of glass and set in a temperature of 55 degrees. The seedlings are potted separately in 3-in. pots, and later transferred to larger pots or planted in hanging baskets. Cuttings of young shoots in summer, 2 in. in length, may be inserted in pots of sand covered with a bell jar until shoots are formed; afterwards they are treated as advised for seedlings.

A Hardy Kind. L. corniculatus, the Bird's-Foot Trefoil, is a hardy kind; a native of Europe and Asia, it is naturalized in North America and is chiefly grown for forage. Its double-flowered variety, named flore-pleno, is an easily grown and charming plant for well-drained soils and full sun in the rock garden. This is a prostrate trailer with attractive three-parted leaves and clusters of double pea-shaped flowers, colored yellow and red, that are borne over a very long period in spring and summer. L. corniculatus flore-pleno is propagated by cuttings taken in summer and inserted in a sand propagating bed in a close cold frame or greenhouse.

LOTUS. A common name applied to Nelumbium and Nymphaea, which see.

LOTUS, EGYPTIAN. See Nymphaea Lotus.

LOUISIANA, GARDENING IN. See Regional Gardening.

LOUSEWORT. Pedicularis, which see.

LOVAGE. See Levisticum.

LOVE-IN-A-MIST. See Nigella.

LOVE-LIES-BLEEDING. Amaranthus caudatus, which see.

LUCULIA (Lucu'lia). Tender shrubs with handsome sweetly scented blooms which open in autumn. The most popular kind, L. gratissima, from the Himalayas, forms a bushy shrub 10-16 ft. tall, has evergreen, opposite ovate-oblong

The Bird's-Foot Trefoil, Lotus corniculatus, blooms freely in early summer. It is a trailing kind which has yellow flowers and is well adapted for planting in rock gardens.

pointed leaves 4-6 in. in length, which are dark-green above and slightly downy beneath. The flowers, produced in large, terminal, rounded clusters on the ends of the young shoots, are tubular at the base and spread out salver-shaped at the top. They are 1½-2 in. across, rosy-pink and deliciously fragrant.

L. Pinceana is similar in appearance, but smaller in stature, and the spreading limbs of the flowers are white. Luculia is derived from *Luculi Swa,* the name given to the tree by the Nepalese. It belongs to the family Rubiaceae.

Hints on Management. These shrubs may be grown in 6-7 in. pots, or planted in a prepared bed in the greenhouse. The latter method gives the best results. The ideal compost consists of equal parts of fibrous loam and peat, with a free admixture of sand and charcoal. The winter temperature should not fall below 50 degrees. Water is applied freely to the soil from April until November; it is then kept much drier, sufficient moisture only being given to keep the foliage healthy.

Pruning and Potting. Early in the New Year, the side shoots are pruned to within two or three buds of the base, and the stems are frequently syringed to assist new shoots to develop. The plants are taken out of the pots, the crocks and a little of the old compost being removed from around their roots with a pointed stick; the plants are then set in slightly larger pots. The pots must be exceptionally well drained, about one third of the depth being filled with crocks. The compost must be made firm with a potting stick and sufficient space left at the top of the pot for watering, as Luculia requires copious supplies of water during the summer.

After potting, the plants are shaded from strong sunlight and the foliage is frequently syringed to assist them to become established in the new compost. During the rest of the growing period the foliage is syringed twice daily and the plants are given more light and air, but they must not be exposed to the fiercest rays of the sun or to cold drafts. When the flower buds are forming, the soil is watered with dilute liquid fertilizer twice a week and, as soon as the flowers show color, the plants are placed in a minimum temperature of 55 degrees. While in flower, they are not syringed; after the flowers have faded, the soil is kept almost dry until the time for repotting comes around. The soil must, however, be watered occasionally to prevent its becoming thoroughly dry.

Large bushes may be obtained by planting the shrubs in a well-drained bed, filled with compost as recommended for potting. The treatment is similar to that advised for pot plants, except that, once planted, they must not be disturbed. They are lightly pruned until they reach the flowering size, after which the side branches are cut back to one or two buds annually early in the year.

When to Take Cuttings. The principal method of propagation is by cuttings. These, which should be 2 in. in length, are removed from the plants in June when the growth is fairly well ripened. They are prepared by removing a few of the lower leaves and making a clean cut just beneath the lowest node or joint. Well-drained 3-in. pots are filled with sandy soil and the cuttings inserted to half their depth around the edges. The cuttings are not easy to root, and to secure the maximum amount of success they must be placed in a propagating case with a bottom heat of 70-75 degrees. The pots are plunged in peat moss, and the atmosphere in the propagating case is kept uniformly moist.

When well rooted, the cuttings are potted singly in 3-in. pots and returned to the propagating case until established in the new soil. They are then placed on the open benches to harden the foliage, after which they are repotted in 5-in. pots and subsequently into larger ones. The tips of the main shoots, and subsequently the tips of the side branches, should be cut off to ensure bushy plants.

LUDWIGIA (Ludwig'ia). Aquatic plants belonging to the Evening Primrose family, Onagraceae, and named after C. G. Ludwig, a German botanist.

One kind, L. Mulertii, said to be a native of South America, is grown in pools and aquariums but is not winter-hardy in the North. It has weak, trailing stems and yellow flowers. It is readily propagated by division and by cuttings.

LUEDDEMANNIA (Lueddemann'ia). Orchids found wild in Brazil, which must be grown in a hothouse in temperate climates. The few kinds known are epiphytal and have somewhat conical, clustered pseudobulbs with evergreen foliage. They are allied to Acineta (which see) and belong to the family Orchidaceae. The flowers, which are on long, pendent spikes, are of medium size with fleshy sepals and petals and a three-lobed labellum or lip. All are summer flowering, though blooms occasionally appear at odd seasons. Lueddemannia commemorates Herr Lueddemann.

Basket Orchids. Orchid baskets are more suitable than flower pans because of the pendent inflorescences. The compost should consist of three parts osmunda fiber and two parts sphagnum moss; the crocks in the bottom of the basket must be so placed as to leave room for the flower spikes. A warm, tropical atmosphere is required during the season of growth; it should not fall below 60 degrees in winter. Water must be given carefully even in summer and only very occasionally in winter. In March, as much as possible of the old compost should be removed and replaced by fresh.

L. Pescatorei, the chief kind, which grows wild in Colombia, bears as many as fifty flowers on a spike; they have orange-yellow sepals and deep-yellow petals and lip.

LUFFA—*Vegetable Sponge* (Luf'fa). Climbing plants with ornamental fruits sometimes called Dishcloth Gourds. They are wild in India and other tropical countries and belong to the cucumber family, Cucurbitaceae. They grow 10-15 ft. in height, and climb by means of tendrils. The leaves, flowers and young fruits closely resemble those of the Cucumber.

A crop of Loofahs or Vegetable Sponges, the fruits of Luffa cylindrica. Luffa is a tender climbing plant closely related to Cucumber.

When the fruits attain maturity the outer skins become dark brown and brittle; the center portion is composed of a network of tissue which furnishes the well-known bath Loofahs, and is also made into other articles of domestic use. The name Luffa is derived from *Lòuff*, the Arabic name for Luffa aegyptiaca.

A Tropical Climbing Plant. The plants are raised annually from seeds and require the same treatment as do Melons and Cucumbers, although they are somewhat more sensitive to cold than either of these.

When the plants are in vigorous growth, the soil must be kept moist and, as the fruits are developing, weak liquid fertilizer is applied twice a week.

The chief kind is L. cylindrica, flowers yellow, fruit brown, cylindrical, smooth.

A plant of Honesty, Lunaria annua, in full bloom in early summer.

LUNARIA ANNUA—*Honesty*, *Moonwort*
(Luna'ria). A well-known hardy biennial, sometimes annual, plant; a native of Europe and western Asia, it is naturalized sparingly in the United States. It belongs to the Mustard family, Cruciferae. It grows 2-3 ft. high and bears purplish-lilac flowers in May and June; these are followed by flat silvery pods, which are valuable for indoor decoration during the autumn and winter months. The name is derived from *Luna,* the moon, and refers to the shape of the seed pods.

Suitable for Poor Soil and a Shady Place. Honesty is of the easiest possible cultivation. It will thrive in poor soil and in shady as well as in sunny places. It is raised from seeds sown out of doors in a nursery bed in May. The seeds are sown thinly in drills ½ in. deep, 12 in. apart. The seedlings need little attention during the summer months, but the soil between the rows must be kept loose and free from weeds by hoeing frequently.

If the seedlings come up thickly, they should be thinned out to some extent to give the remainder room to grow. In September and October the plants should be set out in their final places, where they are to bloom the following year. After the seed pods have been cut, the plants are useless and should be pulled up.

When Honesty has become established in a garden, self-sown seedlings often spring up freely, and it is then not necessary to make further sowings, for the seedlings can be taken up when they are well developed and planted where they are wanted.

For Winter Decoration Indoors. The stems carrying the seed pods should be cut in early autumn and hung, pods downwards, in a cool, airy room for a week or two, to dry thoroughly; they may then be used for filling vases indoors, where they will remain attractive throughout the winter months.

The chief kind is Lunaria annua (biennis), 2-3 ft., with lilac-purple flowers in May and

For winter decorations—the silvery seed pods of Honesty.

June; there is a variety with white flowers named alba, and Munstead Purple is an especially good strain. Lunaria rediviva is a perennial which bears scented, purplish flowers in early summer.

This plant is also a native of Europe.
LUNGAN. Euphoria Longana, which see.
LUNGWORT. See Pulmonaria.
LUPINE. See Lupinus.

LUPINUS: THE LUPINE

Beautiful Annuals and Perennials

(Lupi'nus). These are hardy annual or perennial herbaceous and shrubby plants which are of great decorative value in the garden during June and July. They belong to the Pea family, Leguminosae, and are natives chiefly of North America, though some are found wild in Europe. Lupine is said to be derived from *lupus,* a wolf; the origin of the name may be connected with the deep-rooting character of the plant, which was, wrongly, thought to impoverish the soil.

There are three chief types of Lupine: the annual, the herbaceous perennial, and the tree Lupine.

Herbaceous Perennial Lupines. The chief favorites are the herbaceous perennials, which, in climates where they thrive, provide a glorious show during the month of June chiefly, when their tall spires of bloom make a magnificent display. The parent of these is Lupinus polyphyllus, a native of western North America. The plants reach a height, when in flower, of 3-4 ft. or occasionally, 5 ft., and the flowers have a wide range of coloring. In recent years Lupines have been greatly improved by means of crossbreeding and selection, and the colors of modern varieties, particularly of the Russell type, are exquisite and greatly varied.

Flowers of Many Colors. The flowers range from white through lavender and pale blue to deep blue and purple; from pale yellow through salmon-pink, rose and apricot-buff to crimson. Numerous named varieties are grown in Europe, but a packet of mixed seeds of the Russell strain will provide the American gardener amply with blooms of brilliant and delightful coloring.

Hints on Cultivation. Herbaceous Lupines

The perennial Lupines in bloom in the right foreground of this picture add greatly to the charm of this small garden.

A typical plant of Russell Lupine.

thrive best where summers are fairly cool and winters not too severe, as in the Pacific Northwest. The plants prefer ordinary garden soil that has been dug deeply and enriched with decayed manure or compost; they flourish in full sunshine or in partial shade. In the course of two or three years herbaceous Lupines will develop into magnificent clumps, 3 ft. across, bearing a large number of spikes of bloom.

It is worth while preparing the ground well for Lupines, for that is the only way to grow them to perfection. In deep, rich soil that does not dry out in summer they grow quickly, soon forming large specimens. They may be planted in October or in spring, and should be set 3 ft. apart. They should be planted as one-year-olds, since older specimens do not transplant well.

Herbaceous Lupines cannot be said to be long-lived plants, for after a period of years—two, three or four—they are apt to dwindle and, if they do not perish, they become so weak as not to be worth keeping. When a Lupine plant begins to deteriorate it should be uprooted, for it will not recover its vigor.

Lupines are seen to full advantage in the perennial border. They should be planted towards the back of the border, for after June they become rather untidy and detract from the display of plants which come into bloom in July. If they are set towards the back, other and later-flowering plants can be set in front of them and will serve to hide the fading leaves.

Treatment after Flowering. It is a mistake to cut the stems right down as soon as the flowers have faded; this may force the development of fresh shoots from the base of the plants, yielding a few flowers in late summer, but the display is a poor one, and such drastic treatment weakens the plants considerably. It is, in fact, responsible for the collapse of many Lupines when they are only about two years old, and is not to be recommended.

Raising Perennial Lupines from Seeds. If seeds are sown singly in 3-in. pots of sandy loam in a cold or slightly heated greenhouse or frame, in March, the seedlings will be large enough to plant out of doors, either in the location where they are to remain or on a reserve border, in May. Many of them will bear small spikes of bloom in late summer.

Seeds may also be sown out of doors in July in drills 1 in. deep and 12 in. apart on a spare border. The seedlings will bloom the following year.

The Tree Lupine. Lupinus arboreus, a native of California, in favorable climates soon grows into a large bush, 5 or 6 ft. high; it bears a profusion of yellow or white flowers in May and June, and when in full bloom is a charming sight. Tree Lupines thrive in ordinary well-drained garden soil in a sunny and somewhat sheltered place; they are not usually a success on heavy, clayey soil or in shady positions. The

Lupines are attractive as cut flowers and for garden decoration. They should be cut while the upper flowers are yet buds, before the lower flowers fade.

bushes soon become rather ungainly and straggly unless they are pruned every year. They
are hardy only in fairly mild climates.

The best time to prune is in February or
March; the shoots of the past year's growth may
then be shortened by one third or by one half, as
may be necessary, to keep the bushes shapely
and to prevent their trespassing or crowding
other plants.

The Tree Lupines are too large for the average perennial border, but they look well towards
the back of a large, wide border where room
can be allowed for their full development. They
may be set in the less formal parts of the garden
in association with flowering shrubs.

Tree Lupines resent being moved and should
therefore be set out while small in their final
positions. No attempt should be made to move
large, well-established plants; they are not likely
to recover and, if they do, their growth will be
checked severely.

Raising Tree Lupines from Seeds. The best
way to propagate Tree Lupines is by sowing
seeds in spring or early summer, as recommended for the herbaceous type. When the seedlings
are well rooted, they should be planted out of
doors in the positions in which they are to grow.

Annual Lupines are attractive and easily grown
flowering plants. From seeds sown out of doors
in March or April, the plants will bloom in early
summer. The seeds should be set 3 or 4 in.
apart, the seedlings being thinned out until they
are about 8 in. from each other. They thrive in
ordinary well-cultivated garden soil in full sunshine or in slight shade. The flowers are of
various colors—blue, rose, and yellow, as well as
white. Annual Lupines are easily grown in a
sunny greenhouse having a night temperature of
50 degrees for winter and spring bloom. Seed
should be sown from September to January.

The Chief Annual Kinds. These are L. densi-
florus, 12-24 in., white, yellow or pink (variety
crinitus is 6 in. tall); L. Hartwegii, 18-24 in.,
blue or white; L. luteus, 2 ft., light yellow; L.
mutabilis, 3-4 ft., white, purple and yellow; L.
pilosus, 3 ft., blue; and L. subcarnosus, Texas
Bluebonnet, 12 in., purplish-blue and white.

The Chief Perennial Kinds. The chief species
or wild types of perennial Lupines are these: L.

arboreus is the Tree Lupine, 5 or 6 ft., yellow.
L. polyphyllus, 3 ft., blue, is the type plant of
the now popular race of herbaceous perennial
Lupines, of which there are numerous brightly
colored varieties. Other notable perennials are
L. cytisoides, 3-4 ft., purplish-rose; L. minimus,
6 in., blue, suitable for the rock garden; and L.
nootkatensis, 18-24 in., yellow, rose, and purplish.

LUSITANICUS. A term used in reference to
trees and plants which are natives of Portugal.
Lusitania was the old name of Portugal.

LUTESCENS. A botanical term meaning becoming yellow; it is often used in the names of
plants with yellowish leaves or flowers.

LUTEUS. The Latin for yellow, used in the
botanical naming of many plants having yellow
flowers.

LYCASTE (Lycas'te). Orchids which grow wild
in Mexico, Peru, Guatemala and Brazil. Some
are epiphytal, but others grow on the ground;
they bear showy flowers freely. Lycaste belongs
to the family Orchidaceae, and the name commemorates Lycaste, the beautiful daughter of
Priam, King of Troy.

These orchids have rather hard pseudobulbs,
often furrowed and surmounted by one to three
large leaves which are persistent in some kinds,
deciduous or nearly so in others. The flowers are
borne singly on erect stems, produced from the
bases of the bulbs, often in profusion. The flowers have much larger sepals than petals. Most
of the Lycastes bloom in winter and spring.

Orchids for an Amateur's Greenhouse. With
one or two exceptions, Lycastes are easily managed in a greenhouse in which the winter temperature is from 50-55 degrees. In summer the
temperature will naturally be higher. Air should
be admitted on all favorable occasions in summer, by night as well as by day, but drafts are
harmful.

Summer and Winter Management. A moist
atmosphere is required when the plants are in
full growth, but it is essential that no water be
allowed to lodge in the young growths, as the
enfolded leaves decay quickly. It is safer not to
wet the foliage. Water may be given freely when
the plants are growing; the growths will be
mature by autumn and the plants should then

Lycaste cruenta, a delightful Orchid, is comparatively easy to cultivate in a greenhouse with a winter temperature of 50-55 degrees F.

be fully exposed to the light; at this time less water is required. In winter, the plants must have a decided rest, water being given only occasionally.

The compost should consist of loam, fiber with a little chopped sphagnum moss, and a small proportion of orchid peat (which see). The ingredients must be mixed well together and kept porous by the addition of crushed crocks. The pots should be well drained, for it is important that water pass away quickly.

The best time to repot the plants is as soon as the flowers are over; the young growths, which often appear at the same time as the flowers, will not be too far advanced and new roots need not be seriously disturbed. Plants which show signs of new growth early in the year, and have no flowers, may be potted then. In most cases repotting is only needed every second year.

The favorite kind is L. Skinneri, from Guatemala. The flowers are large, showy, freely produced, and so varied that no two plants produce them in identical tints. In a typical bloom the sepals and petals are light rose, the smaller petals deeper rose, and the tongue-like lip is thickly spotted with rose and crimson; there are white-flowered varieties, and the color range extends from white to deep crimson. This Lycaste blooms in winter chiefly, several flower stems being produced by a vigorous bulb.

With Scented Flowers. Lycaste aromatica, from Mexico, and its variety major, have scented, golden-yellow flowers, much smaller than those of L. Skinneri but produced in greater profusion; L. cruenta is similar, but has slightly larger flowers with a deep red blotch at the base of the lip. All these bloom in spring.

L. gigantea is larger in growth and has flower stems 12 or 15 in. high. The flowers, which are larger than those of any other Lycaste, have brownish-green sepals and petals and a polished waxlike lip of purplish-brown color, its margins marked with orange. L. locusta and its form known as Sander's variety have deep green flowers in May.

L. lasioglossa, from Guatemala, has red-brown sepals, yellow petals and a narrow lip obscured by woolly hair. Other good kinds are L. Deppei, L. macrophylla (better known as L. plana), L. leucantha, L. lanipes and L. macrobulbon.

LYCHNIS (Lych'nis). Annuals and hardy perennials that are natives of the North Temperate and Arctic Zones. Many are very showy garden plants. A number of botanists refer some members of the genus Lychnis to Melandrium and others to Viscaria; the plants are sometimes grown by these names in gardens. The genus belongs to the family Caryophyllaceae. The name Lychnis is the old Greek name given by Theophrastus, and is derived from *lychnos*, a lamp, possibly referring to the brilliancy of the flowers, or to the shape of the seed capsule or the calyx. All are easily cultivated, being content with almost any reasonably good soil. They may be propagated by division in spring, or by seeds sown in light soil in spring in a cold frame.

The Jerusalem Cross, Lychnis, chalcedonica, is one of the most beautiful of perennials. Its flowers are scarlet.

The Jerusalem Cross. Lychnis chalcedonica, or Jerusalem Cross, is an extremely handsome hardy perennial. It is a native of Russia. For long it has been a popular plant for the flower border, and deservedly so, for it is both showy and easily grown. Lychnis chalcedonica grows from 2½-3½ ft. tall, and in summer bears large clustered heads of flowers of an intense pure scarlet. The plant does best in loam soil in which a liberal allowance of a well-rotted manure or rich compost has been dug. It is somewhat sensitive to drought. It is a fine subject for waterside planting as well as for the herbaceous border. The typical kind is very easily raised from seed, which may be sown in sandy soil in a cold frame in spring or in drills in the open ground.

There is a variety, Lychnis chalcedonica alba, with single white flowers, which may also be raised from seeds, and there are several other forms, including double red and double white, which should be propagated by division of the roots in March.

Rose Campion. Lychnis Coronaria, from southern Europe, is a handsome perennial plant for the flower border, 2-3 ft. tall. Its leaves and stems are thickly covered with white wool, and its flowers, produced in July–August, are pink, purplish, or white. It is easily raised from seeds sown in spring in drills in the open garden, the seedlings being transplanted later.

Lychnis coronata, from China and Japan, is a showy perennial, up to 18 in. tall, bearing panicles of flowers varying in color from scarlet to salmon. It likes a sheltered position and is best raised from seed each spring, as it is seldom long-lived.

Ragged Robin or Cuckoo Flower. Lychnis Flos-cuculi, or Cuckoo Flower, is a hardy perennial. A native of Europe and northern Asia, it is naturalized in eastern North America. It grows in damp meadows and streamsides, where its loose heads of rose-pink flowers with deeply lasciniated (fringed) petals are extremely showy. There is a handsome double-flowered variety of Ragged Robin, Lychnis Flos-cuculi pleniflora, which is well worth growing in the flower border where it should be given loamy soil, enriched with well-rotted manure. It grows about 18 in. high.

The double-flowered Ragged Robin should be propagated by careful division of the roots, soon after flowering, for it produces no seeds. It is excellent for the bog garden. The single-flowered type is well worth establishing in the wilder parts of the garden, at pond sides, in damp ground where bog Primulas are naturalized, or in the alpine lawn in the rock garden. It is easily raised from seeds, but these are probably seldom, if ever, offered by seedsmen.

Flower of Jove. Lychnis Flos-Jovis, the Flower of Jove, also known as Agrostemma Flos-Jovis, is a beautiful plant found in the mountains of

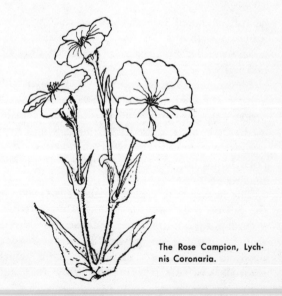

The Rose Campion, Lychnis Coronaria.

Europe, usually inhabiting stony slopes and broken ground or scree. The leaves are white with a beautiful silky down. The flowers are deep rose-pink and of good size. The plant is a perennial, of erect habit, growing about 18 in. tall, and is easily raised from seeds sown in a cold frame in spring. It flowers in June and July.

Evening Campion. L. alba (vespertina) is another beautiful European native plant. It has been naturalized in the eastern United States and is well worth cultivating in the wilder parts of the garden. It grows from 1-2 ft. tall, and blooms in summer. The flowers, which open in the evening and close during the day, are white and deliciously fragrant. There is a handsome variety with double flowers which is very worthy of a position in the flower border, but it is rare in cultivation.

Red or Morning Campion. L. dioica, the Red Campion or Morning Campion, is a native of Europe and Asia and is naturalized in eastern North America. This charming plant delights in growing in half-shady positions, and associates well with such other kinds as English and Spanish Bluebells, Solomon's Seal, and many of the hardy Ferns. It grows 1½-3 ft. tall, and has deep rose-colored flowers during a long summer season. There is a handsome double-flowered variety, and one that has white flowers.

The Arctic Catchfly. L. alpina, a native of Europe, Asia and North America, is most useful in the rock garden. It forms tufts or rosettes of short, narrow, almost grasslike leaves. The flowers, carried in crowded heads, half an inch or so in diameter, are pink, and appear in spring and summer. The plant is 4-6 in. tall, is very easily grown, and makes a bright show in the garden. It is so readily raised from seeds that it is not worth while bothering about any other method of propagation.

Seeds may be sown in a pot or pan of light soil in a cold frame in spring, the seedlings being pricked off into flats of soil and "grown on" until planted out of doors later. The color of the flowers, pink, is rather cold in tone, tending towards claret or magenta, which many people dislike. To these persons may be recommended a pretty variety, L. alpina rosea, with clear rose-pink flowers. This is less common than the

type, but it comes fairly true from seed, which may sometimes be obtained. There is also a variety with white flowers, L. alpina alba, which makes a pleasing contrast with the others.

The German Catchfly. L. Viscaria, the German Catchfly, is a native of Europe and northern Asia. It is a perennial, 12-18 in. tall, with heads of rosy-pink flowers in June–July. The stems are curiously sticky. It is easily raised from seeds sown in spring in pots of light soil, in a cold frame. There is a white variety L. Viscaria alba, but the finest variety is that known as L. Viscaria splendens flore-pleno.

This is indeed a magnificent plant for the flower border, and for cutting for the house. It is of tufted habit and throws up numerous 12-18 in. stems, stiff and erect, each carrying a fine head of completely double flowers of a most brilliant and telling rose-red.

Two Handsome Flower-Border Perennials. Lychnis Haageana is a showy hybrid between L. fulgens and L. coronata. It is an exceedingly fine perennial for the front of the flower border, growing 12-18 in. tall. The flowers, which are 2 in. across, vary through many shades from scarlet to pure white. It is raised from seed sown in pots of light soil in a cold frame in spring.

Lychnis fulgens is a very handsome species from Siberia, growing 6-12 in. tall, with large flowers of vermilion-scarlet. It flowers in spring and summer and is a fine perennial for the flower border. It is raised from seeds sown in light soil in a pan in the cold frame in spring.

The plant sometimes called Lychnis Lagascae is Petrocoptis Lagascae. (See Petrocoptis.)

LYCIUM—*Box Thorn, Matrimony Vine* (Lyc'-ium). A large group of leaf-losing shrubs, often with straggling branches, sometimes climbers or trailers, many of which bear small purple flowers and bright red berries. They are not among the most useful shrubs, and a few kinds only are grown; these form dense, spreading bushes that are very useful in exposed places near the sea, for a large mass provides a good deal of shelter for choicer plants. Lycium is in the Nightshade family, Solanaceae, and the name is taken from the Greek *lykion*, a thorny plant of Lycia.

The Lyciums are easily increased by seeds or by suckers detached from the old plants; in fact, once a plant has become established, suckers appear with considerable freedom. Most of the cultivated kinds succeed in almost any kind of soil. Those in an open, sunny position usually fruit most feeely.

For a Wall, Fence or Trellis. Lycium chinense, the common Box Thorn or Tea Tree, is the best-known kind. It is a native of eastern Asia and has long been an occupant of gardens. It is grown against walls, fences, trellises, and as a straggling bush in the open. Growth is rapid, and it may be expected to grow at least 12 ft. high against a wall. The small purple flowers are usually in pairs and they are followed by bright red or orange fruits, which on different plants vary a good deal in size and shape. In poor soil near the sea this plant forms a dense bush 4-5 ft. high.

The African Box Thorn. L. afrum, the African Box Thorn or Kaffir Thorn, is a native of South Africa. It is suitable for mild climates only and bears purplish flowers freely in May–June, which are followed by dark purple fruits. L. pallidum is a native from Utah to Mexico and is the most attractive of the Box Thorns in flower. It grows 5-6 ft. high and bears greenish flowers tinged with purple, and scarlet fruits. L. Grevilleanum, from the Argentine, and L. halimifolium, from southern Europe, are vigorous kinds with red fruits.

LYCOPERSICON ESCULENTUM. The botanical name of the Tomato, which see.

LYCOPODIUM—*Club Moss* (Lycopod'ium). Tender and hardy mosslike plants from India, the Malay Peninsula, the West Indies, tropical America, New Zealand, Europe, and other areas, including the United States. They have erect or trailing brittle stems covered with scalelike leaves arranged in four or more ranks. As they are closely related to the ferns, no flowers are produced, but they are sexually reproduced by spores borne in little cones at the tips of the shoots.

The spores of some of the species, chiefly L. clavatum, form Lycopodium powder, which is yellow in color and very inflammable; at one time this was used in theaters to produce artificial lighting.

Cultivation of Greenhouse Kinds. The warm greenhouse kinds require a minimum winter

The Ground Cedar, Lycopodium campanulatum, is a native American ground-cover plant of much charm.

temperature of 55 degrees, and the cool greenhouse kinds one of 45 degrees. The best compost consists of equal parts of sandy peat and leaf mold. The plants are grown in well-drained pans, which are kept in a moist, semishaded position. Once established, they must not be disturbed. The soil is kept moist at all seasons of the year, but less watering is required in winter. The plants do best when covered with a large bell jar, under which the atmosphere is kept uniformly moist, and are excellent for growing in a terrarium.

The Hardy Kinds. These are planted in April in a shaded moist position. The best place is in woodlands in a deep bed of sandy peat. The hardy Club Mosses are rather difficult to establish and need a considerable amount of care to get them growing freely.

Taking Cuttings. The greenhouse kinds are propagated by cuttings. The tips of the shoots, about 2 in. in length, are inserted in spring or summer in small pots of peaty soil and placed under a bell jar until rooted; they are then planted in flower pans, as already described. They can also be raised from spores. The yellow powder is shaken off on a piece of paper and then scattered thinly on the surface of pots filled with fine soil. The spores are not covered with soil, but panes of glass are laid over the pots, which are then set in saucers of water.

When the young plants are large enough to handle, they are pricked out, 1 in. apart, in a pan of finely sifted soil. They must be kept moist and shaded from bright sunlight until they are 1-2 in. in height, when they are set in their permanent positions. The hardy kinds may also be propagated by seeds and cuttings, which are rooted or raised in a cold frame.

The Chief Kinds. *For a hothouse:* L. Phlegmaria, 12 in. *For a cool greenhouse or terrarium:* L. obscurum, 9 in. *Hardy:* L. clavatum, creeping; L. complanatum (Ground Cedar), trailing; L. obscurum (Ground Pine), creeping, and L. Selago, 4 in., erect.

LYCOPUS—*Water Hoarhound* (Ly'copus). Hardy perennials that resemble Mints and belong in the Mint family, Labiatae. They are natives of the North Temperate Zone; those occasionally cultivated are native American kinds. Lycopus is derived from the Greek for wolf's foot and refers to the shape of the leaves.

These plants are suitable only for planting in wild gardens and similar places. They thrive in moist soil and are very readily increased by division and by seeds. The kinds are L. americanus, 2 ft., and L. europaeus, 2½ ft.

LYCORIS (Lycor'is). Tender and hardy bulbs which grow wild in China and Japan, and belong to the Amaryllis family, Amaryllidaceae.

They have ovoid, short-necked, tunicated (covered with loose scale leaves) bulbs, 1-2 in. in diameter, strap-shaped leaves, and clusters of red, purple, lavender-pink, or yellow, funnel-shaped flowers, 3-4 in. across, which are produced on the top of a stout scape (flower stalk) 1-3 ft. in length. Some kinds bloom in summer, others in autumn, when the bulbs are devoid of foliage.

The white filaments (anther stalks) and yellow anthers are conspicuous features of the flowers. The name Lycoris is that of a Roman actress, mistress of Mark Antony.

When to Pot the Bulbs. The dormant bulbs are potted in January and are buried to two thirds of their depth. A compost of two parts of loam and equal parts of leaf mold and well-decayed manure is used. The bulbs are set in a temperature of 50-55 degrees; the soil is not watered until it becomes dry, after which it is kept moist until the foliage dies down. Then the compost is kept dry until the bulbs are repotted; this is done annually in January.

The old soil is shaken off and the bulbs are repotted in pots of the same size or slightly larger pots. During the growing period these plants require a sunny position, but when the flowers have faded the pots are stored on their sides on the greenhouse shelf.

Cultivation Out of Doors. The hardiest kinds,

The golden-flowered Lycoris aurea.

L. sanguinea and L. squamigera, are planted in spring. Unless the soil is naturally light and well drained, it must be made so. The bulbs are planted 4-6 in. apart and 2 in. deep. L. squamigera is hardy into southern New England. The tender kinds are hardy outdoors in the far South, and require similar conditions.

Propagation is by offsets. The small bulbs are removed at potting time, potted separately in small pots and subsequently in larger ones until they reach the flowering stage.

The chief kinds are L. aurea (Amaryllis aurea), 12 in., yellow, August; L. radiata, 18 in., scarlet, June; L. squamigera, lilac-rose, 2 ft., July–August; and L. sanguinea, 18 in., red, July.

LYGODIUM—*Climbing Fern* (Lygo'dium). Tender and hardy ferns with twining fronds which grow about 6 ft. in length. They are natives of Asia, the United States, and the tropics of the Old World and New World, and belong to the Schizaea Fern family, the Schizaeaceae. They have thin wiry stems and pinnate (feathery) fronds, 4-5 in. long. When grown on wires fixed to pillars or the wall of the greenhouse, or trained around a tripod of canes as pot plants, they are very ornamental. The name Lygodium is derived from *lygodes,* flexible, and alludes to the twining habit of the plants.

A Hardy Kind. Lygodium palmatum, the Hartford Fern, occurs as a native from Massachusetts to Florida and Tennessee. It is suitable for growing in partial shade in the wild garden and fern garden. A distinctly acid soil that is moderately moist suits it best.

Ferns for the Greenhouse. The hothouse kinds require a minimum winter temperature of 55 degrees and the greenhouse kinds 45 degrees. The best compost consists of equal parts of loam, peat and leaf mold, and one part of equal quantities of charcoal and sand. Repotting is done in February or March, the best time being as soon as new fronds commence to form. The plants are removed from their pots, and the crocks, as well as a little of the old soil around the ball of soil, are removed with a pointed stick. The Ferns are then repotted in larger pots and the soil is made firm by pressing it down with the fingers. A semishaded position and a moist atmosphere are required.

The Climbing Fern, Lygodium palmatum, grows in moist, acid-soil woods in eastern North America.

Water is given carefully until the plants are growing vigorously, when the soil is kept moist throughout the summer. In autumn the fronds of the deciduous kinds die and are cut down to the ground; the soil is kept dry until the following spring. The evergreen kinds are watered only when the soil becomes quite dry. Plants in large pots, 10-12 in. wide, do not need repotting annually, for they can be kept growing vigorously by a top-dressing of compost in spring.

For training on the wall or pillars of the greenhouse, these Ferns are best grown in a bed of soil prepared in the greenhouse floor. Half a cubic yard of soil is removed, 6 in. of drainage is placed in the bottom, this is covered with turfs, and the remainder of the space is filled with compost. The plants are set 2 ft. apart, and treated as advised for pot plants.

Propagation by Spores and Division. These Ferns are increased either by spores or division. Spores are sown as soon as they are ripe in summer, or they may be stored in packets like seeds and sown at any time. To make sure that the spores are ripe, a few fronds are gathered and placed in a paper bag, which is hung up in a dry, airy room for a day or two. Ripe spores are then found at the bottom of the bag, and these are sown thinly on the surface of pots filled with light sandy soil. Just a pinch of the spores is sufficient for a 5-in. pot. The spores are not covered with soil, but a pane of glass is laid over the pot, which is placed in a saucer of water. The pots of spores are set in a glasshouse of the required temperature.

The prothallia, which develop from the spores, are pricked out, ½ in. apart, in pans of sifted compost when they are ¼ in. in diameter. After-wards the soil is moistened and the pans are kept in a closed case until the young Ferns are about 1 in. in height; they are then potted separately in 2-in. pots and subsequently in larger ones.

New plants can also be obtained by dividing the roots at potting time. Each piece should con-tain a portion of rhizome or rootstock and one or more growing points (buds) and should be potted in a pot just large enough to hold it.

The Chief Kinds. L. japonicum, 8-10 ft., pin-nate, feathery fronds (greenhouse, outdoors in the South); L. palmatum, 3-4 ft., palmate (hand-shaped) fronds, hardy; L. circinatum (dichoto-mum), pinnate fronds, needs tropical green-house conditions.

In Ceylon and other countries hats and brooms are made of the frond stems of L. scandens, a native of tropical Asia.

LYME GRASS. Elymus, which see.

LYONIA (Lyo'nia; Ly'onia). Leaf-losing and evergreen shrubs belonging to the Heath family, Ericaceae. The name was given in honor of John Lyon, a collector of North American plants, who lived during the eighteenth and early nine-teenth centuries.

Lyonia mariana, Staggerbush, occurs naturally from Rhode Island to Florida and Arkansas. It is a deciduous inhabitant of moist soils and at-tains an ultimate height of 6 ft. L. ligustrina, Male Berry or He-Huckleberry, grows wild from Maine to Florida and Louisiana. It forms a 6-ft.-tall evergreen bush. Of more southerly distribu-tion is L. lucida, Fetterbush, which occurs wild from Virginia to Florida and Louisiana. This, too, is 6 ft. tall and evergreen.

All of the above bear white or pinkish flowers in spring. They require the same general culture as Leucothoë, which see.

LYSICHITUM—*Yellow Skunk Cabbage* (Lysi-chi'tum; Lysich'itum). Attractive and uncom-mon, though not too pleasant-smelling, hardy plants which are widely distributed, being found wild in eastern Siberia, Japan and northwestern America. They belong to the Arum family, Ara-ceae. The name is from the Greek *lysichiton*, a

A yellow Skunk Cabbage, Lysich-itum americanum. It is a striking plant for the bog garden or waterside. It produces its yellow flower spathes in April-May, and these are followed by handsome leaves.

loose cloak, and it alludes to the flower spathe.

Plants for the Waterside. These plants, which are found wild in marshy or swampy districts, grow 18-24 in. high, and in April and May bear very handsome, pale yellow or white, boat-shaped flower spathes in advance of the leaves. The leaves vary from 1-4 ft. in length and 4-15 in. in width, according to the locality and nature of the soil, reaching their greatest dimensions in deep, moist, loamy soil. They grow freely in moist soil enriched with decayed manure or compost, and are useful for waterside planting.

Propagation is by division of the clumps in September or October.

Two kinds are grown, and for a long time their names were confused. The yellow species, previously called L. camtschatcense, is now identified as L. americanum, and the less common white kind is L. camtschatcense, a native of eastern Asia.

LYSIMACHIA – *Loosestrife* (Lysimach'ia). Hardy and tender summer-flowering herbaceous plants, widely distributed in the temperate and subtropical regions of the Northern Hemisphere; a few grow wild in South Africa, Australia and South America.

These plants belong to the Primula family, Primulaceae. The name is from the old Greek name *lysimachion,* possibly from *lysis,* conclusion or ending, and *mache,* strife, from the reputed soothing properties of the plant, or, al-

The common yellow Loosestrife, Lysimachia vulgaris, a handsome plant for naturalizing by the margins of pools or streams.

The yellow-flowered Lysimachia punctata: it is an erect-growing hardy herbaceous perennial, 1 - 2 ft. tall, suitable for perennial borders.

ternatively, after Lysimachus, King of Thracia.

Few of the Loosestrifes are of great garden value and only a limited number are now in cultivation. They are easily propagated by division in autumn, or spring. Nearly all the Loosestrifes are most suitable for moist soil, for naturalizing by the waterside, or in the bog garden.

Lysimachia barystachys, from China, grows 15-24 in. tall, and bears dense spikes of small white flowers in June. Lysimachia clethroides is a pretty Japanese perennial, 2-3 ft., with long, one-sided spikes of small, white flowers in late summer.

Lysimachia Ephemerum, from southern Europe, 2-5 ft., has spikes of small white flowers each with a dark center at midsummer; the leaves are glaucous (gray-blue). Lysimachia Leschenaultii, a native of India, is of tufted branching growth and has brilliant carmine flowers in autumn; it is 12 in. high. This showy plant, although not hardy in the North, may be grown in light, sandy soil in the border or rock garden in summer, but during winter must be kept in a cold frame or greenhouse.

Creeping Jennie. Lysimachia Nummularia, a very pretty European wild plant, is naturalized in North America; its common names are Moneywort, Creeping Charlie, and Creeping Jennie. The plant is of trailing, creeping habit with large, showy, yellow flowers borne on short stems from the axils of the leaves, over a long summer season. The flowers are fragrant. This is a favorite plant, often used as an edging and for hanging baskets and window boxes, and it is worth noting that it does well in town gardens. Often it is introduced into the rock garden, but there it is rather too rampant except for the very roughest outskirts.

Lysimachia Nummularia grandiflora has larger flowers, and aurea has golden-yellow leaves. Creeping Jennie is of the easiest possible cultivation, thriving in almost any soil or situation, and may be propagated with the utmost ease by division at almost any time of year.

A Handsome Rock-garden Plant. Lysimachia pseudo-Henryi is a creeping plant from Asia. It has thick, rather fleshy leaves and large, rich, golden flowers with darker centers. It is a very handsome plant for a cool, rather moist, position in the rock garden, where it flowers in summer. It is easily propagated from cuttings taken in spring or early summer, and struck in sand in a cold frame; or the plant may be lifted and divided in early summer.

The Yellow Loosestrife. Lysimachia vulgaris, a native of Europe and naturalized in eastern North America, is a handsome plant well worth naturalizing in the garden by the pondside. It grows 2-3 ft. tall, is of erect habit and bears panicles of fine yellow flowers in summer. It is easily propagated by division of the root in spring.

LYTHRUM—*Loosestrife* (Lyth'rum). Hardy herbaceous perennial plants of vigorous growth, reaching a height of about 4 ft., which are suitable for the wild garden, waterside and herbaceous border. In summer they bear tall inflorescences of reddish-purple or rose-colored flowers. Lythrum belongs to the family Lythraceae. The name is derived from *lythron,* black blood, an allusion to the color of the blooms. Some of the Loosestrifes occur in North America, others in Europe, Asia and Africa.

The Purple Loosestrife, Lythrum Salicaria, is naturalized in North America from the Old

A modern variety of Lythrum, an easy-to-grow hardy herbaceous perennial.

World; its spikes of reddish-purple flowers are out in July. A related species from Europe, L. virgatum, is naturalized in Massachusetts. Several varieties of L. Salicaria and L. virgatum are useful plants for the herbaceous border, wild garden or the waterside, where they flourish with a minimum of attention and are very lovely in the summer months. Notable varieties are The Beacon, rosy-crimson; Brightness, 4 ft. carmine-rose; Rose Queen, rich rose; Morden's Pink, deep pink; Robert, deep pink; and Lady Sackville, rose-pink.

Propagation. If an increased stock is needed, it can be provided by lifting the clumps and separating the woody roots into pieces for immediate replanting. This should be done in fall or early spring. If only a few plants are needed, it is unnecessary to lift the whole clump to obtain them; rooted pieces from the outside of the clump can be detached without lifting the latter. It is, in fact, a mistake to disturb old plants of the Loosestrife, for they take a year to become established again.

MAACKIA (Maack'ia). Leaf-losing trees, natives of eastern Asia. About six kinds are known, but with one exception they are rare in cultivation, some of them having been introduced within the last 20 years.

These trees require well-drained, loamy soil and a sunny position. Propagation is by seeds sown under glass in spring. Maackia belongs to the Pea family, Leguminosae, and the name commemorates a Russian naturalist of the last century, Richard Maack.

M. amurensis (Cladrastis amurensis) is a tree widely distributed in Amurland. It has long been in cultivation, and forms a small tree with leaves divided into seven to eleven leaflets, bearing erect inflorescences of densely arranged, attractive white flowers in July. The variety Buergeri is a native of Japan. M. chinensis (M. hupehensis), a closely allied Chinese tree, introduced in 1908, grows 50-60 ft. high in China, and bears white flowers in dense, erect inflorescences in July. M. Fauriei is a small, little-known tree from Korea, and M. Tashiroi is a shrub from Japan.

MACADAMIA TERNIFOLIA—*Queensland Nut* (Macadam'ia). An Australian tree belonging to the Protea family, Proteaceae. The name was given in honor of John Macadam, an Australian physician.

This slow-growing, evergreen tree attains an ultimate height of 50 ft. It produces good edible seeds (incorrectly called nuts) and is planted in southern California and southern Florida. It withstands light frosts only. Fertile, loamy soil, that is not excessively dry, suits it best. It is propagated by seeds, which germinate slowly.

MACARTNEY ROSE. See Rosa bracteata.

MACHAERANTHERA TANACETIFOLIA —*Tahoka Daisy* (Machaeranthe'ra; Machaeranth'-era). An aster-like plant that grows wild from South Dakota and Montana to Mexico and California. It belongs in the Daisy family, Compositae. The name is derived from *machaira,* a dagger, and *anthera,* an anther.

The Tahoka Daisy is suitable for growing in the flower border and for cut flowers. It succeeds in any ordinary garden soil in a sunny location. It is propagated by sowing seeds in fall or early spring. The young plants are set outdoors as soon as the weather has moderated in spring.

MACHAEROCEREUS (Machaerocer'eus). A group of Cacti, family Cactaceae, that are natives of Lower California. The name is derived from *machaira,* a dagger, and Cereus, a genus of Cactus.

There are two species, M. Eruca, a creeping kind which grows horizontally, and M. gummosus, which grows erect to a height of 3 ft., or so. For culture, see Cacti.

MACKAYA BELLA (Mackay'a). Herbs and shrubs from the tropics of the Old World, some of which have very showy flowers, and including the greenhouse plant sometimes called Asystasia bella. They belong to the Acanthus family, Acanthaceae. The name is applied in honor of an Irish botanist, John T. Mackay.

Mackaya bella is a lovely shrub for planting in a cool greenhouse border, for growing in a large pot (in a compost of two parts loam and one part old cow manure), or for planting outdoors in Florida and other warm parts of the

United States. It grows 4-6 ft. tall and bears bell-shaped, lilac flowers in large racemes at the ends of its shoots. When grown in a greenhouse, this plant needs little water in winter, but plenty during the growing season, with frequent syringing. Pruning is done after flowering by slightly shortening the shoots. M. bella can be propagated by cuttings of half-ripe shoots inserted in sandy peat in a warm propagating case.

MACLEANIA (Maclea'nia). Tender evergreen flowering plants, with woody trailing stems. They belong to the family Ericaceae and grow wild in Mexico and Peru. Two or three are in cultivation in Europe, and these have evergreen, ovate, rather tough leaves—those of M. insignis are tinged with red when young—and red or crimson tubular flowers, which are 1½ in. in length, and are borne in the axils of the leaves in spring. The name Macleania commemorates John Maclean, a British patron of botany.

The various kinds are used for different purposes. M. insignis is grown as a pot plant for the beauty of its young red-tinted leaves. M. pulchra is trained to wires for decorating the greenhouse wall or roof, and M. speciosissima makes a fine basket plant. They all require a minimum winter temperature of 45 degrees and a compost consisting of equal parts of loam, peat and sand. Pot plants are pruned back to firm wood in March and frequently syringed until new shoots appear, when they are transferred to slightly larger pots. The soil is made firm and the plants are syringed and shaded until established, when they are set in a well-lighted, airy position.

M. pulchra is planted in a bed prepared on the greenhouse floor. The soil is taken out to the depth of 2 ft.; 9 in. of drainage is placed in the bottom and covered with a layer of turfs. Then the space is filled with the compost recommended for potting and the plant set in position with the roots only just covered. Wires are fixed to the greenhouse wall, to which the shoots are tied as they develop.

M. cordifolia (speciosissima) is planted in a wire basket, the sides of which are lined with moss, and the center is filled with compost as advised for potting. The baskets are hung in a shaded place and the plants must be syringed frequently until they are established.

Water is freely applied to the soil from April to September, but for the remainder of the year it should be given only when the soil becomes quite dry.

Propagation is by cuttings of young shoots 3 in. in length, inserted around the edges of small pots filled with sand and set under a bell jar until roots are formed. They are then potted separately in small pots, and afterwards treated according to the purposes for which they are required.

The chief kinds are: M. pulchra, 10 ft., scarlet-yellow; M. speciosissima, red, trailing; and M. insignis, young foliage tinted red, and scarlet flowers. All bloom in spring.

MACLEAYA—*Plume Poppy, Tree Celandine* (Macleay'a). Two species of bold-foliaged hardy herbaceous perennials, natives of eastern Asia. In gardens they are often grown under the name Bocconia. They belong in the Poppy family, Papaveraceae, and are named in honor of Alexander Macleay, a former secretary of the Linnean Society of London and at one time colonial secretary for New South Wales.

Macleayas are well suited for growing near the rears of flower borders and for naturalizing in less formal parts of the garden. They thrive in any fertile soil and are easily propagated by means of cuttings, suckers, division and seeds. They require no special care.

Kinds. M. cordata grows 6-8 ft. high, has roundish, lobed leaves that are glaucous green

The Yulan, Magnolia denudata.

above and whitish beneath, and tiny buff-colored feathery flowers borne many together in large panicles. This kind is a native of China and Japan. M. microcarpa differs from M. cordata in having bronzy flowers that have 8-12 instead of 24-30 stamens, and leaves that are pubescent (hairy) beneath.

MACLURA POMIFERA—*Osage Orange.* A thorny tree, 60 ft. high, native from Arkansas to Texas. Male and female flowers are on different trees but neither has any decorative value. The orange-like fruits, however, are interesting; they are of large size, with a wrinkled skin, green at first, orange-colored later.

The tree grows well outside its native range, and is hardy in New England and central New York. It is not a particularly fine specimen tree because the leaves have no special attraction except that they turn yellow before falling in autumn; it is, however, valued as a hedge plant, particularly in the Midwest, and also as a tree for windbreaks and poor soils. Propagation is by seeds sown out of doors in autumn and by cuttings and root cuttings.

The curious wrinkled fruits of Maclura pomifera somewhat resemble oranges. Because of this similarity the tree is known as the Osage Orange.

Maclura belongs to the Mulberry family, Moraceae, and the name commemorates William Maclure, an American geologist. There is a variety, inermis, with spineless branches.

MACRANTHA. A botanical term meaning with large flowers.

MACROTOMIA. See Arnebia.

MACROZAMIA (Macroza'mia). Tender, evergreen, ornamental foliage plants from Australia, which belong to the Cycad family, Cycadaceae. They have stout, cylindrical, treelike trunks, covered with the stumps of dead leafstalks, and vary in height from a few inches up to 20 ft. From the tops of the trunks, large rosettes of dark green leathery leaves are formed, which vary in length from 1-12 ft. They are pinnate (featherlike), like those of Cycas, but the pinnae have prominent parallel veins and no midribs.

Very Ancient Plants. These plants do not flower, but bear cones similar to those of the Pines, to which they are closely related. They are usually dioecious—that is, male and female cones are borne on separate plants. These and other members of the Cycadaceae are of great botanical interest, as they are the only living examples of a prehistoric flora.

All Cycads are possessed of remarkable vitality and will withstand a considerable amount of ill-usage. If the stems of large plants are sawn through, they will emit new roots when placed in moist soil. The name Macrozamia is derived from *makros*, long, and *Zamia*, and refers to the long zamia-like fronds. These Cycads may be

The Osage Orange, Maclura pomifera, is valued for planting in windbreaks and hedges. It is native to the Arkansas-Texas area.

Macrozamia Peroffskyana in the Huntington Botanical Gardens at Pasadena, California.

grown outdoors in light shade in the far South.

For a Shady Greenhouse. Under greenhouse conditions these plants require a minimum winter temperature of 55 degrees and should be shaded from bright sunlight. Very little root room is required, the plants being set in pots or tubs just large enough to hold them. Good drainage is needed, and the best compost consists of equal parts of loam, peat and sand. As growth is very slow, repotting is not necessary every year and the plants are best left undisturbed until they show signs of deterioration or the soil exhibits a tendency to become sour. February or March are the best months for repotting, although this work can be done safely at any time during the year.

Winter and Summer Management. During the summer months, water must be applied freely to the soil, and the atmosphere should be kept moist by frequently damping the floor and benches. The fronds are also syringed twice daily. Throughout the winter the soil is only moistened when it becomes quite dry, and less atmospheric moisture is required.

The chief kinds are M. Peroffskyana, M. flexuosa, M. Macleayi, M. spiralis and M. Fraseri.

MACULATUS. A word meaning spotted or blotched, used chiefly in connection with leaves.

MADAGASCAR JASMINE. See Stephanotis.

MADAGASCAR PERIWINKLE. Vinca rosea, which see.

MADDENIA (Madden'ia). A small group of tender and hardy Asiatic trees and shrubs that belong in the Rose family, the Rosaceae. The name commemorates Colonel E. Madden, who collected plants in India.

Maddenias thrive in any ordinary soil and are propagated by seeds or cuttings. Most commonly cultivated are M. hypoleuca and M. hypoxantha. Both grow 20 ft. high and are hardy as far north as Massachusetts. Their flowers are without petals and have little decorative merit.

MADDER. See Rubia.

MADEIRA VINE. See Boussingaultia.

MADIA—*Oil Plant, Tar Weed, Tarweed* (Ma'dia). Dwarf, hardy annual flowering plants which grow wild in North America and belong to the Daisy family, Compositae. They grow about 12 in. in height, are very much branched, have linear (narrow) leaves and yellow daisy-like flowers, about 1 in. in diameter. They are called Tar Weeds or Oil Plants because of their sticky foliage. The blooms of Madia close when the sun is shining on them and open in the morning and evenings. The name Madia is the Chilean name of M. sativa.

For a Shady Border. These plants prefer a position which is shaded from the midday sun, and will grow in ordinary garden soil. If the soil is heavy, it must be lightened by digging in liberal quantities of leaf mold. The seeds are sown in April in the positions in which the plants are to grow. When the seedlings are 1 in. in height they are thinned out to 6 in. apart.

The chief kinds are M. elegans, 12 in., and M. sativa, 12 in. Both bear yellow flowers in summer. M. elegans is the common Tarweed of western North America. M. sativa, a native of Chile and naturalized in western North America, is called Chile Tarweed.

MADONNA LILY. See Lilium candidum.

MADROÑA. Arbutus Menziesii, which see.

MADWORT. One of the common names of Alyssum, which see.

MAGGOT. See Pests and Diseases.

MAGNOLIA: HANDSOME FLOWERING TREES AND SHRUBS

Spring- and Summer-flowering Kinds of Rare Beauty

(Magno'lia). Evergreen and leaf-losing trees and shrubs, many of them having large and attractive fragrant flowers which place them among the most decorative occupants of our gardens. Some kinds flower in earliest spring in advance of the leaves, others flower in later spring, and still others during summer and early autumn. Some have attractive fruits (see Berried Trees and Shrubs).

The hardy kinds are found wild in the Himalayas, China, Japan and North America, but there are also hybrids, some of which can be grown in colder districts than most wild kinds.

Magnolia gives its name to the family Magnoliaceae, and the name commemorates Pierre Magnol, Professor of Botany and Director of the Botanic Gardens, Montpellier, during the latter part of the seventeenth and the early part of the eighteenth centuries.

The fruits of the Magnolias are often conelike and brightly colored. When the seeds are ripe, they are released from the fruits, but are held for a few days by short silky threads before falling to the ground.

Propagation. Rare kinds of Magnolias are sometimes propagated by grafting in winter or spring in a greenhouse, using as understocks M. acuminata or M. tripetala. More usual methods of securing increase are by seeds, cuttings and layers.

Sowing Seeds. Many kinds are increased by means of seeds, but the period between sowing and germination may be as long as 18 months. They should be sown in as fresh a state as possible; if they are allowed to dry much, they are liable to lose their vitality. Sow in a light compost of two parts peat, one part loam and one part sand. The pots or pans may be placed in a cold frame or greenhouse and should be kept shaded.

Taking Cuttings. Many of the leaf-losing kinds, more particularly those of slender growth, can be increased in July by making cuttings of young shoots, about 3-4 in. long, with a slight heel of older wood, and inserting them in a bed of sand in a propagating case in a greenhouse. As soon as rooted, they should be potted singly in a compost of equal parts of fibrous loam, leaf mold, peat and sand; the following spring they should be planted in a nursery border.

Layering. The lower branches of almost any kind may be layered into the soil compost described, this being placed beneath the tree or bush (see Layering). The branches should be

A young tree of the popular Magnolia Soulangeana, of hybrid origin. The flowers are produced early in spring, before the leaves.

The Star Magnolia, Magnolia stellata, is the first to bloom in spring.

The white flowers of the Star Magnolia appear well before the leaves.

tongued or slit and pegged down in spring. They should be left for two years before being disturbed. They may also be increased by air layering (which see).

Not Suitable for Lime Soils. With one or two exceptions, the Magnolias are not well adapted for planting in lime soils, although M. acuminata grows where a fair depth of soil overlies limestone. They like deep, well-drained loam and benefit by a little peat or compost placed about the roots at planting time, in autumn or in spring. They also thrive in peaty soil providing it is well aerated, and they do well in disintegrated granite. Once they have been placed in permanent positions, they should be left undisturbed, for injury to large roots often leads to general ill-health. For this reason plants should not be placed close together but be given

Many Magnolias bloom in spring before their leaves expand. Their large blooms, white, creamy white, pink or purplish red, are produced in profusion.

tender tree from the Sikkim Himalayas, suitable only for warmer parts of the United States. It is said to be one of the most handsome trees of its native country, where it sometimes grows 150 ft. high. It has large oval to ovate leaves and large cup-shaped flowers with fleshy petals, each 4-5 in. long and 3 or more in. wide, the color of the outer side varying from deep rose to crimson. This tree is very beautiful.

M. Delavayi, from China, is not hardy, but is striking by reason of its very large evergreen leaves and large, fragrant creamy-white cup-shaped flowers, which open during summer.

The Yulan. M. denudata (M. conspicua), a Chinese tree, is one of the best known of the leaf-losing kinds. The flowers are white, fragrant and lily-like—hence the common name of Yulan or Lily tree. It is hardy, and forms a tree to 50 ft. high. M. liliflora is a hardy leaf-losing bush with purplish flowers, flowering in spring but bearing a few flowers during summer. It also is a native of China. By intercrossing these two kinds a

enough room for development to their full size.

Planting is best done rather late in spring, just at the time the leaf buds begin to open.

Pruning may be carried out, when necessary, during summer, but it should be confined as far as possible to young plants. The removal of small branches from young plants is not followed by harmful results, but the removal of large branches from old specimens is not recommended. By the removal of large branches large wounds are made and they may not heal well; therefore, decide upon the outline of the future plant in the earlier years and prune and train towards that end. Wounds made in pruning should be protected with tree-wound paint.

The Cucumber Tree. M. acuminata is the Cucumber Tree of North America. At maturity it attains a height of 90-100 ft., with a shapely head of branches clothed with large oblong leaves. The greenish-yellow flowers are not conspicuous, but they are followed by reddish fruits. M. cordata, a smaller tree with yellow flowers, is closely related to M. acuminata.

M. Ashei, a native of the southeastern United States, blooms when young and small in size.

For Mild Climates. M. Campbellii is a rather

Magnolia-Soulangeana Lennei has large cupped flowers that are dark-rosy-purple on the outsides of their petals and white flushed with pink on their inner sides.

Magnolia tripetala, the Umbrella Tree, is a native American kind that bears huge, fragrant, creamy white flowers after it is is full foliage.

The Sweet Bay, Magnolia virginiana, a native of the eastern United States, produces very fragrant blooms in summer.

series of very beautiful and free flowering hybrids has been obtained. They are hardy and rarely fail to flower well.

Beautiful Hybrid Magnolias. The commonest of these hybrids is M. Soulangeana, a large bush or bushy tree bearing, in spring, a profusion of large, white, purple-flushed flowers. Another very attractive hybrid is M. Soulangeana Lennei, which bears very large and shapely flowers slightly later, the color being rosy-purple outside, and white, flushed with purple, within. M. Soulangeana rubra (rustica) is a rather similar hybrid, and other good ones are M. Soulangeana Alexandrina, M. Soulangeana alba, and M. Soulangeana spectabilis, which have almost white flowers, and M. Soulangeana Brozzonii, white, shaded purple.

Yet another fine hybrid kind is M. Watsonii. This originated in Japan as a cross between M. obovata and M. Sieboldii. M. Watsonii attains a height of about 25 ft. and has large fragrant flowers which are pink with red centers. M.

Thompsoniana, a deciduous shrub, is a hybrid between M. tripetala and M. virginiana. The hybrid between M. Campbellii and M. denudata is named M. Veitchii.

M. Fraseri is a tree 30-50 ft. high, a native of the southeastern United States. Its leaves are 9-15 in. long and 6-7 in. wide, and its conspicuous flowers are at first pale yellow, then white.

A Magnificent Evergreen. M. grandiflora, the Bull Bay of the eastern United States, is a magnificent kind which has large leathery evergreen leaves and creamy-white fragrant flowers, which are 8-10 in. across. It may grow 90 ft. high, and it flowers freely in summer. There are several named varieties, notably gloriosa, with large globular flowers, and gallissoniensis, which is hardier than the type. M. grandiflora is hardy at Washington, D. C., and in sheltered places further north.

M. Kobus is a leaf-losing Japanese kind bearing white flowers in spring. M. macrophylla, the large-leaved Cucumber Tree, is a tree 25-50 ft. high of the eastern United States; it bears leaves up to 2 ft. long, sometimes longer on vigorous young trees, and they may be 9-12 in. wide. The flowers are large, fragrant, and creamy white, and open in summer.

Blooms When Quite Small. M. Sieboldii (parviflora) is a leaf-losing bush or small tree, bearing flowers when quite small; these are white and fragrant, and about 3 in. across, and each has a central mass of crimson stamens. M. Watsonii has rather similar but larger flowers and it does not grow so freely. M. salicifolia is a very desirable leaf-losing tree of narrow pyramidal outline, with small willow-like leaves and starry white flowers, 3-4 in. across, produced in spring. It grows at least 20 ft. tall.

The Star Magnolia. M. stellata is a shapely bush, 10-15 ft. high and as far through, bearing, with great freedom, starlike, glistening white flowers in advance of the leaves in spring. It is one of the loveliest for gardens of limited size, and should have plenty of peat mixed with the soil. A variety with pale-pink flowers is M. stellata rosea. M. obovata (hypoleuca) is a tree

A native of the southeastern United States, Magnolia Ashei blooms freely even when the tree is small.

eventually 100 ft. high, from Japan. It has large leaves and large white flowers each with a central mass of crimson stamens.

M. tripetala, the Umbrella Tree, is a white-flowering, leaf-losing tree of eastern North America which bears conspicuous red fruits.

M. virginiana (glauca), the Sweet Bay of the eastern United States, is a bush or tree to 60 ft. tall which may be evergreen, or it may lose its leaves in autumn. The globular white flowers are borne during summer. They are fragrant.

This kind may be grown in soil that is quite swampy.

M. Wilsonii is a shrub or small tree from China introduced in 1908; it bears shapely cup-like fragrant white flowers with a central mass of crimson stamens.

MAHALEB CHERRY. See Prunus Mahaleb.

MAHERNIA VERTICILLATA—*Honey Bell* (Mahern'ia). A lax or trailing subshrub suitable for growing in baskets or pots in window gardens· and greenhouses and out of doors in mild climates. It is a native of South Africa and belongs to the Sterculia family, Sterculiaceae. The name is an anagram of Hermannia, which is a closely related genus.

Mahernia verticillata grows well in sandy, peaty soil. In summer it appreciates a little light shade but needs full sun at other times. The Honey Bell roots readily from cuttings 1-2 in. long. The plants should be pinched occasionally to induce bushiness.

Magnolia grandiflora, a native of the southeastern United States, is one of the most magnificent of fragrant trees. It bears its large white fragrant flowers in summer and is a favorite for planting around southern homes.